Samaskaras

Samaskaras in Indian Tradition and Culture

Ramashray Roy

SHIPRA

ISBN 81-7541-140-6

First Published in India in 2003

Samaskaras in Indian Tradition and Culture

Published by:
SHIPRA PUBLICATIONS
115-A, Vikas Marg, Shakarpur
Delhi-110092, INDIA
Phone: 22458662, 22500954
Fax: 91-11-22458662
E-mail: siprapub@satyam.net.in
www.shiprapublications.com

Laser Typesetting at:
Kumar DTP Systems
Delhi-110091

Printed at:
Choudhary Offset Process
Delhi-110051

Dedication

To the memory of my wife

Dedication

To the memory of my wife

Preface

The present study *'Samskaras in Indian Tradition and Culture: The Case of Marriage in Mithila'* grew out of the awareness of the paradox created by the progressive erosion of traditional values but their greater relevance as the process of modernization makes the individual and social life and relations not only more barren but also more prone to tension, conflict and violence. While the paradox is real and is becoming more painful as days become months and months transit into years, the resources necessary to fight this paradox are either getting increasingly depleted or, if they are available, their knowledge is getting thinner and thinner.

It was this awareness that led me to think of making some effort to bridge the gap that has increasingly grown between traditional and modern knowledge systems. This gap has made it difficult, if not completely impossible, to initiate a meaningful dialogue between the two systems. In the first place, the language both the schools use to articulate their thoughts are incomprehensible to each other. In the second place, the philosophical or theoretical perspectives from which each of the knowledge systems tends to look at the world and devise epistemological means of apprehending, understanding and articulating its understanding are quite dissimilar, almost incompatible. And, lastly, there are few occasions, whether personal or institutional, for the meeting of the proponents and scholars of these two knowledge systems.

In the course of my stay at the Centre for the Study of Indian Traditions, Ranti Deorhi, Madhubani (Bihar), I had an ample opportunity of discussing with the Pandits of Mithila not only the various aspects of Indian culture, in general, but also about its reflection and present status of Indian culture in social life and relations in Mithila, in particular. My stay there also gave me the opportunity of reflecting on and discussing with other scholars at the Centre about possible ways and means of bridging this gradually expanding gap between the traditional and modern knowledge systems.

These discussions impressed upon me the crucial significance of *samskaras* in preserving Indian culture in a living form, a culture whose *arche* can be traced back to the Vedic world-view. Therefore, in order, to understand and appreciate the role of *samskaras* in preserving Indian culture and make it even today a vital force animating the thought-ways and work-ways of the Hindus, it is necessary to, first, have a good acquaintance with the Vedic world-view and, second, to relate Indian culture and different *samskaras* derived from it to their Vedic roots. Persuaded by this perspective, I decided to undertake a systematic study of *samskaras*. However, paucity of fund made it very difficult to do so.

I was, however, able to persuade the Indira Gandhi National Centre for the Arts, New Delhi, to finance the study of marriage *samskara* in Mithila. A grant from this Centre enabled me to undertake the present study. I am, therefore, very grateful to the Indira Gandhi National Centre for the Arts for making it possible for me to complete this study. I am particularly grateful to Baidyanath Saraswati of the Centre for his kind help in getting this grant. Without his encouragement and help in getting the grant to pursue this study, I would never have been able to complete this study.

In the course of completing this study I am indebted to various people for their encouragement, advice and help. I greatfully acknowledge my debt to Babusaheb Shashidhari Singh of Ranti Deorhi and all the memebrs of his family, who provided me not only with hospitality but also gave freely of their intimate knowledge. and deep understanding of *samskara*, in general, and marriage rituals, in particular. I am also thankful to Rajesh who assisted me in many different ways. I am also indebted to the informants who played an important role in making this study possible. I acknowledge their debt thankfully.

to Rajesh who assisted me in many different ways. I am also indebted to the informants who played an important role in making this study possible. I acknowledge their debt thankfully.

I completed the first draft of this study in October 2001. However, I could not find time to edit it and remove the deficiencies that I discovered in the work before I came to Ujjain to stay at the M. P. Institute of Social Science Rsearch, Ujjain at the forceful invitation of Dr. R. S. Gautam, the Founder and Director of the Institute. I am really very grateful to him and his colleagues at the Institute for making it possible for me to remove the deficiencies of the present study.

I am also very thankful to D. Kumar of Shipra Publications who willingly undertook to publish this study despite certain constraints related to the whims of the book market. I must, however, own the total responsibility of the errors I might have committed in interpreting the substantive meaning of marriage *samskara.* I leave it to the readers to judge the merit of the present study.

Ramashray Roy

Contents

Abbreviations

Rigveda	RV
Yajurveda	YV
Samaveda	SV
Atharvaveda	AV
Shatapatha Brahmana	Sh.B
Aitereya Brahmana	AB
Taittiriya Brahmana	TB
Taittiriya Upanishada	TU
Brihadaranyak Upanishada	Br. U.
Chhandogya Upanishada	Chh. U
Manusmriti	MS
Yagyavalkya Samhita	YS

1

Society as Cosmion

What relationship do *samskaras* have with the social order they constitute an integral component of? Also important in this relation is the question: Why are the *samskaras* at all relevant in any social order? Needless to say that *samskaras* have been performed, in one way or the other, in almost all cultures. These *samskaras* are so wide in scope that they encompass both religious as well as secular aspects of human existence. However, they have either shrunken down to a few rites and rituals or are performed perfunctorily as a habit or because their performance, whether at the personal or collective level, is deemed to be respectful. They have, it should also be pointed out, altogether disappeared or become irrelevant in many cultures.

In India, however, they still survive even though they may have lost their salience and may live a precarious life as empty shells of some grand idea or ideal. It is quite possible that they might altogether disappear even in Indian society under the influence and impact of modernisation made possible by the gradual but what seems to be the certain eclipse of the traditional world-view. There may remain only a few traces of *samskaras* like the archaeological remains of the magnificent *Vedic* civilisation from which they sprung to be studied, if at all, as something of historical importance.

The uncertainty about the continuance of *samskaras* in history raises some very important questions whose answers can go a long way in explaining what *samskaras* are and what role do they play in sustaining the social order they form an integral part of.

Additionally, there is also the question of why are s*amskaras* getting depleted and defeated in the battle of survival as history is supposed to move towards a perfect state of human existence on the earth which is coming since historians right from the disintegration of the Middle Age world view have been telling. What are the forces that prove fatal to the continued survival of s*amskaras* as essential part of human life cycle and the cultural ethos of communities of men?

To answer these questions is not possible unless we distance ourselves from the mainspring of ethos of modern culture and look back to primal source of *samskaras* in the dim and distant past. The reason for this is that the mainspring of modern thought-ways and work-ways is radically different, even destructive of the constitutive elements of life that made s*amskaras* an essential part of fruitful and materially and spiritually benign living. Human existence is quite different in terms both of inspirational and structural aspects than what it used to be in ancient and mediaeval times. The main difference lies in the fact that whereas the ancients believed in the idea of the cosmos, the modern man has decisively rejected the idea of cosmos and reduced it to the status of the phenomenal world devoid of the features that made the phenomenal world into a cosmos. The term 'cosmos' conveys three fundamental ideas. In the first place, it denotes that there are several worlds beyond the phenomenal world, all of them linked in an organic relationship with each other. In the second place, cosmos signifies that it is : "...the perfect exemplar of order, and, at the same time, the cause of all order in particulars, which only in degrees can approximate the whole."[1] In the last place, man is just one instance of the particular that compose the whole. As a part of the whole that is larger than the totality of this perceptible phenomenal world, man is not self-complete and, therefore, not perfect. He becomes complete and perfect when, as Cicero observes, he "contemplates and imitates it "[2] particularly the order inherent in it.

For man to be a part of the cosmos he must recognise that his existence is influenced in many different ways by mundane as well as by extra-mundane forces. One can and often does have the knowledge of mundane forces. However, when it comes to extra-mundane forces, they become shrouded in mystery and therefore beyond the ken of discursive logic. What is supposed to be mysterious can be apprehended by seeing through what Ian Gonda calls "heart's eye" and articulated and explained through the process of ratiocination that has its foundation in what the heart's eyes see. And what heart's eye sees is the substratum of reality or the absolute. It is the absolute or Being which gradually gets through procession into what we know as *vishwa* or the world. It is as a result of the process of transformation that Being creates and enters into the flow of time and comes under the sway of becoming.[3]

It is this process of becoming that transforms the One into many. But the many that appears as the result of the procession of the absolute remains the part of the whole and, therefore, retains the properties of the source out of which it has sprung. It is because of this that there exists an essential homology between the larger universe, worlds beyond this world, that is, cosmos and the many that is the micro-cosmos. It is again because of this that man is supposed to be the spark of the divine fire (*yathagne kshudra visfullinga vyucharanti*).[4] Despite this, however, the transformation of man in his natural state, that is, the attainment of manhood in the real sense of the term, is not automatic. It is a possibility that can be realised and translated into reality only by transcending one's lower nature. For this, harmony in the interior of man and harmony with the cosmic order, both are necessary for man to attain his true selfhood as a precondition of harmonious living.

The actualisation of the possibility of man attaining his higher nature depends on the realisation that man is nothing more than a city, a *pura*, whose real resident is the *purusha* that is, the Supreme Being. " On account of his dwelling in all bodies, he (*i.e.* the Supreme Being) is called *purusha*. There is nothing that is not pervaded by him."[5] If man is the abode of the absolute, then, what relationship, we must ask, exists between man, world, cosmos and God? The indwelling God is identified by *Br.U.1.20* as *satyasya satyam*, the truth of truth. Given the identity between the human person and the person in the Sun, it follows that, as long as this identity remains incomplete, only as a possibility, the human person will not be perfect. He will, as a consequence, lack harmony both in his interior and with the external world, both seen and unseen.

The identity between human person and the *purusha* residing in his interior remains unrealised, only a potency, as long as man remains sunk in what in the *Vedic* perspective is called *avidya* (ignorance). *Avidya* (ignorance) or *ajnana*, as Abhinava Gupta says, is twofold: the innate (*pauruasa*), that is, the auto-limitation of God—the consequence of his voluntary decline in time and space, and intellective ignorance (*buddhigata*) increased by man himself.

> Twofold is ignorance, the first intellective and the second innate. The first consists of uncertain and erroneous judgement; the second is nothing else but thought itself; (*Vikalpa*) insofar as it is divine consciousness in its limitation. As such, this is the principal cause of *samsara*.[6]

Avidya (nescience) is the end result, symptomatic of the snapping of the bond of relatedness with the world beyond and its creator. This, in turn, signifies that the human person is enveloped by the darkness of *samsara* and cannot see the light within. To discover this inner light is to be reintegrated with the cosmos and its creator or, to put it differently, to return to the sense of original unity that has been greatly enfeebled, even snapped, by the process of living itself. Reintegration with the cosmos and its creator is possible if three fundamental conditions are fulfilled. First, there must be the awareness of essential relatedness between *pura* and *purusha*. Without such an awareness any effort to know the Supreme Being and relate with it is not possible. Second, one must break the veil of *avidya* (nescience) in order to discover the light within. And, lastly, *vidya* (knowledge), that is, elimination of nescience and to know what one truly is beyond and above what is signified by the empirical self. *Aham*, is, thus, the first necessary step towards reintegration with the divine ground of being. However, this *vidya*, as Tucci puts it—is not dialectical, logical and discursive. Dialectical, logical and discursive knowledge is a necessary framework on which is constructed the instrument with which one works. Real knowledge, that leads to cognition of ourselves and rebuilds the lost equilibrium, is experience, since knowledge to which action is not conformed is not a good but an evil thing. When knowing does not transform life and is not realised in it, disharmony is caused.[7]

Thus the real *vidya* is the one which is transformative knowledge, *praxis,* in real sense of the term. It must, however, be emphasised that to acquire this *vidya* is not possible for all; only a few can ever hope to acquire this *vidya* through self-development. But it is only a few, who experience the divine light existent but shrouded by materiality within them; it is they who gain a glimpse of the true order of things. It is this glimpse that symbolises the fact that these seers have already restored equilibrium in their interior meaning that the different constituents in their interior world are in harmony with each other. The internal harmony then becomes the basis of harmony without, *i.e.* with other beings in the external world and with the cosmos. The glimpse of the true order of things that becomes instrumental in achieving man's reintegration with the larger reality also provides the basis for developing the essential character of a social order. And when a social order is based on the perception of the cosmic order and partakes of its essential characteristics, it becomes a cosmion because it is the replica, albeit on a smaller scale, of the cosmos itself.[8]

As a cosmion social order underlines the fact that society is a civilisational unit and constitutes an arena where human consciousness, intentions and purposes receive definite shapes and direction. But the shaping of human consciousness, intentions and purposes is not haphazard or ad hoc; it is inspired and informed by the vision of the cosmic order. As a replica of the cosmos, the social order is not only inspired by and based on the principles that are seen underlying the cosmos and the meaning man derives from these principles for informing and regulating his life and social relations. It also aims at celebrating in life and the lived world these principles and values, preserving them in institutional arrangements and social practices. Thus, to shape one's life according to these principles and values requires that one knows what these principles and values are and then imitate them in one's life. Thus what is important for human existence is to discern and understand the order and regularity that characterise the cosmos. It is only this understanding that, given the right orientation and impetus, prompts, encourages and sustains man in his endeavour to realise order and regularity in his own life and, through it, maintain and preserve order and regularity in the social universe.

Thus the real significance of the idea of cosmos is that man, as a part of the cosmos, must conform to the pattern of order it displays. That is, man must mould his existence in accordance with the principles that underlie and undergird order and regularity in the universe. Thus, the order in the universe constitutes the paradigm of human existence and establishes the necessary "connection between the apotheosis of the universe and the ideal of the human perfection...." What needs to be emphasised here is the fact that, for most of the people, this connection between the apotheosis of the universe and the ideal of human perfection remains unclear and beyond conscious acknowledgement. As such, the awareness that man is an integral part of a larger order and the making of this awareness an integral part of man's existence are essential, if the contemplation and imitation of the cosmos is to help man become perfect becomes progenitive of a deep commitment of complying with the constitutive principles of this larger order. This awareness, as we shall see later, is kept alive by the culture of a society and by arranging pragmatic affairs of life and relations in the light of the higher principle grounded in culture.

To recognise some higher principle as the ordering element of man's pragmatic affairs is to radically change the meaning of human condition which refers today only to the temporality of human being. "It is this temporality", as Eliade notes, " that makes all other conditionings possible and that, in the last analysis, makes man a conditioned being, an indefinite and evanescent series of conditions." It does not need to be pointed out that to be enmeshed in the structures of temporality is to let oneself be completely situated in phenomenality and allow oneself to be conditioned biologically, psychologically and sociologically. To be so conditioned is to be completely cut off from the divine substratum of reality and snap attunement to this *substratam* which alone can endow human existence with meaning and value. In other words, when man is supposed to be nothing else but a biologically, psychologically and sociologically conditioned entity, he becomes completely unaware of his connection with the world beyond this world.

This unawareness induces a state of mind that rejects, ignores or induces forgetfulness of the existence of the imperishable, unchanging Being that lies concealed under the layers of the plurality of the phenomenal world. The experience of the enshrouding plurality of the phenomenal world, devoid of the conscious recognition of the unity out of which the plurality has sprung and in which ultimately it merges, breeds particularism and therefore excessive concern with personal good. Knowledge of things that change in the process of becoming is necessary. However, exclusive concern with this knowledge does not conduce to a realistic attitude either towards one's own self or towards the external world. This is so for the simple reason that things that change lack substantiality. The knowledge of changing things does not yield that knowledge which helps man transcend the claims of his narrow existence and contingent experiences. It is not, therefore, surprising that action based on the knowledge of changing things leads only to existential troubles. As Zimmer notes, "naïve unawareness of the hidden truth of the self is the primary source of all the misplaced emphases, inappropriate attitudes and consequent torments of auto-intoxicated world."[9]

Self-torments of the auto-intoxicated men in this world and the sufferings of the others caused by auto-intoxication can be avoided if man consciously acknowledges the mystery that permeates the cosmos and is persuaded to accept the sanctity of his relatedness with the substratum of reality and let this relationship inform and influence his life activities. It is in this sense that we can appreciate the fact that the mystery associated with the cosmos signifies the impingement of certain mysterious forces on human existence. It is through the effort to understand, even if only vaguely, the nature of these forces and relate oneself with them in a meaningful way. It is this relationship that allows man to give meaning, substance and direction to his existence in the phenomenal world. In other words, it is this relationship that provides anchorage to the ship of his life which otherwise floats aimlessly and helplessly in the vast sea of insatiable desires, appetites and passions. It is by being firmly anchored in the divine ground of being that man can rise above the mere animal existence and give to his life a semblance of meaning. It is in this sense that man does not merely live, he leads his life in accordance with an ideal vision of life derived from his linkage with the divine ground of being.

To lead rather than live life, in this perspective, is not only to recognise the world as linked with the divine ground of being and, as such, it forms an integral part of the cosmos to be pervaded by mysterious forces. Also, it is to treat it as the exemplar of proper human conduct. And as an exemplar, it gives a definite direction to man's thinking and everyday activities. *Samskaras* are, as we shall see later in greater detail, an integral part of the worldview that is embedded in the conscious acknowledgement of the divine ground of being and treat every life activity as the vehicle of refreshing and renewing man's attunement to this divine ground of being. It is in this context that we can appreciate the fact that classical Indian thinking treats man's existence as well as the social order as *yajna* (sacrifice).

> In the sacramental order there is a need and place for all man's work: and there is no more significant consequence of the principle, work is sacrifice, than the fact that under these conditions...every function from that of the priest and the king down to that of the potter and scavenger; is literally a priesthood and every operation a rite.[12]

To treat every function as priesthood and every operation as a rite pertains undoubtedly to the individual's attitude towards his own self and its relationship with the external world both seen and unseen. But this is possible only when a social order is organised and functions in a way that not only encourages and sustains the individual, no matter what his place in society and his vocation, to embrace a view of life which incorporates *samskaras* as integral to a good life. This raises the important question of the form of society that offers a hospitable habitat for *samskaras*. It needs to be pointed out that *samskaras* assume significance not in all forms of society; they have significance only in societies that claim to be modelled on the cosmic order. To be so modelled is to articulate a two-tier view of life. What is important in this perspective is that while it recognises the importance of fulfilling ordinary life needs of acquiring wealth, power and prestige, it also gives allegiance to higher life purposes, such as, self-realisation, aspiration of becoming a good man, etc.

Given these two important life purposes what needs to be pointed out is that while fulfilment of ordinary life purposes pertains to the needs of a natural man, that is, man who has still not transcended his animal nature, the pursuit of higher life purpose is meant to make the transcendence of animal nature and attainment of true humanity possible. It should also be pointed out that these two different life purposes are not dichotomous and, therefore, not antagonistic. As a matter of fact, both of them are recognised in all traditional world views as necessary. And as a necessary component of good life, the pursuit of both the life purposes is considered as *sine qua non*. The only stipulation that traditional cultures make in respect of the pursuit of these purposes is to subject the fulfilment of ordinary life needs to the over-lordship of the pursuit of a higher life purpose. As such, these two purposes are hierarchically organised. It is against this background that we can appreciate the insistence in the classical Indian thinking on the need to subordinate the pursuit of *kama* (desires) and *artha* (resources necessary for satisfying a particular desire) to *dharma* (righteousness). The pursuit of a higher life purpose is considered in all cultures to be absolutely necessary; without it life is considered as lacking, a desert.

What needs to be emphasised here is that the pursuit of higher life purpose makes it necessary for anyone to rise above the contingencies of his narrow existence and relate himself with an entity that is larger than his own finite existence. The need to relate one's finite existence to something larger makes it incumbent to get freedom from what Plato calls the slavery of many mad masters. By this he means a state of affairs in which the individual is not motivated by his natural desires in engaging in action. Since desires are numerous, fickle and difficult to satisfy, and are not pacified even if satisfied, to become their slave is to lose control of oneself, that is to become, what *Chhandogya Upanishad* (*Chh. Up. vii.25.2*), calls *anyarat.* When a person becomes *anyarat*, his soul loses its discriminating, regulatory and disciplining power; appetites and desires fill the gap created by the withdrawal of the higher ordering element in his interior. Integration of different faculties and capacities of the individual as well as his relatedness with the cosmos is disrupted; the consequent disorder in the interior of man results in what *Chh.Up.* calls *kamachara.*

This leads to the merger, in Freudian parlance, of id and ego exemplifying Freud's saying : " Where id was, there ego shall be." It does not mean : " the ego shall replace the id but that the id should come to exist in the realm of the ego—that is, it should shed the illusion of integral, controlled selfhood and dissolve into these associative chains normally repressed into the unconscious."[13] This also means that the self emerges, as Rieff suggests, "as a subject of struggle between two objective forces, unregenerate instincts and overbearing culture. But in these two forces there may be compromise but no resolution. Since the individual can neither extirpate his instincts nor wholly reject the demands of society, his character expresses the way in which he organises and appeases the conflict between the two."[14] This struggle is real and escape from it is either surrender of the self to the id or to the super-ego. In the case of the former, it is ruled by appetites and desires and, in the case of the latter, it is governed by oppressive traditions, conventions, customs or regnant fashion of ideas and opinions. The individual has, in this situation, no other choice than what euphemistically is called adaptation. In any case he is not his own master, he is ruled either by his passions or impersonal social order in whose making he has had no hand.

The situation leads to loss of freedom, making man *anyarat.* "If they are ruled by others and live in perishable worlds, they are not free to act as they wish in all worlds" (*Chh. Up. vii.25.2*). This suggests that integrated, controlled selfhood cannot be attained if the individual surrenders either to his id or to his super-ego. In either case he loses the capacity of self-rule and, as a consequence, come into conflict with himself and with his external environment. For integrated, controlled selfhood, it is necessary to install a superior ordering entity which can quell the rebellion of desires and appetites.

The rebellion of desires and appetites can be quelled only when the fulfilment of ordinary life-needs is controlled, disciplined and regulated by the pursuit of some higher life purpose. By the same token the pursuit of a higher life purpose, whether it is self-realisation through self-knowledge or the Aristotelian ideal of the life of a good citizen, must be free of the influences of the considerations of self-interest and be governed by a superior element that forms an integral part of man's being. And this integral part is none else that the soul which is considered as the sensorium of divine. This divine has been identified, as already pointed out, by *Chh.Up., 8.1.1*, as the *Purusha* who dwell's in all bodies. It is this indwelling *Purusha* whose rulership must be accepted by the individual if he wishes to be at peace with himself and the external world. This indwelling *Purusha* is *Atman* who is "free from evil, free from old age, free from death, free from sorrow, free from hunger, free from thirst, whose desire is for truth (*satyakamah*), whose resolve is of truth (*satyasamkalpa*), *Chh. Up.,8.1.5.*

> It is this *Atman* which is everywhere, is all, "Verily, he it is who sees thus, and understands thus, has pleasure in *Atman*, délight in *Atman*, union in *Atman*, joy in *Atman.* He becomes self-sovereign (*swarat*); he becomes free to act as he wishes in all the worlds (*Chh.Up. 7.25.2*).

The pursuit of the higher life purpose is, thus, possible only when the rulership of the soul as the sensorium of divine is accepted, established, and its commands are consciously obeyed. To obey its command is to mould one's life in accordance with the requirements of keeping the soul attuned to the divine ground of being. This means that all life activities must be treated as the medium through which this attunement is celebrated, kept alive and renewed if its consciousness gets dim. Thus the importance of *samskaras* is recognised only in a social order which, because it is modelled on the principles of order presumed to be inherent in the cosmos, is capable of keeping man attuned to the divine source of order.

In contradistinction to the conception of society as a cosmion, there is entirely a different conception of society that explicitly denies the existence of worlds beyond this world. As such, this conception of society also denies that the world we see, live and work in has any mystery. This view projects a perspective on this world that forcefully posits the idea that this world is nothing more than an accidental concourse of cause and effect. As such, the world can be easily apprehended once we know or calculate what these causes are and what effects do they produce or are likely to produce. We can know these causes and their effects, that is, the operation of the cause and effect relation, if we can discover the laws that determine, govern and regulate their functioning. And since natural sciences are meant to be concerned primarily with discovering these laws, man can gain perfect understanding of this world, how it is constituted, how it works and how its working can be manipulated and transformed in order to serve the needs of mankind.

Needless to say that it is this perspective on the world that has proved fatally injurious to the philosophical approach to the apprehension of the world. Natural sciences have gradually replaced philosophy and have assumed greater significance for man's existence. This has been possible because of what Max Weber calls disenchantment of man with the world that traditional thinking supposed to exist. As long as the world was shrouded with mystery, the understanding of what this world is, how it functions and how it impinges on man's existence in its functioning—the understanding of all these factors depended on philosophical insights. However, when this world was demystified, it also paved the way for de-divinisation of the world. Philosophically speaking, even when the notion of cause and effect relationship was retained as an important aid in understanding the world, the Aristotelian concern with the prime mover was discarded. With it also was banished the creator of this world to the uncertain and perilous world of theological contestations.

The denigration of the philosophical or, what is the same, theoretical perspective, meant not only the rejection of God as the substratum of reality but also the changed outlook of man towards the external world. As Becker observes:

> We necessarily look at our world from the point of view of history and from the point of view of science. Viewed historically, it appears to be something in the making, something which can at best be only tentatively understood since it is not yet finished. Viewed scientifically, it appears as something to be accepted, something to be manipulated and mastered, something to adjust ourselves to with the least possible stress. So long as we can make efficient use of things, we feel no irresistible need to understand them.[15]

The assumption of prominence by science is symptomatic of an outlook that treats knowledge not as something that must be sought for the delight of the mind or for self-transformation but something that can produce some concrete results insofar as human purposes are concerned. This transformation of the conception of knowledge became possible when the need to pursue higher life purpose was considered to be irrelevant and therefore redundant. As a consequence, the fulfilment of ordinary life needs involved with the process of production and reproduction came to occupy the center-stage of man's life. Satisfaction of desires became the pivot of human existence in the sense that it was considered to be instrumental not only for the attainment of felicity but also for the self-making of man and for the progress of the civilisation. Self-making of man signifies the fact that man makes himself in the process of fulfilling his needs. Fulfilment of needs propels man to interact with nature with the help of technology. In interacting with nature with the help of technology man realises the potentialities slumbering in his breast. As his potentialities are progressively actualised, man establishes institutions, develops customs and conventions, makes law, creates culture and makes history. It is in this process that man's personal and collective identities are shaped and formed.

It is in this process, again, that civilisation ceaselessly advances on the path of progress. This can be easily appreciated if we consider the fact that the fulfilment of human needs requires the help of technology; the use of technology proliferates needs; proliferation of needs requires further advancements on the technological front; further technological advancements proliferate needs further, and so on. As a result there comes to be established a dynamic relationship between need fulfilment and technological development. This relationship is seen to have initiated a process of progress that is supposed to be open-ended. This further means that, as Kant argues, history has a *telos*, that is, the history of mankind has an end towards which it is unceasingly moving. This end is the realisation of the good life of modern conception. Supposedly, then, once the good life of modern conception is realised, history will stop.

The modern conception of good life, as has already been pointed out, rests upon the fulfilment of ordinary life needs. There exist at least two versions of how to go about the fulfilment of desires. In one version, the primacy of the satisfaction of various desires is recognised. However, it is also recognised that they must be satisfied under rational control. What is distinctive about this view is that rationality does not, in this perspective, mean the Platonic *Sophia*, that is, wisdom that is gained as a result of the contemplation of the Form. It means nothing more than Aristotelian *phronesis*, that is, the rational calculation of end-means relationship. What this signifies is that one must consider dispassionately and clairvoyantly all the possible ways of achieving a given end and selecting the one, most effective means that promises to be the least costly and most beneficial. In this perspective, rationality simply means an instrumental, calculative, and expediential reason; what is also important in this regard is that human purposes need not be put before the bar of reason; it is only the means that can be subjected to rational calculation and control.

In contrast to this, there is the view advanced by Rousseau, that advocates to treat the fulfilment of biological needs itself as the highest moral aspiration. What is distinctive about this perspective is that it considers it very necessary to free desires from the control of reason whether in transformative or calculative sense. These desires, it is argued, must become the ground of their own legitimation. This means that they should no more be submitted either to the bar of reason or judged with reference to any higher life purpose. They have, in short, become endless in two important senses. First, they are no more linked with any higher life purpose or higher end of life; they have become autonomous and have, as a result, acquired auto-legitimacy. And since man's felicity depends on the satisfaction of whatever desire the individual happens to harbour at any particular moment, desires become endless in yet another sense; they proliferate endlessly. Two additional factors need to be noted in this connection. In the first place, it is undoubtedly the fact that the goal of realising good life has been a dominant concern of man in every age. However, there is a radical divergence between the traditional and the modern conceptions of good life. If the various ends of life are hierarchically organised in the traditional world-view, there now occurs a fusion between them in the modern times. Traditionally, the conception of higher purpose of life underlined the need to rise above the claims of everdayness and cultivate one's life in the light of certain values; values that can make life more meaningful than is possible by sinking in animal existence. Also, as already pointed out, it is the higher life purpose that governs the selection of other purposes, mostly those involved with pragmatic affairs of life, and the manner of realising them so that ordinary life needs do not become autonomous and acquire auto-legitimacy. What has happened in modern times is that the concept of higher life purpose is interpreted in the sense of the fulfilment of ordinary life needs. Thus, both higher life purposes and ordinary life needs have been fused to create one unitary purpose in life, that is, the satisfaction of one desire after another unceasingly.

In the second place, with coming into prominence of the fulfilment of ordinary life needs, man's outlook on and orientation towards the external world has undergone a thorough sea-change. In all traditional world-views, the external world, both nature and society, each was considered to be significant in its own right. Both nature and society were supposed to be fully ordered by virtue of their being integral parts of the cosmos, and, therefore, meaningful with their independent existence beyond the whim, caprice and wishes of individual persons. As such, both of them exerted considerable influence on the thought-ways and work-ways of men. They were supposed to be something that cannot be looked at from an instrumental perspective. This conception of the external world was jettisoned fully and completely in the modern times in favour of a view that considered the external world as nothing more than a potential means for the realisation of human purposes. The external world is there simply to be exploited for serving man's ends; it can, therefore, be manipulated and/or transformed so that it can help in the realisation of goals men set out to achieve. It is against this background that we can appreciate the fact that man in the modern times has developed a purely utilitarian outlook on the external world, both nature and society.

Since the concept of utility has become regnant in modern times and since it has pushed aesthetic and/or spiritual stance towards the world, science has been able to push philosophy to the background. As Descartes puts it:

> In thé place of speculative philosophy taught in the schools, we can have a practical philosophy by means of which, knowing the force and the actions of fire, water, air, of the stars, of the heavens, and of all the bodies that

> surround us—knowing them as distinctly as we know the various crafts of the artisans—we may in the same fashion employ them in all the uses for which they are suited, thus rendering ourselves the masters and possessors of nature.[16]

It does not need to be pointed out that this eminently exemplifies a very strong Faustian overtones of conquering and mastering nature not only for creating the most appropriate condition for establishing sustaining and ensuring the good life of modern conception. It is also to fulfil the expectations of a virtuous and a harmonious socio-political life and relations. If truth can be apprehended through the use of scientific method by laying bare the secrets of nature, so can individuals uncover and identify the true patterns of behaviour in society because scientific method can be equally fruitfully used to discern moral facts as well. Man is endowed with the faculty of reasoning and can, employing the scientific method of knowledge construction, effectively bridge the gap between what is and what ought to be. "The revolution of knowledge encompasses knowledge of the 'ought' as well as the 'is'. It would guarantee that men who appropriated the new method would be able to know with unprecedented clarity what they should do as well as what was the case."[17] The light of reason, if appropriately directed, will amply illumine the valley of life enabling men to clearly discern its topography and to steer his way in it by the help of the landmarks of morality. As Locke assured, the candle (of reason) that is set up in us shines bright and is sufficient for obtaining "the conveniences of life and information of virtue."[18]

In addition to the disclosure of virtue to individuals, scientific knowledge would also make public life harmonious. Public life becomes tension-ridden and conflict-prone because opinions tend to overshadow the truth discovered by the use of scientific method. Public life tends to be pervaded by doctrines and ideologies that are narrow, variable and context-bound. They proliferate and self-interest makes it quite difficult to negotiate between them. These doctrines are usually founded upon scientific errors. In the words of Condorcet, "all errors in politics and morals are based on philosophical errors, and these, in turn, are connected with scientific errors."[19] Scientific knowledge would prevent committing these errors. As a result, public life would improve in quality since individuals would, under the influence of knowledge constructed through the use of scientific method, rise above their petty self-interest and work for the good of all. They would fight exploitation, domination and oppression and thereby rid public life of all those factors that tend to create tension and conflict in society. As such, individuals would work for a harmonious and tension-free public life.

Thus, the knowledge derived by the use of scientific method will not only produce all the conveniences of life that are vitally necessary for successfully translating into reality the modern conception of the good life. Also, it would yield truth that makes man free of ignorance and superstition and rid public life of all those factors that cause tension and conflict. Crafted by scientific knowledge, the world of knowledge bearing a new truth will no more create philosophical befuddlement but yield clarity of perception and cognition. It would overcome and defeat the power of prejudice, oppression and tyranny. What must be emphasised here is that if the knowledge yielded by the use of the scientific method of investigation is claimed to free man from his proneness to fall a prey to opinion, superstition and prejudice and, if by gaining this new truth, he becomes capable of throwing aboard arbitrary authority, unreasonable traditions and stultifying orthodoxies, by the same token it paves the way for progressively increasing manipulation/transformation of nature for serving man's ends.

When the end of life comes to be equated with life itself and when it is emphatically stressed that good life must be attained here and now on this earth by man guided solely by the light of reason and experience, "the freeing of men's mind from the bonds of ignorance and superstition, and their bodies from the oppression of the constituted social authorities"[20] becomes the first essential condition. This signifies, among other things, the rejection of tradition as something that limits human freedom and restricts human choice.[21] To get release from the bonds of ignorance and superstition, common men must now become philosophers. But it is not philosophers in the Platonic sense; it is rather in Baconian sense which insists on finding what is truth on the basis of examining empirically and inductively various objects and events that are supposed to be its instances. It is practical philosophy made possible by scientific knowledge that holds the key to good life. " The reason is that common men take up philosophy, if at all, not as an exercise in dialectic but as something that holds for them the assurance of a better way of life."[22] The relevance of practical philosophy is to reveal truth, truth that is uncorrupted by opinion, uncorrupted by prejudice and that holds out the promise of making men free. But it is, as Becker points out, "a special brand of truth, a truth that is on their side, a truth they could make use of in their business,"[23] that is, the business of everyday life.

This is a truth, it must be stressed, that transforms knowledge as wisdom into knowledge as power. It is only knowledge as power that can help men in using, even abusing, the external world, both society and nature, as potential means for the realisation of their self-defined purposes. It is knowledge as power that proves immensely helpful in manipulating/transforming nature so that it can yield its hidden riches for the use of man. We can therefore understand that, when the good life of the modern conception becomes the pivot of human activities, the idea of an ordered and meaningful cosmos must go by default. With it also has been eclipsed the idea of looking beyond this world to a larger world as the source of meaning and value. This has also the consequence of freeing life activities from their tutelage to religious or spiritual considerations. As a result these activities have become completely secular based on the value of utility. And when utility reigns supreme, man becomes afflicted by *hybris*; he does not really need any God to protect and help him. In a sense, he has already replaced God and has taken his place in the universe. In view of all this, it is not surprising that *samskaras* have lost their legitimacy in modern times and have either become rituals torn of their animating energy based on the quest of transcendence or are getting extinct.

It is a well known fact that the *samskaras* have formed an integral part of Indian culture since the inception of the Indian civilisation. They are still practised with zeal and enthusiasm. It is not, however, certain whether they are practised with equal devotion and understanding. It is not also certain whether people who do see the need of performing these *samskaras* have any clear idea as to where they have sprung from, why they are important and what precise role they play in the preservation and sustenance of the cultural ethos that animates and gives a particular shape to Indian civilisation. With a view, therefore, of assessing what *samskaras* are and what role do they play in personal and social life and relations and to throwing ample light on their significance that exploration of these questions becomes absolutely necessary. We propose to do so by focusing on the institution of marriage in Mithila as it functions among three important caste groups, Brahmans (Srotriyas), Bhumihar Brahmans and Rajputs. The marriage *samskara* is embedded in the *Vedic* cosmogony and a substantial part of this *samskara* is inspired by and reflect the *Vedic* cosmogony. However, it has also accumulated a large number of secular and semi religious ideas. As such, marriage *samskara* consists of both *shastra*-stipulated and *laukika* (local) *vyavahara* (practices). Both of these aspects will, while exploring the phenomenon of marriage *samskara*, receive proper attention.

References

1. Hans Jonas, *The Gnostic Religion: The Message of the Alien God and the Beginning of Christianity* (Boston: Beacon Press, 1963), p. 242.
2. *De Natura Deorum*, II.II.II., quoted in Jonas, op. cit., 245.
3. For a fuller discussion of the process of transformation of the absolute into *vishwa*, see Ramashray Roy, *Beyond Ego's Domain: Being and Order in the Veda* (Delhi: Shipra Publications, 2000).
4. Br. U. II.i.20.
5. *Ibid*, II.v.18; YV 31.19; Mund. U. II.1.1. Mund. U. II.1.7 treats the many as the extension of the Supreme Being. What is also interesting to note is that, according to Tait. U. *sa yaschayam purube. Yaschayaditya sa ekah* (He that is here in the human person and He that is is there in the sun, are one).
6. Abhinavagupta, *Tantrasara,* p. 3 quoted in Guiseppi Tucci, *The Theory and the Practice of the Mandala* (London: Reider & co., 1974), p. 12.
7. Tucci, *Ibid*, p. 14.

8. Eric Voegelin, *The New Science of Politics: An Introduction* (Chicago: University of Chicago Press, 1987), p. 54.
9. Heinrich Zimmer, *Philosophies of India*, ed. Joseph Campbell (London: Routledge & Kegan Paul, 1952), p.12.
10. Cicero as quoted in Jonas, op. cit.,. p. 246.
11. Mircea Eliade, *Yoga, Immortality and Freedom,* tr. Willard Trask (Princeton: Princeton University Press, 1969), p. XVI.
12. Zimmer, op. cit, p. 120.
13. Ananda Coomaraswamy, *Hinduism and Buddhism* (Delhi: Munshiram Manoharlal Publisher, 1975), 27.
14. L. A. Sass, "The Self and its Vicissitudes: An Archeological Study of the Psycho-Analytic Avante-garde," *Social Research*, 55 (1988).
15. Philip Rieff, *Freud: The Mind of the Moralist* (New York: Anchor Books, 1961). P.29.
16. Carl L. Becker, *The Heavenly City of the Eighteenth Century Philosophers* (New Haven: Yale University Press, 1952), pp. 27-28.
17. Rene Descartes, *Philosophical Writings*, ed. and tr. Norman Kemp Smith (New York: Modern Library, 1958), pp. 130-31.
18. Thomas H. Spragen, Jr., *The Irony of Liberal Reason* (Chicago: University of Chicago Press, 1981), p. 61.
19. John Locke, *An Essay Concerning Human Understanding*, Introduction, Section 5.
20. M.J. A. N. C. de Condorcet, *Sketch for a Historical Picture of the Progress of Human Mind*, tr. June Barraclough (London: Weidenfeld and Nicolsan, 1955), p.200.
21. Becker, op. cit., pp. 102-103.
22. It is interesting to note here that past with which tradition is inexorably linked loses its traditional meaning. It is usually interpreted in the West either a condition for the appearance of the present or as the womb out of which present comes. In either case, when present makes its appearance, the past loses its significance. So is the case with tradition.
23. Becker, op. cit., p. 59.
24. *Ibid*, p. 42.

2

The Substance of Society

The term social order signifies a particular arrangement of the essential components of a society. It is this arrangement that is symptomatic of the way these different components are inter-linked with each other. It is this inter-linking that is supposed to rid social life and relations of tension, conflict and disorder. The need of order in society will and should not arise if individual persons were naturally endowed with the disposition of pursuing their different life purposes in a way that did not prove detrimental to the pursuit of similar purposes by others in the society. This means that individual persons must somehow be attuned to the needs of others and should not consciously do anything to obstruct and block the fulfilment of the needs of others. Needless to say that this calls for the adoption of the strategy by the individual such that the adopted strategy ensures compatibility between the quest of happiness by one individual with that of the quest of happiness by all individuals.

It does not need to be argued that the necessary condition of compatibility can be satisfied only when the individual has the conscious appreciation of his essential relatedness with other members of society he is a part of. This, in essence, means that the way he opts to go about realising his life purposes affects the possibility of the realisation of life purposes by others and *vice versa.* But this awareness in itself is not a sufficient condition for ensuring compatibility between the quest of happiness by one individual and such a quest by all individuals. What is also necessary is that this awareness must be reflected in translating a project into practice and the process of this translation must be informed, supported and sustained by appropriate cultural ethos. The role of social order thus consists in ensuring this compatibility by promoting and diffusing values, creating institutional arrangement, and evolving practices that are immensely appropriate for and supportive of this.

The question immediately arises: What kind of social order is capable of doing this? This is a question that cannot be answered satisfactorily without looking closely at the form, to be particular, the external form, a particular society assumes and the substance that gives meaning and relevance to that external form. This substance is inexorably linked with the notion of who man is.[1] The question who man is can be interpreted in two different ways, each radically different from the other. One view of man can be interpreted to mean that man is a self-complete entity and, therefore, autonomous in the sense that he alone, independent of the determination of his life purposes by any authority or source external to himself, can and should determine what he wants to be and do for whatever he wants to become. He is, to begin with, a natural man. As a natural man, he has certain desires and appetites; he has certain needs that must be fulfilled in order for him to ensure his survival and, going beyond that, his well being in accordance with a particular vision of what good life means.

Another way of looking at the entity called man is to treat him as something more than a natural man, as something more than a bundle of desires and appetites. He must be viewed as something more than a natural man concerned exclusively with the fulfilment of the needs of his animal existence. Beyond these needs are the needs whose fulfilment enables him to transcend the limitations of his lower nature. This transcendence alone makes him truly human; he can, then, acquire higher range of values and abilities. By acquiring higher range of values, he can become capable of looking beyond the need of fulfilling his own needs and appreciating the need to resolve the possible tension between his own good and the good of others in society.

Given these two rival conceptions of who man is, it is quite likely that only the conception of man as a natural being is accepted as the most appropriate characterisation and, therefore, the only legitimate and viable basis for evolving and organising a society and creating its institutional structure. If this view of man becomes the regnant idea that provides the mainspring of the motivation of creating and sustaining a social order, the rival conception underlining the need of the cultivation and acquisition of higher abilities generally associated with the pursuit of higher life purposes, such as, self-knowledge through self-development, can very easily get side-tracked and may even be finally jettisoned. Needless to say that to recognise as vitally essential the need to acquire higher range of abilities and values in order for man to become man in the real sense of the term, it becomes necessary, first, to acknowledge the reality of the soul and, then, to prevent it from getting polluted by the thick incrustations of pollution generated by the immersion in materiality, in everydayness of fulfilling ordinary life needs.

To allow the soul to become impure and, therefore, make it incapable of resisting the drive of appetites to usurp the power to rule over man is to obey the dictates of passions. To obey the dictates of passions is to engage in actions that are motivated by the needs of his own earthly existence ignoring the claim of his soul. This is also tantamount to ignoring or driving out of consciousness the consideration of the good of others. As a result, the moral sense of man gets beclouded by the fog of cupidity. This, in turn, creates a situation in which compatibility between the efforts to pursue happiness by one individual with that of other individuals receives a setback. The loss of compatibility is symptomatic of the fact that everybody does, in fact, actively seek to acquire and enhance his happiness alone. But while doing so, he does not take into account whether his exclusive concern with his own happiness is good for others or not. He also tends to ignore the question whether it is possible that, in a situation where everyone seeks to acquire and enhance his own happiness when there is an acute scarcity of resources that are unavoidably necessary for acquiring happiness, his own efforts will meet with success. Exclusive concern with one's own happiness breeds intense competition for access to and control over scarce societal resources.

That this happens to be the case can easily be demonstrated. If the existence of the soul is denied and if its suzerainty is overthrown by passions even if its existence is accepted, the idea of happiness degenerates into that of pleasure, in fact, the pleasure of the body. What is distinctive about the pleasure of the body is that it cannot be shared with others, as is the case with, say, a pleasant scene or a beautiful sunrise. Another distinctive thing about it is that only the goods and services that can help in acquiring pleasure can really be shared with others. But the resources that can be transformed into goods and services for meeting the needs generated by the pressure to acquire pleasure always lag behind. This creates a situation of competition, even conflict. It is in this context that we can appreciate the fact that the utilisation of these goods and services depends on the extent to which a person has access to and control over scarce societal resources. This tendency, if it becomes widespread and pervasive, generates competition and often conflict. This, in turn, paves the way for the erosion of social concord, making it possible for violence to be pervasive.

The search for pleasure, it must be emphasised, assumes central importance only when the substantive definition of man rejects the idea of the cosmos. The idea of nature as an ordered entity endowed with intelligence was replaced by the ascendance of what Collingwood calls renaissance cosmology. This cosmology rests on "the denial that world of nature...is an organism and the assertion that it is devoid both of intelligence and life."[2] As such, nature cannot order its own movement in a rational manner; as a matter of fact, it is quite incapable of moving at all. It is true that nature does display regularity of movement and manifests orderliness. But both regularity of movement and orderliness we associate with nature are due not to its intelligence; whatever intelligence it seems to have is external to nature itself. The regularity it exhibits and orderliness it displays have their genesis in "laws of nature" imposed from outside by a *deux ex machina.*

Needless to say that renaissance cosmology projects a mechanistic view of nature. Instead of being seen as an organism, as in the Greek view of nature, or as is the case with the traditional

Indian view, the natural world is supposed, in the renaissance cosmological perspective, to be a machine; that is, it is seen as an arrangement of bodily parts designed and put together and set going for a definite purpose by an intelligent mind outside of itself. Order in this perspective is equated with mechanical intermeshing of various parts of the machine which ... instead of seeing nature as expressing meaningful order, equates order with system without distortion or conflict. As Taylor points out:

> Order is one which has to be explained in terms of interlocking elements whose relation can be explained in terms of efficient causation. The order (as against disorder) in things... consist in their meshing without conflict and distortion.[3]

It is obvious that it is this model of order that finds its fullest expression in the Newtonian view of natural order expressed through the concept of equilibrium. In Newton's view, nature comprises a myriad of autonomous and unconditionally viable forces which are in constant interaction with each other. Equilibrium signifies stability within a system composed of autonomous forces. But this equilibrium, despite its relative durability, is tenuous; it is frequently disturbed "either by an outside force or by a change in one or other elements comprising the system...."[4] However, inherent in nature is the property that restores the old equilibrium or creates a new one. Thus the natural system is self-regulating even though created by intelligence external to it.

It is this conception of order that is projected on to the human world. Individuals in the world are treated as autonomously given entities, self-complete, autonomous and self-defining. What is central to individual life is the search for felicity. It is this search for felicity that generates energy impelling individuals to satisfy their desires as and when they make their irresistible appearance. Impelled by this energy, individuals interact with each other and with the external world, both society and nature, for ensuring their felicity. Hobbes, for example, identifies felicity as the central, if not the exclusive, concern of individuals as natural beings. Felicity consists in satisfying one desire after another for which generation and exercise of power is not only for retaining what one has but also for acquiring and possessing what one thinks is necessary for his felicity becomes *sine qua non*[5]

The search for felicity as the central driving force of individual action assumes importance only when God is banished from his own creation. As a result, the significance of the pursuit of a higher life purpose as a necessary step towards attuning the soul to the divine ground of being, too, comes to be eclipsed and given up. Its place is taken by a secularised, democratic ideal of a moral life which is considered to be possible only as an act of will helped by the process of adjustment to ever-growing complexity of social environment forcing upon man the constant need of adaptation.[6] Through the process of adaptation, man continually transforms himself. The displacement of the pursuit of higher life purpose opens the way for the fulfilment of ordinary life needs involved with the process of production and reproduction and impels men to create appropriate socio-economic conditions that can render this fulfilment possible. These needs pertain to the acquisition of wealth, power and prestige.

It is believed that if everyone is driven by the energy of his desires to seek what he wishes to have, personal as well as collective good will be adequately served. On this view, the one dynamic entity available in society is the self-defining individual who, as the centre of energy, enterprise and creativity, serves to promote collective good by promoting and realising his own self-defined purposes. On this view, collective good is nothing other than the sum-total of individual goods. In this perspective, then, vitality, vigour and dynamism of the social order of which the individual is an integral part depend on the extent to which he performs his role well as an entrepreneur. The extent to which the individual becomes a successful entrepreneur, he contributes to collective good. In performing his role as an entrepreneur, the individual must not encroach upon or become a hindrance to the performance of a similar role by other individuals in society. On this view, man, as Taylor observes, "comes to realise natural order when the company of desiring subjects comes to achieve full satisfaction (happiness), each compatibly with others. This perfect compatibility of desires is the goal which nature and reason prescribe to man."[7]

Needless to say there is a profound similarity between what Edgeworth calls "mechanique celeste" and "mechanique social." If the law of self-interest (generating a psychological energy and motion) rules the moral universe, the law of physical motion rules the physical universe. As he says:

> Mechanique social may one day take her place along with mechanique celeste throned each upon the double-sided height of one maximum principle, the supreme pinnacle, the principle of moral as of physical science. As the movements of each particle, constrained or loose, in a material cosmos are continually subordinated to one maximum sum total of accumulated energy, so the movement of each soul, whether selfishly isolated or linked sympathetically, may continually be realising the maximum energy of pleasure, the Divine Law of the Universe.[8]

Needless to say that this perspective regnant since the enlightenment offers a particular account of human nature according to which "action are the expression of our will caused by desire and according to which the chain of parochial reasoning always terminate in some 'I want' or 'it pleases me."[9] This is indicative of the fact that the individual decision of what desires to satisfy, when and how to satisfy is essentially that of the individual alone. This decision must remain uninfluenced by what tradition, conventions and opinion of influential persons in society may suggest or demand. It is in this sense that the modern identity of man as a self-defining subject assumes significance. Actions that please individuals need not satisfy the condition that they prove compatible with actions that other persons may like to engage into. This is quite likely to incline individuals to sidetrack completely the issue of compatibility. As a consequence of this, social concord will certainly be disturbed. This is all the more likely in view of the fact that since the key to felicity is held by the satisfaction of desires, the only consideration for the individual is how his desires are to be satisfied. This exclusive concern with the satisfaction of his own desires does not induce the individual to take into account whether whatever he wishes to do is harmful for others or not. In such a situation, auto-control is sure to erode leading again to the possibility of the disruption of social concord.

Society, in this perspective, is nothing else than a mechanical aggregate of self-defining subjects; it receives its particular form and distinctive substantive nature from the need to allow private passions to shape and give definite direction to man's life activities. It is the endeavour to satisfy passions that gives the essential shape social order assumes; it is this particular shape that determines the structure of social institutions, practices and processes. Thus the creation of social order, culture and history is the direct consequence of the process of what Giambatista Vico calls "self-making of man." By this is meant the actualisation of potentialities inherent but in a state of slumber in man's breast; it is made possible by his interaction with nature with the help of technology for fulfilling his material needs. It is in this sense that the distinctive features of social order, its form and substance—all these are inspired by man's need for doing everything possible under his power to ensure for himself the good life of modern conception. As such, social institutional arrangement takes its inspiration from the need to help man in satisfying his desires.

It does not need to be argued that such a perspective on society takes into account the external form of social order alone; it does not recognise that society is significant in itself and, therefore, it signifies something more than the mere instrument of man in his endeavour to realise his self-defined purposes. Denying this, it also denies that society is anything more than an arena where individuals engage into the game of pursuing their own private concerns. Undoubtedly, it is conceded that society is composed of a diversity of human nature and is characterised by a plurality of individual purposes. These two factors make society heterogeneous; however, it drains it of its capacity to integrate these diverse elements into a well-knit unity, a complete whole. The integration of these diverse elements is left to the good sense of the individual who, it is believed, usually takes note in his own actions of the need of maintaining compatibility between the pursuit of his own happiness with the pursuit of a similar objective by others. If individuals fail in this, it is further believed that the state will then intervene to maintain compatibility. But, as we have already seen, erosion of auto-control proves inimical to compatibility. Also, state action in regulating the interaction pattern of individuals for maintaining compatibility lacks effectiveness in want of necessary support from individuals.

The perspective on social order ignores the fact that society is not, nor can it be, defined solely by its external aspect or dimension, that is, institutional arrangement no matter how unique it is in social practices and processes. These are only the formal aspects of society. Society has yet another aspect or dimension; this aspect or dimension pertains to its internal substance that shapes society's external form and gives it meaning. It is this internal substance or aspect or dimension that alone makes it a valued and meaningful entity, that is, a cosmion. It is as a cosmion that society constitutes an arena where human consciousness, intentions and purposes receive definite shapes and direction. As a cosmion, the true significance of society cannot be confined to all that is given to our perception. What is given to our perception is only the external, visible or easily discernible aspect or dimension, *i.e.* its institutional arrangement. Society has an internal, not easily discernible aspect or dimension, that makes it a meaningful entity. It is the internal aspect or dimension that, when embodied in what Heraclitus calls *xynon* (shareable commonality) or what Gobind Chandra Pande calls *samana-chittata* (likemindedness), endows its members with an overpowering sense of belongingness even while they exhibit a large degree of biological, psychological and sociological diversity.

It is only when man becomes imbued with the sense of belongingness, that is, when he is imbued with the sense that he is a member of a larger entity meaning society that his finite existence gets linked with an entity larger and more durable than his own existence. It is this linkage that endows his life with meaning, value and truth. What this internal substance is can be made explicit only when we project anthropological perspective on man and his world. This anthropological perspective signifies, to paraphrase Plato, that society is man writ large. This refers to two different but organically linked dimensions of man's being pertaining to his existence in this world. First, it refers to the tripartite division of his being. These three divisions are *adhibhautika* (biological), *adhyatmika* (psychological) and *adhidaivika* (spiritual) aspects of his existence. This tripartite division points to the fact that, even though man is a biologically, psychologically and sociologically conditioned entity, he is not totally bound by these determinations. His ultimate nature is not that of a closed being; as a matter of fact, he is endowed with the capacity to transcend the givens of society and nature. To transcend these givens is to look beyond the phenomenal world, that is, to a larger order which, when man is consciously attuned to it, can give a semblance of meaning to his finite existence. The triple dimensions of human existence thus lend man a dual character. If he is immersed in materiality and conditioned by biological, psychological and sociological factors, he is also capable of breaking free of the limits imposed on him by nature and can, if he is so inclined, explore the depths of his spiritual being and shape his spiritual destiny.

The dual nature of man underlines the fact that man has both material and non-material needs. The social order inspired by the ideal of satisfying material human desires does not take note of man's non-material needs. As such, such a social order takes into account of only a part of man's being and elevates this part into a whole, a whole that turns the individual, as Jacques Maritain puts it, into a demi-god and the need to fulfil his needs constitutes the foundation of the social order. In order, therefore, to apprehend the reality of social order it is necessary to focus on the totality of man's being as the proper concern of the social order.

The totality of man's being is defined both by his material and non-material needs. But what these needs are and what can be the appropriate means of fulfilling these needs cannot be determined apart from resolving the question of who man is. Without the proper idea of who man is, an idea that takes note of both material and non-material needs of man and their inter-relationship, we can have no frame of reference for the designation of human phenomenon as relevant or irrelevant insofar as the determination of the form and the substance of society is concerned. To talk of the dual nature of man is to point to the need to rise above the givens of both society and nature and seek to link man's finite existence with the absolute as the source of meaning and value. It is this linkage that, on the one hand, conjoins the external aspect or dimension of man's existence, the dimension that has mainly to do with actions aimed at fulfilling material needs, with man's interior and, on the other, establishes a particular relationship between the vital forces in his interior with his perceptible external activities.

Without taking these aspects or dimensions of man's existence into account, man can have only what Aristotle calls "*apaulistic* life." It is a life that destroys the uniqueness and preciousness of man that he can attain only when he explores the depth of his spiritual nature or what Jacques Maritain calls "the metaphysical centre." That is why the traditional view of man treats man as an ethico-religious entity; it underlines the fact that man has the capacity of overcoming his limitations as a conditioned being and of realising the possibilities that can get actualised only when he explores the depth of his spiritual nature buried deep in the crevices of his being and veiled by his immersion in everydayness. It is only the exploration of his spiritual nature that enables man to transcend the contingent experiences of his narrowly conceived and confined existence. Thus the outstanding mark of man, as traditional world-views conceive of it, is "the superiority of the possibilities over the actuality of his being," to use Heschel's felicitous phrase.[10] It is in this context that man is understood, in the classical perspective, as a complex of opportunities and a bundle of facts."[11]

This complex of opportunities and a bundle of facts is what makes man the resident of two realms. One of these realms is the one that is defined by his being a biologically, psychologically and sociologically determined entity. The other realm is defined by the opportunities that beckon him to break out of his determination by natural and social forces and explore new avenues and acquire new experiences made possible by the opening up of the spiritual frontier of his existence. This becomes possible only when man recognises the importance of the spiritual dimension of his being. To recognise the spiritual dimension is to be cognisant of the fact that man essentially belongs to a larger order and that the meaning of this awareness becomes explicit and assumes transformative power only when man attunes his soul to the divine ground of being.

The larger order is defined, in Indian traditional thinking, by the idea of *sapta loka* (seven worlds) hierarchically ordered. At its apex is the creator himself. The idea of *sapta loka* thus signifies a hierarchical cosmos with layers of graded worlds one within the other with all of them forming one and a unique cosmos. As Needleman puts it, "...man stands before a universe which extends him in quality as well as quantity. The spheres which encompass the earth... represent levels of conscious energy and purpose which "surround" the earth much as the psychological function of an organ such as the heart "surrounds" or permeates each of the separate tissues which compose it....."[12]

The network of purposes or purposeful energies constitute a concentric circle, each circle of which happens to be the locus and repository of energy or possibilities which are compatibly inter-related and which, taken together, constitute a state pregnant with the possibility of transiting from one stage to another which is different but organically linked with the preceding stage. Each of these centres is the locus of a particular state or outcome which, in turn, is the outcome of certain antecedent forces occupying a particular circle. Even while the forces occupying a particular circle have been engendered by certain antecedent forces, they are uniquely constituted and have a particular role to play which uniquely belongs to itself.[13] Despite this, the forces occupying different circles are organically interconnected and functionally inter-related and integrated. These circles or spheres or *lokas* do not refer to actual spatial locations or description of the cosmos; they are meant to be understood symbolically. To put it again in Needleman's words:

> ...the word "sphere," used in describing the forces and purposes at different levels, is never meant merely to be taken literally. The very idea of circularity of movement in "the heavens" can be understood to mean not only the encompassing nature of these progressively higher influences, but their eternal nature. The circle is, among many things, a symbol of that which "eternally recurs," that which is not subject to time and change as we know them.[14]

It is quite clear, then, that the *sapta loka* contains forces that not only provide the elements out of which man's being is carved out and created. They also remain active in influencing man's thought-ways and work-ways. Needless to say that these forces appear in the process of the absolute undergoing the process of transforming itself into *vishwa*, that is, the cosmos. It is in this context that we can appreciate the question the *Vedic* seer-poet, Dirghatamas, asks: "What is that one alone, the unborn one, who has upheld the six spheres or *rajamsis* or *lokas?*"[15] Needless to say that this unborn one is none else than *Swayambhu* (the self-born), *satyasya satyam* (truth of truths) as *Br. Up. II.i.20* puts it. It is true that man can and often does consciously or unconsciously disown his linkage to and membership in this larger cosmic order. But, then, he becomes the slave of his lower nature forfeiting, perhaps forever, his right to be called a man in the real sense of the term. He then lets slip all the opportunities that are or can be available to him for attaining his higher nature and higher abilities that he can claim to be his own; he is reduced merely to a bundle of facts.

But when man does recognise the need to cultivate his higher nature, he acquires, in addition to his external aspect or dimension, an inner substance. He is, then, sustained in his actions aimed at fulfilling his material needs, also by an internal aspect or dimension to his existence. This internal aspect or dimension requires that man remains "awake" to his essential relatedness with the ground of being, the prime source of spiritual consciousness. To remain awake requires self-effort which wilts and withers away in the lack of certain important conditions. These conditions are: (a) a paradigm of social order engendered and articulated as a consequence of a primordial insight into the structure of order; (b) a social order along with its institutional arrangement derived from and based on this primordial insight into the structure of order; and (c) practices and procedures of performing religious as well as secular life activities in conformity with fundamental tenets of the primordial insight. It is the sum-total of all these components that constitutes a social order.

The primordial insight into the structure of order is not available to all and sundry. It is an insight that comes as a flash of eternity to a few chosen philosophers, saints, mystics and *kavirmaneeshis* as a result of their spiritual explorations and meditations. It is this insight that constitutes a paradigm for deriving the organisational, structural and other related principles for creating a social order. What is distinctive about such a social order is that it is grounded in and reflects the fundamental properties of the primordial insight. The fact, however, remains that the primordial insight that is gained by spiritual explorations provides only a vague, indistinct and the barest outline of the social order based on this insight. But, then, it is elaborated in certain definite constitutive principles and finds its detailed, if not the fullest, articulation and expression in social institutional arrangement, and is reflected, to a very large extent, in individual and social thought-ways and work-ways. It is this primordial insight that, when articulated through institutions, social practices and processes that are treated as legitimate and proper for guiding and regulating individual lives and social relations, constitutes the ground of what Heraclitus calls *xynon* (shareable commonality) or what Pande calls *saman-chittata* (like-mindedness).

It is this *saman-chittata* that undergirds and joins together the thought-ways and work-ways of the members of a particular society. Both together form the ground of the self-identity of the members of that society anchored firmly in self-knowledge inspired by the primordial insight into the structure of order. Self-identity of the members of the society thus straddles over two distinct but inter-related dimensions of human existence. If one of these dimensions pertains to the constitutive principle of the social order, the principle embedded in the primordial insight and the fountainhead of the structure of the self-identity of individual members of society, the other dimension refers to the external, easily identifiable aspect of the social order exemplified by its institutions, practices and work processes. It is the combination of these dimensions–one beyond the domain of the eye and the other perceptible and visible, that is, the external—that determines the nature of human consciousness. It is this combination, again, that becomes the basis for formulating and embracing a two-tier view of man's life-purposes incorporating, on the one hand, the pursuit of higher life-purpose and, on the other, the fulfilment of ordinary life needs.

The recognition and adoption of a two-tier view of life-purposes does not by any means signify that these two life purposes are of equal significance or occupy the same rank of importance. All societies that are informed by the importance of pursuing these two life purposes also order or grade them in importance. There is an implicit ordering of these purposes in a hierarchical fashion such that the fulfilment of ordinary life needs is subjugated to the need of pursuing higher life purpose. As a matter of fact, a life not given to the pursuit of a higher life purpose, be it self-knowledge or better citizenship, is considered to be devoid of any value and meaning and, therefore, like a desert.

It is in this sense that, as Pande observes, knowledge about man cannot be adequate and real if man is treated as an object. In other words, knowledge of man cannot be limited to that of objects and object-relations. In addition to this, there is also the phenomenon of man's consciousness of and linkage with the spiritual world.[17] It is for this reason that human consciousness exhibits a dual character. If, on the one hand, his consciousness is linked with and directed towards the invisibly existent source of truth, meaning and value, it is, on the other hand, involved with and focused on objects and object-relations in the external world whose significance lies in their instrumentality for and usefulness in fulfilling man's ordinary life needs. This does not, however, mean that this duality of human consciousness implies any opposition between the internal and external aspects or dimensions of his social existence and therefore his consciousness. This is so for the simple reason that invisibly existent ends impregnate, underlie and animate human actions men engage into for managing their pragmatic affairs.

It is against this background that we can appreciate the fact that the proper understanding of what society substantively means cannot be obtained just by focusing our attention on its external aspect or dimension. The external aspect or dimension refers simply to the institutional arrangement of society, its practices and procedures of action. All these are the direct products of human action which takes a concrete shape in the emerging relationship between ends and means. Thus, human action is meaningful action directed towards the attainment of certain goals. These goals arise from the inherent needs of man whose realisation must compete with other goals. Given the plurality of goals human beings must seek to realise them in order to ensure their well being, the question as to how to justify the selection of particular goals as against certain others or fix their hierarchical ordering assumes crucial importance. Social situations that give rise to needs are not unchanging; nor are they an end in themselves. The condition of social life strives beyond itself because it is in need of completion with reference to something higher than itself. It demands justification of its factuality which can be provided by spiritually and philosophically sound principle of order alone. This is necessary because human action is always an unfolding of power ranging from psychological persuasion to sanction by force.[18]

The use of naked power is likely to disturb social concord since it is usually used to influence the will of and dominate others. As such, power and its use must be justified in terms of certain higher principles—principles that protect and preserve the integrity and the wholeness of man, on the one hand, and safeguards social concord, on the other. This is possible if human action in the social world is inspired and informed by spiritual truth, embracing which the individual can order his own soul that has become as a consequence of the diseased by the rebellion of appetites and desires. When human existence is inspired and informed by spiritual truth, society becomes something more than the mechanical aggregate of self-defining subjects. It becomes, as Immanuel Kant notes, a society of ends, that is, it is the social order that predefines what goals individual persons must pursue and the means for the realisation of predefined goals they must choose.

A society of ends cannot be fully and properly understood if we treat society only as an association whose sole purpose is to provide and make available to its members perceptible but material means for realising perceptible ends. On the contrary, society must be treated as something that, as Pande notes, conjoins visible means and higher ends, ends that have their origin in the spiritual aspect or dimension of man's existence. It is only on this basis that the relationship in any society between science and knowledge, craft and art, politics and morality, economic organisation of society and detachment and disciplined life is shaped and established. The particular character this relationship assumes determines the distinctive form of different societies. [19]

It is obvious, then, that it is this relationship defined and determined by the spiritual dimension of man's existence that establishes an intimate and dynamic pattern of interaction between the external form and internal substance of a social order. What is also obvious is that this relationship has, at its roots, the transcendental source of order which provides the paradigm of social order; as a copy of this paradigm the social order becomes the replica of the larger order exemplified by the term cosmos. It is this transcendental source of order articulated through and made explicit by the insight of seers, philosophers and mystics that represents the self-interpretation of society. It is this self-interpretation that shapes the society's institutional structure. This self-interpretation is articulated with the help of symbols that give concrete expression to the ineffable experience of the divine source of order. It is as the result of the " interpretations of institutions and experiences of order that a society's form is unique and authoritative articulation of the truth of being."[20] This articulation through a constellation of symbols, myths, rites etc. constitutes a society's self-interpretation of truth and order. It is this self-interpretation is that literally constitutes a society and orders it in a distinctive way.

As such, it is the symbolic form of existence that creates a society. In the course of being preserved and reaffirmed through ritual observances, the symbolic form sustains the society by harmoniously securing the attunement of its members to the divine ground of being. This is through this means that a society attains and retains its identity in the flux of history. A society's civilisational form is, therefore, "its mode and allotted measure of participation in the world-historic process of experience and symbolisation of order that extends indefinitely into the future."[21] It is in this sense that society's civilisational form has historical singularity that can never be absorbed by phenomenal regularities, because the form itself is an act in the drama of human beings striving towards the truth of being.

This makes it quite clear that the form and substance of society cannot be fully understood if we focus our attention only on the external aspect or dimension of society. It is true that the external aspect or dimension is most visible and, therefore, easily discernible and apprehensible. However, what needs to be stressed in this connection is the fact that a particular form of society assumes the characteristics that it does because it is rooted in and arise from the society's self-interpretation of its linkage with the sub-stratum of reality. This self-interpretation forms the fountainhead of the concrete expression of this linkage in a particular pattern of order. It is this pattern of order that undergirds, informs and is reflected in social institutional arrangement and practices. All these—that is, the primordial insight into the structure of order, its expression in social institutional arrangement and practices governed by and reflecting the principles of order yielded by the primordial insight of those who are called, in the *Vedic* parlance, *sura-chakshush* (sun-eyed)—constitute, sustain and reinforce *saman-chittata,* that is, the fundamental consensus that ensure and safeguards the viability and vitality of the social order.

In this perspective, social order signifies the coupling of the finite and the absolute, or the infinite and the celebration of this coupling in various facets of the social order. As an instance of the coupling of the finite and the infinite, the social order performs a shelter function. It is a function with the help of which man attempts to give to his life a semblance of meaning.[22] Such a social order is capable of reaching the emotional and spiritual centre of man's existence and makes it possible for its members to outlive their fragmentary personal lives by a projection into the life of a larger community. As such, the social order provides a structure of meaning into which the single human being can fit the results of the biologically and spiritually productive, (procreative) energies of his personal life, thereby (relieving) his life from (disordering) aspects of existence that always spring up when the possibilities of life ending in annihilation is envisaged.[23]

The shelter function of the social order aims primarily at impregnating man's world with meaning so that man succeeds in transcending his own finitude, on the one hand, and acquires, by being attuned to higher realities, sufficient strength and courage to resist and overcome temptations that threaten to disturb order in his interior and make him the slave of many mad masters, that is, his numerous desires. More important in this regard is the fact that it provides the opportunity to man to attain *sarvata* (wholeness) by blocking the advance of what the Veda calls *nirriti*, that is, inner disintegration because of the immersion into materiality. It is this coupling of the finite and the infinite that assumes a concrete expression in the social order and is reflected in the elaborate symbolisms, communicating the fundamental consensus of the society and shaping the fabric of its institutional life and personal and public lives of its people. It forms the belief structure which is the distinctive foundation of association in society; and it also shapes the essential humanity of the individual members of a society by supplying meaning in their existence as participants in a reality which they experience as transcending merely private existence.

What is distinctive about the social order is that, while immersion into materiality is considered to be inimical to the pursuit of higher life purposes, the fulfilment of ordinary life needs is not considered undesirable as long as it is only supposed to be infra-structural to the pursuit of higher life purposes. Such a society, thus, permits both the fulfilment of ordinary life needs and the pursuit of higher life purposes. The former pertains to the satisfaction of desires and the mobilisation of requisite resources necessary for satisfying myriad desires, while the latter is concerned primarily with regulating and controlling the satisfaction of desires in such a way that it does not allow *pleonexia,*[24] one the one hand, and ensures social concord, on the other. If the ends-means relationship involved with the life of enjoyment sustained by the satisfaction of desires can be called *artha-Tantra* (*oikonomia,* economic life and relations) and the set of principles that regulate the management of pragmatic affairs of life related with the fulfilment of ordinary life needs must be characterised as *dharma-Tantra* (the rule of righteousness).[25] The subjugation of the conduct of pragmatic affairs of life (*artha*) to *dharma* is what provides the constitutive principle of social order.

In disciplining and controlling human behaviour, *dharma* conjoins two realms of human existence, the realm and that of freedom. It is the sense of freedom induced by accepting the rule of *dharma* that enables man to escape the tentacles of the realm of necessity. As such, the social order manifests itself in two layers. One of these layers, the external layer, is constituted by a net-work of rules and procedures of performing actions. It is this layer that comprises the organisation of interests, principles of justice, and considerations of morality. The other, the internal layer, is symptomatic of self-knowledge and ideals and spiritual explorations intrinsically related with self-knowledge. It is the intermingling of and dynamic interaction between these two layers that shapes and informs social consciousness. As Pande notes:

> Social consciousness can be distinguished by the fact that it regulates, as a partially manifest order of things, understanding, *samskaras,* memories and beliefs of its individual members in a relatively longer temporal framework.

> In this sense, society can be understood as the deeply embedded soul of all individual members (as reflected in the sub-stratum of their life and life activities); it is because of this that society is capable of making and sustaining the awareness of its members of their identity, ideals, rights and duties and provides them with the opportunity (and the means) of living their lives and engaging in action in ways sanctioned by it. Every individual finds himself related with a tradition of knowledge and understanding as well as a network of relationships that are larger than their finite existence. If this tradition of knowledge and understanding can be characterised as culture, then, the network of relationships can be called society. Man, as a being who is endowed with consciousness, is, in this sense, a resident of a socio-cultural cosmos that has an external form and internal consciousness.[26]

What this perspective on society underlines sharply is the fact that, externally, society is truly a network of relationships that gets established in the process of living in a community of human beings. But these relationships evolve and receive definite institutional shape in the process of articulating and institutionalising internal meaning structure which becomes explicit in different life activities. It is the articulation of this meaning structure and institutionalisation that constitute and form tradition. It is, again, this meaning structure that gets transmitted and renewed through the continuance of tradition. And tradition, in turn, gets expressed, preserved and extended through the performance of rites and rituals which form a body of *samskaras.* It is in this sense that *samskaras* are instrumental in reminding the people in a particular social order of their essential relatedness with the world beyond, the world of the infinite. Thus the performance of *samskaras* enables man not to live but to lead his life according to certain higher principles. It is, again, the commitment to and performance of *samskaras* that provides the fulcrum, a reliable and sustaining foundation, to the primordial quatenarian community between God and man and world and society.

References

1. This does not mean that the question "what man is," is an illegitimate question. As a matter of fact, for the last three hundred years at least, it is this question that has received the utmost attention and has been installed upon the highest pedestal. This is reflected in the fact that political and philosophical thinking, the creation of socio-political order, etc. all these have taken their inspiration from discussion about the essential nature of man. But in all these discussions, there has been emphasis not on "who man is," but on "what man is." To ask "what man is" is substantively a scientific question; what becomes necessary in this connection is the assumption of a scientific attitude in determining the essential nature of man. Such an attitude must rely on description for understanding what man is. But, as Heschel persuasively points out, definition of man cannot be scientific; it can only be creative and transformative because man has the capacity to become what he imagines himself to be. As he puts it, "the truth of theory about man is either creative or irrelevant, but never...descriptive. A theory of man enters his consciousness and modifies his very existence. The image of man affects the nature of man." *Who is Man?* (Stanford: Stanford University Press, 1965), p. 8.
2. R. C. Collingwood, *The Idea of Nature* (London: Oxford University Press, 1976), p. 5.
3. Charles Taylor, *Hegel and Modern Society* (Cambridge: Cambridge University Press, 1970), p. 75. Cf. David Hume in *Dialogues Concerning Natural Religion:*
4. Look around the world. Contemplate the whole and every part of it. You will find it to be nothing but one great machine, subdivided into an infinite number of lesser machines which again admit of subdivisions to a degree beyond human senses and faculties can trace and explain. All these various machines and even their most minute parts, are adjusted to each other with an accuracy which ravishes into admiration all men who have ever contemplated them. The curious adoption of means to ends through out all nature, resembles exactly, though it much exceeds, the production of human intelligence.
5. Hans Morgenthau, *Politics Among Nations: The Struggle for Power and Peace* (New York: Alfred A. Knopf, 1964), 3rd ed., p. 168.
6. Thomas Hobbes, *Leviathan* (New York: Dutton, 1952), p. 79.
7. Se Maurice Mandelbaum, *History, Man and Reason: A Study of Nineteenth Century Thought* (Baltimore: The John Hopkins University Press, 1971), p. 142.
8. Charles Taylor, op. cit. Also see Elie Halevy, *The Growth of Philosophic Radicalism* (London: Faber & Faber, 1972), p. 15.
9. Francis Edgeworth, *Mathematical Physics,* 1881, quoted in George J. Stigler, "Economics or Ethics," in Sterling McMurrin, ed. *He Tanner Lectures in Human Values, II* (Salt Lake City: The University of Utah Press, 1981), p. 168.
10. Alisdair McIntyre, *Whose Justice? Which Rationalituy?* (London: Gerald Duckworth & Co. Ltd., 1988), p. 21.
11. Abraham J. Heschel, *Who is Man?* (Stanford: Stanford University Press, 1965), p. 40.

12. Loc. Cit.
13. Jacob Needleman, *A Sense of the Cosmos: The Encounter of Modern Science and Ancient Truth* (Garden City, New York: Doubleday & Co., Inc., 1975), p. 17.
14. On this point, see Madhusudan Ojha, *Vijnana Vidyut* (Jaipur: Rajasthan Patrika Pvt. Ltd., 1990), p. 24.
15. Needleman, op. cit., p. 18.
16. *Rigveda I.164.6.*
17. Gobinda Chandra Pande, *Bharatiya Samaj: Tattwika Aur Aitihasik Vivechana* (New Delhi: National Publishing House, 1994), p.14.
18. *Ibid.*, p.10.
19. What needs to be emphasised in this connection is the fact that the term "power" signifies in modern times the Weberian meaning of it. According to Weber, power (*macht*) signifies the bending of the will of others to one's own. That is, it is the opportunity of asserting one's will, the necessity of justifying the subjugation or elimination of another will.
20. Pande, op. cit., pp. 13-14.
21. Eric Voegelin, *Order and History: Israel and Revolution* (Baton Rouge: Louisiana University Press, 1957), I, p. 60.
22. *Ibid.*, p. 13.
23. Eric Voegelin, *History of Political Ideas: Hellenism, Rome and Early Christianity* (Columbia: University of Missouri Press, 1997), I. p. 225.
24. *Ibid.*, p. 226.
25. Elis Sandoz, *The Vogelinian Revolution: A Biographical Introduction* (Baton Rouge: Louisiana University Press, 1981), p. 116.
26. Aristotle defines *pleonexia* in terms of (a) self-aggrandisement, that is, the inclination to acquire more than one deserves or one's merit allows one to have, and (b) the inclination to tolerate injustice voluntarily. See his *Nichomachean Ethics*
27. Pande, op. cit., p. 37.
28. *Ibid.*, p. 12.

3

Society and Samskara

"Every nation which has reached a certain stage of development," writes Jaeger, "is instinctively impelled to practice education. Education is the process by which a community preserves and transmits its physical and intellectual character. For the individual passes away, but the type remains."[1] As we have already pointed out, the management of the pragmatic affairs of life does begin with the individual. However, it soon takes upon a group character. Even the fulfilment of ordinary life needs of even the solitary individual, that, too, in a very rudimentary and inelegant style, assumes a larger trans-individual significance. As already pointed out, this larger trans-individual significance assumes two substantive dimensions, that is, temporal and spatial.

The temporal dimension to the individual need for provisioning develops as a result of the transmutation of the concern for the self, that is, "I" into the concern of the progeny, that is, "mine." The other dimension, that is, the spatial dimension, is added to the individual existence by the extension of the self into a family and eventually into a society. It is this extension that establishes a very important relationship between the individual and society whose distinctive character can be safeguarded and preserved if individuals are cognisant of and are committed to the continuity of the form and substance of the society they are members of. This is possible only when individual members are attuned, first, to the inescapability of the dependence of the individual on a group of which he is an integral part of for sustenance and support for living his life well and, then, to the need of preserving the essential characteristics of the group of men he belongs to as a necessary condition of a meaningful existence. To live well and to live meaningfully are two different things; however, they are neither antagonistic nor incompatible.

As we have already seen, there are two different purposes of life underlining two different but necessary aspects or dimensions of human existence. One of these pertains to the fulfilment of ordinary life needs, the sustenance and care of the body. The other has to do with the need of the soul. The former requires the fulfilment of such ordinary life needs that are involved with the process of production and reproduction, needs that can be fulfilled only by acquiring, gaining access to and control over such societal resources as wealth, power and prestige. The fulfilment of these needs becomes instrumental in ensuring what Thomas Hobbes calls felicity. The search for felicity forces man to interact with the external world, both society and nature on a continuous basis, use them as potential means for the fulfilment of his diverse needs, if he is to ensure the fulfilment of his ordinary life needs. In the process, man is compelled to externalise himself as the only way possible for him to ensure his material needs, needs that define his essence and whose fulfilment is considered to define his essential humanity. It is also quite likely that the more man externalises himself, the more he becomes forgetful of or gets alienated from the divine ground of reality; it is also likely that he even becomes disdainful of the needs of the soul.

The exclusive concern with the fulfilment of ordinary life needs is, however, likely to produce three very profoundly debilitating ill consequences. In the first place, the exclusive concern with the fulfilment of ordinary life needs signifies the utmost importance of the quest for pleasure. What is distinctive about this quest is that, as an object of the highly subjective experience of the individual, it cannot be shared with others as is the case with, say, the enjoyment of the setting of the sun or a vastly beautiful natural scene. What can, however, be shared are the resources that are vitally necessary for fulfilling these needs. In the second place, these resources are scarce, not only in the sense of their availability but also in the sense of their exhaustibility. As a result of these two limitations, there naturally ensues a stiff competition for access to and control over these scarce societal resources. This competition gets all the more accentuated when the pleasure of the body is supposed to be, as is the case with modern times, the vehicle of individual and social development, social concord and harmony, and civilisational progress. As a result, self-interest pushes the consideration of the good of others out of man's active concern. And, lastly, to be concerned primarily, even if not exclusively, with the pursuit of one's own interest is the sure indicator of the loss of auto-control and, therefore, of morality signifying the onset of disorder not only in man's interior but also in the external world, particularly society.

It is against this background that we can appreciate the need to turn to the soul and be attentive to its call. It is true that to turn to the soul makes it necessary for the individual to attune himself to the world beyond this visible world in order to regain autarchy (in the Socratic sense) or become *swarat* (in the sense *Chhandogya Upanishad* uses this term) by virtue of this attunement. It is true that the experience of the world beyond is also very subjective. However, the distinctive characteristic of this experience is, to begin with, self-transcendence as a consequence of this experience. The experience of self-transcendence engenders an orientation that inclines the individual to take into account the well being of others in ensuring his own. It is self-transcendence in this sense of the term that constitutes the foundation of culture and morality. Culture in this regard assumes entirely a different and ennobling significance than its modern, anthropological understanding.

The word "culture" has, Jaeger notes, "sunk to mean a simple anthropological concept, not a concept of value, a consciously pursued ideal."[2] Needless to say that the simple anthropological concept of culture is modern, as is evident from the writings of Tyler, and is inexorably linked with the modern concept of man. According to this concept, man is primarily, even exclusively, concerned with the fulfilment of ordinary life needs. This makes it necessary to develop an economic system that must do everything possible to satisfy the ever-proliferating needs of man. In order to satisfy these needs, it is unavoidably necessary to initiate the process of technologically induced and sustained economic growth adequate to fulfil the ever-proliferating needs of man. It is as the result of this production system that the material and non-material aspects of human existence take on distinctive characteristics. The material aspect, characterised as civilisation, signifies the ever-rising level of living standards and rising affluence. This generates the belief in open-ended growth and the idea of progress denoting the ever-escalating level of human achievements, capabilities, and accomplishments.

In contradistinction to this, there is the non-material aspect, symbolised as culture, which refers to the creation of social institutions, laws, religion, etc. What is interesting to note here is that all these are created in the process of the fulfilment of ordinary life needs of man and are, therefore, concomitantly and causally related to different stages of technologically induced and sustained economic growth. It is in this sense that the fundamental attributes of culture are governed by the changing characteristics of the economy. It is also in this sense that culture has become dependent on the changing nature of economy and has, as a consequence, lost its educative, prescriptive and evaluative authority and has emerged as something whose usefulness lies in providing entertainment. This sense of culture is diametrically opposed to traditional understanding of it which identifies it with something that plays an important educative role. This educative role consists in providing guidelines about what is proper to do in a particular context of action. It is in this sense that culture has frequently been identified with education, as Jaeger points out.

It is also apparent from the discussion above that culture in the traditional sense is considered to be educative insofar as it functions to make man attune himself to something larger than his own finite existence and its pragmatic concerns. To be attuned to something larger and be attentive to its claims is to promote self-transcendence as the basis of social life and relations. It is also clear that self-transcendence as well as the elevation and ennobling of social life and relations is not possible as long as man remains immersed in everydayness and prefers the pleasure of the body against the bliss of the soul. It is, therefore, necessary not to reject the pleasure of the body but to submit its quest to the stricter control of certain higher values. These values are not objects that can be grasped and possessed just by extending one's hand to grab it before it slips out of reach. They have to be cultivated by training the soul by attuning it to the ground of being so that it can develop or regain, if it has been lost, the capacity to rule over passions.

It is this attuning of the soul to the divine ground of being that enters into the definition of who man is and, through it, makes a decisive impact on the essential form and substance of society. It is also because of this that man becomes a resident of two realms, one defined by his location in the factual order, the world of here and now, and his responsibilities flowing from his residence in the phenomenal world. The other realm is defined by his relationship with the world beyond the visible world that is necessarily shrouded in mystery because of its nature as something that cannot be perceived; it can only be "seen" through the "heart's eye." While the former constitutes the external part of man's existence, the latter is internal. It is these two dimensions—internal and external—of man's existence that define the totality of human being and are reflected in the form and substance of society. Thus, society, too, exhibits two dimensions, one external defined by the network of relationships that come into existence as a result of man's endeavours to fulfil his ordinary life needs and the other internal symbolising values that lift man up from his immersion in animal nature and endow his life with meaning.

It is this internal aspect that, as we have already seen, signifies culture and prescribes the ways in which responsibilities pertaining to the external dimension of man's existence and their character are determined by the soul's attunement to the Unknown which cannot be either perceived or cognised; it can only be experienced by rare souls who set upon this quest. The origin of *darshana* symbolises a particular way of apprehending the Unknown which, when elaborated, defines the nature of culture and becomes the basis of creating institutional and other structure that undergird it. As such, culture plays the important role of making men conscious of their essential relatedness with their fellow-beings as a result of the conscious acceptance of the influence of the Unknown on the way they must lead their life. But this consciousness needs to be kept alive by means of educating members of the society about what action is proper in personal and social life and relations.

It is in this sense that the traditional significance of culture is quite different from the modern understanding of it. It is in this sense that Jaeger uses the term culture. Culture, according to him, is practised by every nation that has reached a certain level of development with a view to preserving and transmitting its physical and intellectual character.[3] This is necessary to ensure the continuance of the human race. But even while the human race is marked by certain typical attributes unique to itself, this type is differentiated by so many factors. One of the most important of these factors is, of course, culture which makes every society distinctive because the constitutive principle of each culture type is different. The preservation of the type or the human race means, in effect, the preservation of the type differentiated by culture.

The preservation of the type, even when differentiated by cultural factors, means, first, the perpetuation of physical characteristics of the human race. This, however, also applies to animals. But since man is different from animals because of his intellectual and spiritual endowments, the preservation of the type also means the transmission of intellectual and spiritual properties that distinguish one culture from another. The transmission of intellectual and spiritual properties is not, however, something that is random and ad hoc. It cannot be transmitted through what is today known as formal education because it does not cater to the needs of anything other than brain and brawn. It helps man to fully exploit brain and brawn power with a view to creating and sustaining those conditions that conduce to the realisation the good life of modern conception. Even informal education is no different from formal education except in terms of coverage and depth. Moreover, none of these categories of education creates the situation in which "men can transmit their social and intellectual nature only by exercising the qualities through which they created it—reason and conscious will."[4]

A little thinking is enough to suggest that the word reason is quite ambiguous since it straddles over three different senses in which the term is used. It is used, in the first place, to refer to a process of discursive reasoning in which legitimate conclusions are arrived at following a particular procedure of making inferences from a given premise. It is also used, in the second place, in the sense of instrumental reasoning that analyses the comparative costs and benefits of pursuing alternative means of attaining a particular goal. This calculative reasoning only projects an instrumental perspective on the external world. Obviously, then, these two senses of reason is only of limited value in transmitting the social and intellectual nature of man. This is so for the simple reason that rationality in both these senses does not recognise any authority outside itself in performing whatever task it is assigned. It is because of this that they can serve any purpose whether good or bad, virtuous or sinful since both types of rationality are value-neutral.

It is, therefore, necessary to make a distinction, as the Greeks do, between *phronesis* (calculative reasoning) and *Sophia* (*prajnana*). This distinction is necessary insofar as *phronesis* cannot judge a particular end as right or wrong; it treats ends as already given and is, therefore, concerned with determining the means that are least costly and maximally beneficial for realising a particular end.

In concrete social situations pursuing a particular end in a particular manner may affect the well being of others. It, therefore, becomes necessary to submit ends themselves to certain evaluative standards on the basis of which the propriety or impropriety of a particular end can be determined. But what should be these standards? It is quite usual to judge an act or thought as right or wrong, as sinful or virtuous, with reference to a universal idea of proper and improper. This, however, proves unhelpful since contextual variations of action call for making exceptions with a view to safeguarding the possibilities inherent in a particular situational context as well as the integrity of the persons who are likely to be affected by a particular action.

In view of this consideration, it is necessary to relate the idea of propriety of action to two different referents: the well being—material, moral, etc.—of the individual and that of the community the individual is an integral part of. But the idea of propriety itself has to be grounded in something that authenticates, justifies, validates and legitimises it. And since the domain defined by the management of man's pragmatic affairs is diverse and not infrequently heterogeneous, the application of the idea of propriety in concrete action situations must also be determined by situational imperatives. This requires discriminating judgement because a willing acceptance and self-imposed universal principle of action, even if such a standard is necessary, is not helpful in deciding what kind of action is proper so that both the spirit of the standard pertinent for adjudging any action virtuous or sinful and the situational imperative remain inviolate.[5] Seen from this perspective,[6] it is quite clear that no universal statement of what is right and what is wrong can reliably yield the discriminating judgement that can discern what ought to be done in a particular situation.[7] What is essential is discriminating mind sharp enough to discern and strong enough to act. It is necessary to train the mind in such a way that it can cut through the dense fog of contrary opinions, conventions, outlooks, etc. and see the light of wisdom (*prajnana* or *sophia*) which illumines action choices—choices that safeguards the well being of both the individual and the community. In the third place, therefore, it is the knowledge that helps in reconciling the claims of the private and the public. This knowledge is *prajnana.*

Needless to say that it is this knowledge—the knowledge that helps man to steer the ship of his life through the seething and surging sea of the attractions and snares of the phenomenal world—that is helpful in organising and successfully managing the pragmatic affairs of life. The act of managing the pragmatic affairs of life takes place in a situation where other individuals are also engaged in doing the same. Needless to say that pragmatic affairs of man has a double orientation. If, on the one hand, they are rooted in and are shaped by the pressure of fulfilling different life needs, their fulfilment is linked with and dependent upon the fulfilment of the life needs of others in the society, on the other. It is these double referents of the need fulfilment of the individual,—uniqueness and reciprocity, its compatibility with the well being of others, that is, that constitute the warf and woof of the external aspect of the social order, an aspect acquiring a particular structure as a result of the manner in which individuals go about managing their own separate pragmatic affairs. And since the process of the need fulfilment by different individuals is related to and inexorably involved with each other, the question of what needs the individual ought to fulfil and how to go about fulfilling them cannot be left to individuals to decide. The reason for this is very simple. Man *qua* natural man tends to give the utmost priority to his own need fulfilment without taking into account whether or not the action he contemplates to take with a view to realising a particular purpose would be harmful to others.

It is, therefore, necessary to move away from the individual as the source of such decisions to some principle or authority that is trans-individual and, therefore, capable of providing the proper standards for judging the merit of both the purpose the individual plans to realise and the action he contemplates for realising that purpose. It is only on this basis that the individual can rise above the petty concerns of his limited existence. And as long as the individual remains fully committed to the need to pursue his own good without any consideration of the good of all, the claims of the private and the public aspects or dimensions of man's existence will work at cross-purposes. As a consequence of it, neither the individual existence nor social life and relations can attain that degree of orderliness and normalcy which is absolutely necessary for well calibrated social order. As such, a complete fit between the need to ensure the good of the individual and the desirability of safeguarding the integrity, viability and vitality of the social order becomes pressing.

This is possible, as already indicated, only when a trans-individual standard of judging which needs must be fulfilled and in what ways they ought to be fulfilled is evolved or deduced from the primordial insight into the structure of order. Obviously, such a standard cannot be derived from needs themselves because, in the absence of a criterion situated outside them, every need claims to be the most important and, therefore, worthy of receiving the utmost attention and priority. Instrumental, calculative reasoning, too, cannot provide a reliable criterion since it does not enjoy the authority of judging the propriety of needs and declaring which of them should or should not be taken seriously. Instrumental, calculative reasoning can only suggest the costs and benefits of pursuing alternative means of realising different purposes. It is, therefore necessary to go beyond instrumental, calculative reasoning for determining what needs are legitimate and what actions must be taken to attain a particular legitimate goal. In view of this, the determination of the criterion for judging the merits of both the purpose and the action for realising that purpose must be anchored in something that makes it possible not only to reconcile the claims of the private and the public dimensions of the individual existence but also to link them together in a mutually supportive and reciprocally beneficial and harmonious relationship.

Compatibility between what is good for one individual and what is good for all individuals is possible only when a person is either capable of rising above the contingent experience of his limited existence and relate himself to a reality larger than his own limited existence by his effort or acquires an orientation in a social setting where he trains and disciplines his thinking and action that keeps him attuned to the larger reality. Needless to say that no amount of information about himself or about the world he is located in is helpful to a person for acquiring or training and disciplining his orientation in a way that helps him in refraining from upsetting the delicate balance that a social order seeks to maintain with the help of a particular institutional arrangement and a pattern of everyday practices. For this, training of mind, formal education as we know it today, is of no help since it aims at preparing man for using his brawn and/or brain power skilfully and effectively for participating in the creation or sharing in the good life of modern conception. Formal education or education in formally organised institutions of learning does not in any sense help individuals in acquiring and acting according to certain higher values.

The training of mind in such a way that keeps the individual keyed up to the requirements of a pattern of life most propitious for maintaining the delicate balance between the good of one individual and the good of all individuals needs entirely a different kind of education. This type of education must be able to meet the special conditions most appropriate for the maintenance and transmission of those values that must be embraced and acted upon by the members of society for ensuring the continued vitality of the internal mainspring of the social order. Needless to say that the meeting of these conditions requires man to be exposed to forces that impose on man a special set of formative processes—physical, mental and spiritual—that can be characterised as education.[8] Education in this sense implies the formation of man in a way that makes him receptive to a particular mode of thinking and acting, closing his mind to certain other ways. This further means that the education most suitable for this kind of formation of man is inevitably and necessarily such that it serves two essential functions. It is true that the form of education is inspired by the creative and directive force that impels every natural species to maintain and preserve its own type. However, it also aims additionally at raising it "to a far higher power by the deliberate effort of human knowledge and will to attain a known end."[9]

It is this known end that distinguishes one society from another insofar as every society defines this end in its own way. Even while this end may be the same for all societies, the mode of realising this end differs from one society to the other. But common to all societies that seek to fashion their institutional arrangement and practices in the light of certain transcendental values must devise and develop a system of education that helps their members to learn and internalise those values that give them a distinctive character. This means that the significance of social order lies in its ability and effectiveness in moulding the expectations and behaviour patterns of its members in such a way that help realise the values underlying it. This further means that the creation of a social order signifies, at one and the same time, the wholesale "murder" of incompatible possibilities in the character of man. Also, what additionally it implies is that the community of men constituting a particular social order must make it difficult for conflicting and antagonistic values to exist and produce disturbing effects. What must also be added here is the fact that the suppression of incompatible possibilities and conflicting values is justified because it allows man to grow in stature towards the rank of the best. A social order that aims at allowing, or to be more precise, insisting on making man grow in stature towards the rank of the best, performs the function of what Voegelin calls a "shelter" with the help of which man can attempt to give his life a semblance of meaning.[10] Such a social order is capable of reaching the emotional and spiritual centre of man's existence and of making it possible for its members to outlive their fragmentary personal lives since it is projected into the life of a larger community. As such, the social order has the responsibility of providing this shelter function.

But the possibility of life annihilation does not refer to physical annihilation. In the *Vedic* perspective, what is perceived to be most threatening is not the loneliness of man in the vastness of a universe supposed to be nothing else than "a realm of merely contingent correlations utterly devoid of human meaning and subject only to purely causal laws and modes of explanations."[12] For the *Vedic Rishis*, the universe is well ordered and structured: it is governed by *Rita*. If there is anything that terrorises "the *Vedic* seer-poets, it is *Nirriti*, inner disintegration, the falling apart that destroys the domain of possibility itself ... It is *abhvam,* the black abyss of darkness ... It is *ambas,* the sense of being hemmed in and trapped, constriction, the anguish of space closing in."[13] The feeling of constriction, of inner disintegration overtakes man when his connection with the source of divine light is cut off and his soul gets diseased as a consequence. This connection can be re-established if man conforms to *rita*. It is only then, the *Vedic* perspective insists, man can terminate his disjunction from the divine light and allow his inner world to be illumined. It is only when the inner world of man is illumined by divine light that he can specify the pattern of his relationship with a well ordered and structured world, as an aspect of his mode of being, his being-in-the-world, as an unified play of *Prithivi, Dyau, Amartyas* and *Martyas*. It is a mode of being in which, to quote Mehta again,

> Man dwells on earth in his home, under the heavens, in friendly commerce with the gods, with his fellowmen and with things. Keenly and intensely aware of his finitude, man is always the moral (*martah*), exigent, desirous of earthly goods, needing help in the conduct of his life, unable to see clearly through the perils of living, to know the truth of what is within him or of things beyond.[14]

Thus, for the *Vedic* seer-poets, it is as a result of conformity to *Rita* that man can hitch the wagon of his finite and fragmentary existence with the Absolute as the source of truth, value and meaning. It is in this sense that the social order inspired in its constitution by the interpretation of this coupling that performs the shelter function. The main purpose of this shelter function is to impregnate man's world with meaning and values so that man can transcend his finitude, on the one hand, and acquire, by being attuned to higher realities, sufficient strength and courage to resist and overcome temptations that threaten to disturb order in his interior and thus make a willing servant of his lower nature. This shelter function can play its proper role only when a system of education is devised to deliberately mould man's character in accordance with an ideal. And the ideal of man that the *Vedic* seer-poets conceived and upheld was the protection and preservation of the essential characteristics of the quatenarian primordial community of man and God and society and world.

The import of this primordial community points to the acceptance of the world of everydayness not as illusory but as something real. As such, its claims on man must be recognised and given effect to. But this recognition does not by any means signify either the autonomy of the phenomenal world or immersion in materiality, that is, in the concerns of everyday life. It rather signifies the conduct of pragmatic affairs of life in the light of values derived from linkage of the finite with the absolute. To put it differently, the subordination of the concerns of this world, to the need to keep this linkage alive and active is the core of the *Vedic* world-view. Such a subordination signifies the pursuit of *kama* and *artha* under the harsh discipline of *dharma*. It does not, however, mean that the *Vedic* perspective on man and his world rejects fully the idea of man *qua* natural man. Similarly, it recognises that even though man is a member of a social group, he also possesses an independent personality. However, over all these stands man who is, or can be, fully aware of and committed to the need of attuning his soul to the divine ground of being and organising and managing the pragmatic affairs of his life in accordance with the requirements of keeping this attunement alive and vital. It is this ideal that inspires, animates and sustains Hindu culture and provides the basis for formulating and organising education as the prime means of forming man in the light of the ideal referred to above.

Education in this sense is the surrogate of culture since it aims at shaping man in accordance with the ideal dear to the *Vedic* seer-poets. As a formative process, its central objective is to train man's mind in a way that he becomes receptive to the ideal of man the *Vedic* perspective espouses and projects as something that is beneficial and ennobling; this receptivity inclines him to engage in activities that are necessary for realising this ideal in life. And since it requires the deliberate pursuit of an ideal, education as a formative process touches upon each and every aspect of man's residence in the phenomenal world. From this point of view, each and every act that man embarks upon is seen as an integral part of a whole defined as the spiritual destiny of man in the world of here and now, a world that tends to lead him astray from the path of virtue. It is this whole that links every isolated act with each other and with itself and holds everything together in an organically linked system. Culture as an expression of this organic whole and articulation of thought-ways and work-ways grounded in this whole, represents the entire complex of all the ways and expressions of life in a particular society. By virtue of this, education, too, reflects the essential attributes of culture it is inspired and is charged with the responsibility of safe-guarding its continuity amidst the flux of change.[15]

Insofar as the *Vedic* world-view is concerned, it treats the world as the emanation of the Absolute. As *Yajurveda* 31.19 puts it, "In the womb (of every being) moves Prajapati; he, never being born, is born in sundry figures. The wise discern the womb from which he springeth. In him alone stand all existing creatures." It is, then, clear that, unlike the Platonic universe, the universe of the *Vedic* conception is not something that is separate and separated from its Creator. As *Isopanishad* underlines, the universe is the abode of the God and is, therefore, not only well-ordered but also sacred. To put it differently, the visible world or the *idam sarvam* is the result of the One or the Absolute undergoing the process of becoming many. The One becomes many through the process of *yajna*, that is, the transformative process in which the One, the Unchanging, or Being enters the stream of change and assumes numerous *nama* (name) and *rupa* (form. As such, the transformation of Being into Becoming, a process in which Idea becomes embodied (or *enhylon eidos* as Plato calls it) or the process in which *asat* transforms itself into *sat*,[16] is characterised in *Rigveda I.164.35* as *bhuvansya nabhih* (*cf. Yajurveda 23.62* and *Atharveveda IX.1.14*), *omphalos of the world.*

Since the universe is the act of creation, the process of *yajna* goes on forever unceasingly. As Agrawala notes, *yajna* signifies a creative act at all levels; on the biological plane, it is the creation of new life in matter that is *yajna*, a union of *Agni* and *Soma*; whenever there is such a creative process, there is the centre of universe, the meaning being that the entire mystery or the potentiality of the cosmic process becomes inherent in the centre of that *yajna.*[17]

The created world is the *vivarta*, the manifestation of Brahma or Prajapati.[18] To quote Agrawala again:

> The created worlds stand for the *mahima* of *Prajapati* or of the *Devas*, *i.e.* the divine powers inherent in creation, and that also is *yajna,* but the real *yajna* is the controlling centre or the Navel of Immortality whose force is inexhaustible in time and space. Thus we witness in the cosmic process a two-fold *yajna*, the one that is archetypal and divine and the other which descends to the plane of Matter. Such is the primeval plan according to which cosmic creation has been ordained....[19]

Before his manifestation as *idam sarvam* (this all or, as Aristotle puts it, *tode ti*), the Absolute was *apraketa* (without any visible sign), only a potency, protean, full of infinite possibilities of names and forms. These possibilities are actualised through *yajna* and the actualised possibilities represent the *vishwa*, the *idam sarvam.* The transformation of the One does not, as already indicated, mean either that the God is partitioned in order to become many or the *vishwa* has become something else than its maker.[20] As a matter of fact, the relationship between the One and the many is understood in the *Vedic* perspective as not One or many but as one and many.[21] But even while the One becomes many, the *idam sarvam* remains one with its maker (*vishwam ekam, Rigveda III.54.8*) and, therefore, it is true (*vishwam satyam, Rigveda, II.24.12*). In order to emphasise the identity between the created world and its creator, it is made explicit in *Rigveda VIII.41.6* that the One is that in which all created beings (which can be likened to the felly of a wheel) are concentrated in Him, who is the navel of the wheel. Similarly, *Rigveda X.82.6* speaks of the gods who are deposited on the navel of the unborn in which all beings abide.

In this *yajna* the Unborn One is transformed into many, threads of life are spun, the cloth of existence is woven and spread all over *idam sarvam.* Spreading out the sacrifice (*yajna*), (the gods) follow the illuminator of the world (the sun); protect the luminous paths (of the gods) constructed by sacred acts (*tantum tanvo rajaso bhanumanvihi jyotishmutah pantho raksha dhiya kritan, Rigveda X.53.6*). This *yajna* is coeval with *vishwa* and is extended all around and never ceases. One hundred and one gods have worked to extend this *yajna* and Pitris weave it, weaving forward, weaving backward (*RV X.130.1*). This *yajna* is the vehicle through which the God creates beings and makes them his abode (cf. *AV XI.8.13*). It is, therefore, not surprising that the *Vedic* perspective considers man to be modelled upon Prajapati himself (*purusho vai Prajapainedishtam*). Since Prajapati is the model of man, he is endowed with essential powers in order to make him as close to the original model as possible.[22] Given the homology between man and his creator, it follows that, as long as this identity is not total, the human person will not be perfect.

Lacking perfection, he will also lack harmony within his interior and with the world outside.

It is true that man is the spark of the divine. However, what is also distinctive about man is his bivalent nature underlining the fact that man combines in him both *martya* and *amartya* (*durita yo bhudumrito martyeshu, Amaveda 1515*). In him live two *atmans* (souls), *jivatma* and *paramatma,* referred to respectively in *Rigveda I.164.20* as *bhoktri suparna* and *sakshi suparna,* that is, the enjoyer and the silent witness. Of the two residents in human body (*Brahmapura* as *Chhandogya Upanishad* calls it) representing two different aspects of human existence, *martya* and *amartya,* mortal and immortal, *paramatma* is the elder and *atma* is the younger *sakha* (friend). Even though the elder stays with the younger (*asti jyayana kaniyasa upae, RV VII.86.6*), the younger does not often acknowledge the presence of the elder. As a result of this, the soul forfeits its right and authority of driving the horses (that is, senses) of the chariot of the body.[23] This authority is usurped by the senses themselves. However, the trouble with them is that they can only look outside and see only the things that are outside and not the divine being who is within (*paranchi khani vyatriswayambhoo-stasmatparangapashyati nanantaram, Kath. Up. II.i.1*).

When the senses look out, they see a multitude of objects and get entrapped in them. And since they become attached to these objects, they become immersed in materiality. And, as a consequence, the indwelling *atman* also gets immersed in materiality. Being immersed in materiality, "as it does and acts, it becomes; by doing good, it becomes good, and by doing evil, it becomes evil; it becomes virtuous through good acts and vicious through evil acts" (*Yathakari yathachari tatha bhavati; sadhukari sadhurbhavati papkary ppapi bhavati; punya punyena karmanabhvati, papah papena*).[24] Driven by the willful horses of the senses, the maker of the chariot, that is, the indwelling *amartya,* gets caught up in the snare of pleasure and pain. "Verily, the embodied self is held by pleasure and pain. Surely, there is no cessation of pleasure and pain of one who is embodied" (*vai sasharirah priyapriyabhyam na vai sasharrasya priyayorapatih, Chh. Up8.12.1*). Caught up in the web of pleasure and pain, the embodied self tends to become *kamachara* (one who is moved in his actions by his desires) and turns out to be *arthasamgrahi* (one who goes on accumulating the means of satisfying desires, that is, wealth). And God does not become the friend of those who become acquisitive and possessive (*naki revantam sakhyaya vindase*), because "those who are puffed with wine" offend him (*piyante te surashah, Rv VIII.21.24*).[25]

This is symptomatic of the fact that a *kamachari* sinks to the level of the natural man and, therefore, cannot seek to cultivate higher values in life. He becomes, in effect, spiritually blind.[26] That is why he cannot make a distinction between the Sun that everyone sees and the Sun which not all know with the mind (*pashyanti sarve chakshusha na sarve manasa vida, AVX.8.14*). In order to acquire higher range of values that give life its meaning, it is necessary to see the Sun, the other Sun than the one we customarily behold with our physical eyes. To see the Sun that can be seen only through the eye of the mind is to develop the power to discriminate between what is right and what is wrong and what is good for one individual and what is good for all individuals. Obviously, no universal statement of what is wrong and what is right can generate the discriminating power to discern what ought to be done in different contexts of action. What is needed is the discriminating mind sharp enough to discern and strong enough to act. This makes it necessary to train man's attitude in a way that he can cut through the dense fog of contrary opinions, conventions, outlooks, etc. and see the light of wisdom (*prajnana*) which alone can illumine action choices.

This is what *samskriti* (culture) does; it trains man in proper action in different contexts and keeps him on the proper course of right action by exercising its prescriptive and evaluative authority on him. But culture is not a set of fixed rules or procedures which can be reliably followed by a person to safely cross over the perilous sea of life. As already indicated, its proper function is to train the mind or keep it attuned to certain higher values in such a way that individuals are always conscious of the need, on the one hand, of serving their own good compatibly with the good of all and, on the other, ensuring the flow of uninterrupted commerce between the mortals and the immortals. What needs to be emphasised in this connection is that it is the uninterrupted flow of commerce between mortals and immortals that provides the firm, reliable and salubrious basis for compatibility between the good of one individual and the good of all individuals. And the friendship between the mortals and the immortals can be sustained only by the performance of certain rituals aimed at making everything sacred.

To keep the bond of friendship between the mortals and the immortals intact and uninjured is the central concern of Hindu culture.

> Let the threads that bind us to divinity not be broken, let the sacred threads by which we weave the coloured web of our song remain intact. May we not loose the track of the paths that run between the gods and men, nor fail in our contractual hospitality to the immortal that has come as a guest in the mortal's house.

This thought is scattered all over in the *Rigveda,* the *arche* text of the Hindus. It is this bond that, again, constitutes the foundation of Hindu culture. Being true to this sacred bond and all the norms of proper action constitutes the common sacred measure and guiding principle for man's relationship with the gods, to nature, to other men and to oneself. As Mehta puts it:

> The breaking of these bonds is a lie; keeping and cherishing it is truth, integrity, loyalty, fidelity, faith, truing and troth. Truth is the origin and source, the *arche* and ruling principle, of all bonds, of all *religio* and sacrality. The immortals born of truth, 'are truth' and provide the measure of truth to man, according to the *Vedic* conceptions, and the mortal estate, taken by itself, is one of untruth; only participation in a sacred order, *religio*, and through that in the Great Truth, enables man to be led from darkness to light, from untruth to truth.[27]

And, of course, it is through participation in the sacred order, that is, religion, that man is led to a life, that is, from the death of the spirit to its regeneration as a source of happiness, *sukha,* in the true *Vedic* sense of the term. It is, again, this participation that keeps the channel of communication open between the mortal and the immortal, the message of invocation to be carried above to the gods and paths to be built for the divinities to reach man's dwelling and, more importantly, his *manas,* that is poorly translated as mind. And this participation is made possible through basically two sacred paths—one of them is *yajna* and the other generically labeled as *samskara. Yajna,* as already pointed out, is *bhunasya nabhih;* that is, a process through which the One becomes many characterised as *idam sarvam,* the abode of the gods. It is in the process of the One becoming many that a complete homology is established between man and the God, the universe and society. Given this homology, it is necessary to support and sustain the process of *yajna* by constituting a social order patterned on the principle of *yajna* itself. This condition is sought to be met by organising the social order on the basis of *varnashrama* system. However, the *varnashrama vyavastha* is a necessary but not a sufficient condition.

What is also additionally necessary is to continue the process of *yajna* at the level of individual members of society. By this it is meant the performance of certain rites and rituals as a part of life cycle. But the mere performance of rites and rituals is not what the *Vedic* world-view insists upon. There is, in the *Vedic* thinking, a clear distinction between the mere performance of *yajna* and *yajna* as a means of inner spiritual transformation or, at least, the living awareness of the spiritual dimension of man's existence. For example, *RV VII.70.3* underlines the fact that none attains Him (Indra) by works or sacrifice.[28] As such, what is important in the *Vedic* perspective is not what is enacted outwardly, but what is accomplished inwardly by the understanding sacrificer.

The emphasis in the Veda is on *adhyatmika antaram agnihotra* (the inner *yajna*). In this *yajna* no external *havya* (offering) is used insofar as *vihavya* (without any external oblation) *yajna* is superior (*astinu tasmadogiyo yad vihavyenegire, AV VII.5.4*). In this *antaram agnihotra,* the sacrificer, *RVV.46.1* declares, yokes himself like an understanding horse (*swayam ayuji hayo na vidwana; cf. GeetaIV.27*).

And when the sacrificer engages in *antaram agnihotra*, he becomes the ladle for the gods (*ayam yaschamaso devepanah*) who drinking from it, revel (*tasmin deva amrita madayantam, AVXVIII.3.53*).

It is in this context that the distinction the *Shatapatha Brahman* makes between *satisad* and *satrasada* assumes importance. While *satisada* signifies a sacrifcer who is seated in the *yajna* in reality, that is, he performs the *yajna*, by supporting it with his mind (*manasa adhavayati, SB*11.2.4.8), and he is seated, in essence, among the gods (*satisu devatasa sidantah*), the latter, that is, the *satrasada*, refers to a sacrificer who just sits at the sacrificial session without yokig his mind to the *yupa*, that is, divine. The *satisad* himself is transformed into a *yajna;* he offers oblation only as a symbol of himself becoming the oblation (cf. *RVX.124.6*; *SB12. 5.2.13*; *ABII.4*; *Br.Up.VI.ii.14*). In contradistinction to the *satisada,* the *satrsada* goes on performing *yajna* offering not himself as oblation, as the sacrificial beast, but external oblation to please gods to acquire sons, riches, prowess, etc. This brings into play another distinction, that between *atmayaji* and *devayaji,* the former referring to the sacrificer who performs *yajna* to transform himself and the latter only brings tributes to the gods (*SB11.2.6.13-14*).

Needless to say that, in the *Vedic* perspective, to become an *atmayaji* is the essence of *yajna.* Without this *antaram agnihotra,* without offering oneself as the sacrificial beast, self-transformation on the basis of self-knowledge is not possible. However, the external aspect of the *yajna*, that is, different rites, rituals and works that comprise the externality of *antaram agnihotra*, are necessary for many since, on the one hand, the path of self-transformation on the basis of self-knowledge (*jnana prasadena, Mund. Up. III.i.8*) is out of the question and, on the other, it is only through the external works that the internal attunement to the larger reality is possible for many. The performance of *yajna,* even by those who are nothing else but *devayaji*, signifies the recognition and acceptance of the important place of the shining ones, that is, the gods in man's existence and the offering of oblation to these gods is the conscious acknowledgement of their existence and the need to make obeisance to them, if for nothing else, then, at least for expressing in concrete terms the realisation that man's existence is finite and, therefore, incomplete. Its completion requires the help and grace of the shining ones.

It is to make this realisation an integral part of man's normal life that it is necessary to cleanse, through the performance of certain *samskaras,* the mind of its pollution that immersion in materiality causes. The performance of these *samskaras* is an integral part of *yajna*; these *samakaras* are instrumental in attuning the individual to the higher reality and, through it, making him attentive to his worldly and other responsibilities and obligations. These *samskaras*, as we shall see later, cover different stages of the life cycle of the individual and instill in him the need to make sacred all the important events and happenings in his life. But, more importantly, *samskaras* also open the way to the realisation that while man is located in a world characterised by diversity, what is most important for him is to reach out to unity. "For each individual human being, what is given to begin with in his experience is multiplicity, the darkness of error, from where he can take off as a task to be accomplished, and the very purpose of living, and reach out to unity, to more light, to truth."[30] *Samskaras* are the vehicle of this reaching out to unity.

Seen in this light, *samskaras* constitute an integral part of education as a formative process, a process that helps man to acquire higher range of values when he links his finite existence to the absolute. They form a part of a living culture. As such, education as a formative process is not a process that concerns the individual alone; it is essentially the function that concerns the whole community. But the character of the community is expressed through its individual members who realise in their lives the essential attributes of culture and thereby sustain not only the culture itself but also the essential characteristics of the community they are a part of. For man as an ethico-religious entity, social order as a cosmion is the source of man's attitude and behaviour, both secular and sacred. The formative influence of the community on its members is constantly active in its deliberative endeavour to educate each new generation of individuals for making them in its own image. *Samskaras* are the components which enliven this educative process.

References

1. Werner Jaeger, *Paideia: The Ideals of Greek Culture*, trans. Gilbert Highet (Oxford: Oxford University Press, 1965), Vol. 1, p.xiii.
2. *Ibid.*, p. xvii. It is interesting to note that Jaeger identifies the idea of culture with the Greeks. As he notes,

   We are accustomed to use the word culture, not to describe the idea which only the Hellenocentric world possesses, in a much more trivial and general sense, to denote something inherent in every nation of the world, even the most primitive. We use it for the entire complex of all the ways and expressions of life which characterise any one nation. Loc. Cit.

   He further notes that "in this vague analogical sense it is permissible to talk of Chinese, Indian, Babylonian, Jewish or Egyptian culture, although none of these nations has a word or an ideal which corresponds to real culture." Loc. Cit. It must be emphasised here that it is as far removed from reality as it is an example of ethnocentrism that attribute everything—culture, philosophy, history, and what not to the ancient Greece. This Hellenocentric perspective has blinded many a perceptive student of philosophy, culture, etc. to the real merit of the nations that scholars adjudge to be bereft of the virtue they attribute to Greece.
3. Jaeger, op. cit. p. xiii.
4. Loc. Cit.
5. Cf. *Kathopanishad* I.ii.10.
6. Max Weber identifies three principal modes of evaluating any action: traditional reasoning, sensible reasoning, and rational reasoning. He gives the impression that these are three distinct, easily separable and need-to-be-separated action choices. However, a moment's consideration is enough to suggest that they are aspects of one rational deliberation.
7. For a discussion on this point, see Ramashray Roy, *Samudayikata ka Adhar* (Delhi:Vani Prakashan, 1994).
8. This is precisely the definition of education (*paideia*) that Jaeger offers. See op. cit. p.xii.
9. *Ibid.*, p.
10. This is the characterisation that Voegelin ascribes to political order. See his *History of Political Ideas: Hellenism, Rome and Early Christianity* (Columbia: University of Missouri Press, 1997), vol. I, p. 225. But it applies with greater force to social order.
11. *Ibid.*, p. 226.
12. L. A. Sass, "The Self and its Vicissitudes: An Archaeological Study of the Psychoanalytic Avant-garde," *Social Research,* 5 (1998), p. 558.
13. J. L. Mehta, *Philosophy and Religion: Essays in Interpretation* (New Delhi: Indian Council of Philosophical Research, 1990), p. 279.

14. *Ibid.*
15. Jaeger claims erroneously that the Greeks created culture in the sense of the pursuit of a known end. The *Vedic* perspective, too, uses the term "culture" in the same sense.
16. For a fuller discussion on this point, see Ramashray Roy, *Beyond Ego's Domain: Being and Order on the Veda* (Delhi: Shipra Paublications, 1999), chaps. 3-6.
17. Vasusdeva Sharan Agrawala, *The Thousand Syllabled Speech:Being a Study in Cosmic Symbolism in its Vedic Version* (Benares: The Author, Vedaranyaka Ashrama, 1963), p. 126.
18. As *Yajurveda* 31.2 underlines, *Purusha e vedam sarva yadbhutam yaccha bhavyam,* that is, *Purusha* is, in truth, this all, what hath been and what yet shall be.
19. Agrawala, *Vedic Lectures* (Benares: Benares Hindu University Press, 1967), p. 148.
20. Plato uses the term "*gignomenon*" to denote the process of becoming. But this process for Plato is symptomatic of the otherness of the created world. This separation between the Absolute and the created world is sought to be mitigated by introducing the concept of imitation and participation. In the *Vedic* cosmogony, the created world is not, strictly speaking, *gignomenon*; it is one with the One as well as something else underlining the process of individuation.
21. In answering the question whether *Mrityu* (Death) is one or many, it is said, "Both one and many, for inasmuch as he is that (man in the sun) in the yonder world, he is one: and inasmuch as he is numerously distributed here on earth among beings, there are also many of them." *SB 10.5.2.16.* Needless to say that this equally applies to the creator.
22. According to *Aitereya Upanishad* I.i and I.ii.1-4, the absolute Self created this world including the gods who demanded an abode, staying where they could eat food. A cow was brought but was rejected as inadequate. A horse was, then, brought, but it, too, was rejected. Finally a man was brought. The gods said, " This one is well-formed; man indeed is the creation of God Himself." Then different gods entered their respective abodes in the body of man.
23. *Kathopanishad* I.iii.3.
24. *Brihadaranyak Upanishad* IV.iv.5.
25. *Cf. Kathopanuishad* I.ii.6
26. Ananda Coomaraswamy, "Windows of the Soul" in *What is Civilisation?* (Delhi: Oxford University Press, 1989), p. 53.
27. Mehta, op. cit. p. 115.
28. For a very fruitful discussion on this, see Coomaraswamy, "Atma-yajna: Self-sacrifice," in *Selected Papers,* II, p. 108.
29. Cf. *Jaimjiniya Upanishad Brahman* I.xiv.1: "He should not be one whose gods are far away. Verily, it is insofar as he approaches the gods with himself (*atmana devat upasate*) that gods become for him;" and Br. Up. I. iv.10: "So whoever approaches a deity as being other, thinking ' He is one, and I another,' does not comprehend, he is a mere victim of them."
30. Mehta, op. cit, p. 280.

4

The Significance of Samskaras

The significance of culture lies in the fact that it helps man to commit himself to a vision of life according to which he can regulate and discipline his pattern of living with a view to realising the vision of good life he embraces. As we have already pointed out, culture is the trait not of individuals as separate, separated, and autonomous members of a human group. It is a group property. But groups differ from one another in terms of world-view, orientation, structure, and processes. The most crucial factor in differentiating one human group from another is the world-view. And world-views do not grow on the tree of whims and caprices, fashions or arbitrary preferences of individuals, nor it is a conscious group decision. They grow out of primordial insight of saints, mystics, and philosophers, and *kavirmanishis* into the structure of order.

Needless to say that the term "order" has different and sometimes polar connotations. The one connotation of the term "order," most strikingly the characteristic feature of traditional societies, underlines its distinction from other conceptions because of its rootedness in the concept of a higher order, an order that derives its essential characteristics from being linked with a transcendental source. According to the perspective contained in this conception of order, the idea of order posits the existence of a super-sensuous transcendental entity which becomes the source of the *idam sarvam* either through imitation, as is the case with Plato who spins the "likely story" of creation in his *Timeaus* or through transformation or *vivarta* as recounted in the *bhavavrttam* or the *Vedic srishtividya.* This transcendental source itself is the exemplar of order. It, therefore, offers the best paradigm for order that comes into being as a result of the Absolute entering or assuming the transformative mode. And since the Absolute itself is the paradigm of the world he creates, the world also displays perfect order as exemplified by the term *Rita.* That is why the world created through the transformation of the Absolute, is called cosmos.[1]

The meaning of the term "cosmos" as an ordered world is well illustrated by the term "the great chain of being" which has a two-fold significance. It signifies that it is not simply an organic whole, it is also a network of relationships that relates each unit, each entity of the whole with others in a reciprocal bond of interdependence, cooperation and harmony. Organically organised societies are by necessity hierarchical and draw their legitimacy from the old conception of cosmic *logos.* Different groups are seen as expressing complementary principle; different classes and functions correspond to different links in the great chain of being. Each is necessary for the other and the whole is necessary for the links in the great chain of being, and the place of each relative to the place of others is thus natural, right and according to the order of things.

In contradistinction to the organic conception of order, there is the mechanical conception which is completely at variance with the former in one very important sense. While the former recognises the existence of a world-transcendent divine entity, the latter does not recognise any such authority and projects a mechanical perspective on the world. Inspired by the mechanical analogy of the world as a clockwork entity, the world, too, is seen as a great machine with innumerable parts which mesh with each other without any conflict or distortion.[2] Needless to say that the mechanical conception of the world rejects the soul as the sensorium of the divine and, therefore, with it, also the relevance of the pursuit of any higher life purpose. With it, felicity in the sense of satisfying one desire after another in a ceaseless fashion, assumes a central importance in the life of man. The mechanical conception of order projects compatibility between the search for felicity of one individual and the search of felicity by all individuals, it has of necessity to rely on the idea of the meshing of different components constituting the whole without disorder or distortion. This is necessary because the pursuit of felicity, that constitutes a purely individualistic goal, boils substantively down to competition and, not infrequently, conflict, for access to and control over scarce societal resources. But compatibility between the search for felicity by one individual and that by all individuals proves elusive. It has, therefore, to be shored up by instituting certain external controls that are supposed to moderate the virulence of individual tendency towards self-aggrandisement. The chief among these controls is, of course, the state. But, for many reasons we do not have to go into, here in greater details, these controls, however, do not work effectively or even benevolently. One of the reason for this, is not very far to seek. Since the pursuit of self-interest depends on the extent to which individuals have access to and can bring into play the power resource they have available to them or can easily mobilize, the existence of compatibility between different and not infrequently antagonistic goals depend on the extent to which different contesting individuals and groups interact and succeed in establishing at least a working balance that ensures a semblance of order. Order, therefore, proves to be only a possibility since it has to depend on the relative power positions of actual or potential competitors for privileged access to and control over societal resources. But what is distinctive about the balance of power existing at any moment in society is subject to change, sometimes very radical change.

Needless to say that all traditional world-views consciously reject the mechanical conception of order in favour of the organic one. But since the organic conception of order seeks consciously to link the finite existence of man with a transcendental absolute source of truth, meaning and value, two questions assume central importance. First, since the transcendental entity is beyond the range of discursive logic, how is this transcendental entity conceived and articulated? And, second, no matter what the conception of the transcendent entity one forms, what is necessary is to elaborate and elucidate the way in which this entity is seen to be related with the world and the beings in it. And since this entity cannot be apprehended with the help of the senses, the only way to apprehend this trans-mundane reality is to rely on what Jan Gonda calls the "heart's eyes." But what the heart's eyes see may not describe the reality as it actually is. In the lack of exact knowledge of what the un-manifested reality is like and how this visible world, *the idam sarvam*, has come to be, one can only speculate about or have a fleeting glimpse of the transcendent entity as a result of some spiritual experience of the Un-manifest. One can only tell, as Plato underlines, the most likely story which is as close as possible to the reality it purports to depict.[3]

The likely story of the creation that Plato recounts cannot be authoritative and definitive unless it is grounded in and backed by a spiritual experience of the Unknown. Such a likely story of creation is recounted in the *Vedic bhavavrittam* or *srishtividya* which flows out of the deep and exhilarating spiritual experience of *kavirmanishis* or the seer-poets. The primal source of this likely story is *Tadekam*, that One, who, overcome by the desire of creation to terminate the condition of his solitude, begins the process of his self-transformation through the process of *yajna* and gets finally transformed into *vishwa*, the *idam sarvam,* or the phenomenal world as we know it. The transformation of the One into many through the ever-pervasive and ever-occurring process of *yajna* is what is recounted through myths and symbols in the *Vedic* likely story of creation.

The *idam sarvam* represents an ensemble of a multiplicity of *nama* (name) and *rupa* (form). But this does not mean either that the God has been partitioned in order to become, many or that the *vishwa* that is totally different and totally separated from its maker. Even while the One becomes many, the *vishwa* remains one with the Maker (*vishwam ekam, RV III.54.8*) and, therefore, it is also true (*vishwam satyam, RV II.24.12*). That the *vishwa* is *ekam* as well as *satyam* is due to the fact that the Absolute is also the omphalos of the world (*vishwam garbham, RV X.121.7*). To make the identity between the One and many clear, *Rigveda* uses other mataphors. For example, in *RV VIII.41.6* it is explicitly stated that the One is that in which all created beings (who can be likened to the felly of a wheel) are concentrated in Him (who is the navel of the wheel). Similarly, *RVX.82.6* speaks of the gods who are deposited in the navel of the Unborn in which all beings abide. What it all amounts to is that the God creates the beings but does not desert them. Or, to put it differently, as *Chhandogya Upanishad* (*Ch. Up.*) underlines, the *Purusha* resides in the *pura* (city), that is, all embodied beings. As *Yajurveda* (*YV 31.19*) puts it, "In every womb moves Prajapati; he never being born, is born in sundry figures. The wise discern the womb from which he springeth. In him alone stand all existing creatures."

But man's nature is bivalent and tends, when the superior element in his interior to discipline and curb the excesses of his base, animal nature is driven out of its position as the ruler, to become what Plato calls "the slave of many mad masters" or what *Ch. Up.* calls *kamachara"* (i. e. a person who is swayed by his desires to realise them). To become a *kamachara* is to lose auto-control or to become *anyarat,* as *Ch. Up.* calls it; erosion of auto-control means the annihilation of the distinction between right and wrong, making, in the process, the interior of the individual a veritable playground of riotous appetites. With it, he loses peace of mind and is compelled to do the bidding of his appetites. He must, then, treat the external world, both nature and society, as a potential means of realising his self-defined purposes.[5] This is the sure indication of the fact that when the individual turns or degrades himself into a *kamachara*, he must live lustfully.

When a person begins to live lustfully, he becomes "dead," entombed in his passions and becomes the subject, willing or not, of the frenzy of his body, dead to the call of the superior element in his interior that always warns him against his surrender to his passions. He also becomes dead to the real significance of the external world, both society and nature. And, above all, he does not even know which good to pursue. In the absence of the knowledge of what is the greatest good and, lacking the basis of choosing reliably among the multiplicity of apparent goods, it becomes very difficult to achieve completeness or wholeness of existence and the integration of his being. He is, therefore, forced to welcome them all and fails to determine in what manner and to what extent they all might fit together. Fitting together is difficult in want of what Plato calls "synoptic vision," that is, the capacity to establish a principled relationship among various goods as well as among various components of the external world. Without it, the soul loses its discriminating power; appetites and desires fill the gap created by the withdrawal of his soul from the position of stewardship of lesser components of man's interior and loses its ordering function. Integration of different capacities of the individual person as well as that of the relationship between him and the cosmos is distorted and disrupted; the consequent disorder of the soul leads to the disorder of the social order. With it, the road to *matsya nyaya* is paved.

The way out of this disorder lies in becoming What Ch. Up. VII.25.2 calls *swarat*, self-sovereign; that is, by submitting himself to the God dwelling inside him, he regains his freedom to act judiciously. But the question that assumes importance in this connection is: How does it become possible to surrender to the in-dwelling God? One answer that is usually given in different religious texts is to turn away (*periagoge,* as Plato calls it, or *pratiyantam* as the Veda declares it, or *paravritti* as Buddhists call it) from the world of senses, and turn inward and engage in self-development by acquiring self-knowledge.[6] But to devote oneself completely to developing one's what is called the true self and be attentive to its needs alone is to treat the visible phenomenal world, the *idam sarvam,* as devoid of any essence. But such an attitude is anathema to the *Vedic* world-view since it treats the world as the *praket* (sign, signature) of the *apraketa* (the Un-manifest). It is because of this that the world is divine, ordered and the fit instrument, a cosmion, of keeping men attuned to their maker. This it does so if it is organised on principles derived from the primordial insight of the seers and philosophers into the structure of order. This structure is articulated in the *Vedic* cosmogony which must be contemplated and imitated, as Cicero points out,[7] if man is to conquer his base nature and become a man in the true sense of the term as well as a better and worthy member of human association he belongs to.

The need to imitate the order inherent in the cosmos, that is, to embrace this order and allow it to mould one's life pattern is necessary because, as *Aitereya Brahman* (*At. Br.*) 1.6 puts it, *satya samhita vai deva, anrit samhite manushya iti* (gods embody truth, man only untruth). Culture, impregnated as it happens to be with the possibility of transforming man into *deva,* projects the vision embracing which man cannot live his life, but lead it in accordance with that vision to become godlike. But culture represents only un-embodied ideas, that is, ideas or principles, that are only abstract. They need a medium through which any specific culture can articulate and express itself and become an integral and dynamic part of man's being and regulate his life activities. It is the transformation of thought-ways in such a way that they become capable of determining what kind of life must animate every person of a particular human association he happens to be a member of and adopt work-ways that make culture alive and authentic and endow it with educative powers. The concrete forms that this transformation assumes in Hindu society are *yajna, samskaras, vratas,* etc.

As has already been pointed out, *yajna* plays a central role in the process of the transformation of the *Tadekam* into *vishwa.* It is *yajna* that is the soul of the Hindu *samskriti*, that is, culture and *samskaras.* But *yajña* means more than the mechanical performance of certain rites and rituals. In its externalised, routine form, it does signify *atmayajna*, that is, a *yajna* in which a person sacrifices himself in lieu of making offerings to gods as an external act, that is, *devayajna.*[8] In this perspective, *yajna* is primarily a means of self-transformation through which man seeks to do what the gods did in the age before the beginning of ages. At. Br. VI.27 makes a distinction between *devashilpa* (Gods' craft) and *manushashilpa* (man's craft) which has a deeper connotation than the mere making of things, that is, *techne.* When projected on to the level of man, it also signifies *praxis*, that is, *shastra* in its double sense, that is, contemplation and self-discipline in the light of the truth yielded by contemplation. *Yajna,* too, is an instance of *devashilpa* with the help of which man seeks to purify his soul of all its impurities, corruption and distortions (*atma samskritrvava shilpanichchadamayam va etairyajanam ataman samskurute,* At. Br., *Ibid.*). But the act of self-purification means 'murdering" all those tendencies endowed to man by nature that, when active, prevent him from becoming truly human. *Samskaras* are the means through which these tendencies are sought to be checked and, then, obliterated. As such, *yajna* and *samskaras* are organically linked and reinforce each other.

The *yajna* is the gateway to heavens is well illustrated by *At. Br. II.1*:

> Gods ascended to the heaven with the help of *yajna.* They feared that men and sages, too, will do the likewise and become like them. They therefore joined earth and heaven with *yupa* (pillar).[9] But while doing so, they buried the foremost part of the *yupa* in order to prevent men and sages to make their way to the heaven. When men and sages went to the place of the *yajna,* they found only the wrong end of the *yupa.* They therefore came to realise that the gods have hidden the *yupa.* They therefore uprooted the *yupa* and stood it with its topmost part pointing towards the heaven. They then performed the *yajna* in the manner prescribed by *shasras* and attained heaven.[10]

The import of this is very clear. If men wish to become like gods, they will have to do the *tapas* as the gods did as a precondition of translating the vision of life as sanctified by culture. One of the components of this precondition is the performance of *samskaras.* The word "*samskara*" has been interpreted in different ways in different areas of knowledge. Note, for example, that, according to the Mimamsa school of thought, the main purpose of *samskaras* is to purify different objects and components, such as, *purodash, etc.* used in *yajna* because without them the *yajna* cannot be performed.[11] But in the Nyaya system *samskaras* are assigned entirely a different function, which is related to the power of expressing ideas forcefully, clearly and precisely.[12] In the field of Samskrita literature, they refer to the cultivation of abilities that can be acquired, developed, or refined or sharpened involving expression of ideas grammatically correctly and linguistically elegantly.[13] And for the Vedant school of thought, *samskaras* main function is related with the process of purification of corrupting elements that leave their effect on the body of a person when he engages in certain physical actions.[14]

Given the different purposes that different authorities assign to *samskaras*, one thing that is common to all the areas of life-activities, emerges clearly and sharply. This factor pertains to the fact that *samskaras* refer to the act of purification so that particular acts related to different areas of life activities could be performed in a manner that is pure and clean. It is true that several ideas of quite a diverse nature have been attributed to the phenomenon of *samskaras*. However, it is also quite clear that they refer essentially to the process of purification as a precondition of performing certain physical, psychological and religious acts or states. It is in this sense that *Viramitrodaya* (*Samskara Prakash I, p. 132*) interprets the essential function of *samskaras* when it says that *atmasashariranyatarnishtho vihitakriyajanyo'tihashyavisheshah samskarah* (All those acts that purifies body and the interior of man for special purposes are *samskara*). It is thus clear that related as they are with the process of purification, they are germane to different dimensions of man's existence. These dimensions constitute the totality of man's being and cover all the areas of life activities We shall return to this aspect of *samskaras* in the next chapter.

As is clear from the above, the substantive purpose of *samskaras* is thus to purify or refine. As such, they refer essentially to those acts that are performed for physical, psychological and intellectual purification and refinement. Given this, it is quite clear that, while the performance of *samskaras* is prescribed for specific purposes by different schools of thought and different authorities, the connotation of *samskaras* cannot by any means be delimited and restricted to only particular areas of human activity. In their generalised sense, *samskaras* signify purification, elevation, refinement, etc. It is, then, entirely a different matter that they are referred to as being germane to and relevant for particular areas of life activities in particular ways most relevant for a particular area of life activity. In their generalised, universal sense, *samskaras* refer to all the acts of purification and refinement of physical, psychological and intellectual dimensions of man's existence. They pertain to the totality of man as a journeying self in the phenomenal world. It can thus be seen that to restrict the significance of *samskaras* to a particular constellation of life activities is to narrow down their real purport as has been done by the Mimamsa school. It is in this sense that the Mimamsa school refers to all the acts of purification of those objects that are used in performing *yajna*, particularly those objects used in the process of making offerings in the sacred fire lit at the beginning of the sacrifice.[15] By doing so the Mimamsa school restricts the significance of *samskaras* to certain acts that are, to say the least, external. As a result, the significance of *samskaras* tend to be divorced from their engendering spiritual experience, the source that constitutes their omphalos, endows them with meaning, and provides them with legitimacy. As has already been pointed out, this spiritual engendering experience is, of course, the experience of self-transcendence on the part of seers, sages and philosophers that constitutes the source of apprehending the sub-stratum of reality. It is this experience that provides the ground of the thought-ways, work-ways and the social institutional arrangement of a society that forges a reliable link between man's finite existence and the absolute source of truth, meaning, and value.

Needless to say that the fundamental problem concerning human existence is the conflict between the finiteness, the givens of nature and society that flow from it, and transcendental values related with the realm of the absolute. In seeking the solution to the riddle of life revolving around this fundamental problem, any meaningful perspective on man and his world has to be grounded in Ontology. By being so grounded, the linkage between the finite and the absolute becomes capable of performing a "shelter" function with the help of which man attempts to give his life a semblance of meaning. Such a linkage reaches the emotional and spiritual centre of man's existence and makes it possible for individuals to outlive their fragmentary personal lives by a projection into the life of a larger conceptual or real order.

The shelter function of the linkage between the finite existence of man and the absolute is to impregnate man's world with meaning so that the individual persons can transcend their finitude, on the one hand, and acquire, by being attuned to higher realities, sufficient strength and courage to resist and overcome temptations that threaten to disturb order in their interior and make them *kamachara*, on the other.[16] It does not mean that desires must be ruled out of court by a superior faculty in man's being and completely annihilated. What is meant is that the desires must be ruled by a superior faculty in man's being so that the depredations of desires are checked from dragging the soul into the mire of corruption.[17] This superior faculty is none else than the soul which happens to be the sensorium of the divine. In order to perform its role as a superior faculty, that is, to be the ruler of all the elements in the interior of man, and rule over them fairly and effectively, the soul must submit to the suzerainty of the *Purusha* (lierally, the citizen dwelling in the *pura*, that is, beings in this world) for man to become what *Chhandogya Upanishad 7.25.1* calls *swarat.* It is only on this basis that man can be at peace with himself and the external world. It is also on this basis that man's interior can be well ordered and, therefore, capable of providing a firm ground for installing benign order in the external world.

To establish this linkage between the finite and the infinite and to make this linkage the active principle of life in terms of subjugating thought-ways and work-ways to it means to know the One beyond the flux of changes. This source of the phenomenal world, the transcendent entity, has been identified by the *Atharveveda X.8.37* as the *sutrasya sutram* (thread of threads).[17] But how does one know this *sutrasya sutram* and to know this entity is necessary in order to establish the much needed linkage between the finite and the infinite. It is true that man is the abode of God (*shariram brahma pravishachharire'dhi prajapati, AV Xi.8.30*) and as *Yajurveda* (*YV 17.14*) puts it, *yebhyo na rite pavate dhamakinchan* (no abode can ever be sacred without the gods). To have the seed of the transcendent entity deep inside one's being, and to let it grow into a fine sturdy and restful tree are two different things. Insofar as man is the combination of both *martya* and *amartya* (*durita yo bhadramrito martyehu, Samaveda* (SV) 1515), in him live two *atmas, jivatma* and *paramatma.*[19] Between them, *Paramatma* is the elder and *atma* is the younger *sakha* (friend). It is true that the elder stays with the younger (*asti jyayana kaniyasi upare,. RV VII.86.6*). However, the younger *sakha* does not often acknowledge the presence of the elder except, perhaps, the times of troubles when he cannot find any other support, succour, or help.[20] This is a clear indication of the fact that the nature of man is bivalent containing the possibility of travelling either the path of virtue or vice. The embodied self is, in the words of *Chhandogya Upanishad* 8.12.1, held by pleasure and pain. Surely there is no cessation of pleasure and pain of one who is embodied. Being held thus, man tends to become *kamachara* and becomes forgetful of the *sutrasya sutram.* As such, natural man is spiritually blind.[21] It is for this reason that he cannot make the necessary distinction between the Sun whom everyone sees and the Sun which not all know with the mind (*pashyantisarve chakshusha na sarve manasa vida,* AV X.8.14). This inability to behold the sun through the mind's eye is consequent upon the incapacity to conform to *rita,* that is, the principles of cosmic order. It is this incapacity that leads to a willing or unwilling, conscious or unconscious, infringement of deviance from the ways of God and, therefore, nonconformity to the principle of cosmic order, that is *rita,* in personal lives and social relations. It signifies disjunction of man from the light that illumines his inner world and, through it, make vivid and clear the pattern of his relationship with a well structured world, as an aspect of his being, his being-in-the-world as the unified play of *Prithivi, Dyau, amartyas* and *martyas.*[22] To bring this disjunction to an end is the purpose of *yajna.*

But what kind of *yajna,* it must be asked? The answer that we get from the *Vedic* literature is clear. It is not the mechanical performance of rites and rituals because they are only the external aspects of *yajna.* It underlines, as already pointed out, the need of performing *adhyatmaka antaram agnihotra* (the internal *yajna* of self-sacrifice, that is, self-transformation). Needless to say that, in the *Vedic* perspective, to perform the *adhyatmika antaram agnihotra* is the essence of *yajna.* It is this internal process of self-transformation initiated by the soul's attunement to the divine ground of being that facilitates self-knowledge. And it is self-knowledge that constitutes the basis of self-transformation (*jnana prasadena, Mund. Up* III.1.8) It is, then, clear that the ritual enactment of this self-surrender to the divine ground of being as a means of self-transformation is the precondition without satisfying which man cannot lead his life according to some ideal vision of life. The emphasis by the Mimamsa school of thought on *karmakanda* can be understood only if performance of external rites and rituals is considered to be the necessary instrument of *yajna* which evokes and sustains internal transformation. Without the leavening of the evocation of the need of initiating the process of internal spiritual change, a change that radically transforms man's orientation towards himself, his world and beyond, the mere performance of the rites and rituals tends to degenerate into something that has lost its power to evoke the engendering experience of a worth while spiritual quest. Without the evocation of the engendering spiritual experience, it is not at all possible to initiate the process of self-transformation. As Baldeva Upadhyaya puts it, "the significance of *karmakanda*, that is, *yajna* in its externality, can be understood only as something that helps in *antaram agnihotra.* Without this internal spiritual change, rites and rituals degenerate into religious orgy or religious extra-vaganza."[25]

The emphasis on *yajna* as an act that helps man in self-transformation is central to the *Vedic* world-view. This world-view is inspired and informed by the realisation that 'the truth of life and experience is necessarily transcendent" which calls for "the continuous effort to transcend the empirical level...."[26] There is no doubt that the act of self-transformation has a great value. It enables a person to put different forces in his interior in a definite order by restoring to his *atman* its long lost sovereignty over the psychic powers so that it can effectively rule the unruly mob of desires and appetites. It is, again, this act of self-transformation that plays a crucial part in, to quote Zimmer, "a radical changing of man's nature and, therewith, a renovation of his understanding both of the outer world and of his own existence; a transformation as complete as possible, such as will amount when successful to a total conversion or rebirth."[27] The immense value of the personal experience of the Beyond and the consequent self-transformation is the beginning, not the end in itself. It is a process that must, in addition to paving the way for the attainment of *dwijahood* and renovation of man's understanding of himself and his world, guide and direct man in organising his pragmatic affairs in such a way that is informed by and sustains *rita* or the cosmic order. This simply means the ordering of society in a way that it caters to both material and spiritual needs of its members. It is in this sense that society is organised for survival in the world and, at the same time, for partnership in the order that has its origin in world-transcendent divine Being; it has to cope with the problems of its pragmatic existence and, at the same time, it is concerned with the truth of its order.[28]

Needless to say that the *Vedic* world-view pertains to both of these dimensions of man's existence. This is evident from the system of *varnashrama dharma* that has, for centuries formed the backbone of the Hindu social order. The division of the social order into *varnas* and that of the phases of man's life into four stages refer to certain religious or *parmarthika* and secular or *laukika* responsibilities that must be discharged by all the individuals constituting the Hindu social order. The determination of *varna*-specific responsibilities or duties and *ashrama*-specific duties or responsibilities is motivated and inspired by the idea of both ensuring the continuity of the social order as well as the reconciliation of the individual good and collective well being. It is the effort of matching the good of one individual and the good of all individuals, on the one hand, and the safeguarding of the dynamic existence of the quatenarian primordial community of man and god and society and world that is reflected in both the world-view undergirding the Hindu social order and the need to make the structure of the social order itself sacrosanct. The idea of the social order as symptomatic of the cosmic *yajna* is what makes the social order sacrosanct. But this requires, as already pointed out, a radical renovation of man's attitude towards himself and his external world. Needless to say that *yajna* is the primary means through which this radical renovation of man's attitude becomes possible. As such, *yajna* signifies that action which, as Upadhyay points out, "makes participation of body, senses, ego sense and intellect possible; whose fruit is meant not for promoting self-interest but the good of others; which does not form or create fresh layers of Karmic bonds but removes them; which imparts to man the knowledge that paves the way for his all-round well being."[29] Thus, the real significance of *yajna* is the transformation of man, a transformation that makes him a man, a whole man, in the true sense of the term. However, the performance of *yajna* requires, that, on the one hand, the materials that are to be used in the performance of *yajna* (in the Mimamsa sense of the term) and, on the other, persons performing the *yajna* must become worthy of performing the *yajna* by purifying themselves through the performance of certain rites and rituals prescribed by the *shastras.*[30]

The fitness of things or persons (that is, *patrata* meaning worthiness) for a particular religious purpose, *i.e.* the performance of *yajna,* to be specific, as *Tantravartika* points out, are of two kinds: one, the taints already acquired and, two, generation of fresh qualities or *vikaras.*[31] The identification of these two kinds of taints (*doshas*), one pre-existing and the other that may be eventually acquired or that still lie in the cavernous womb of possibilities, is due to the fact that man is considered, in the Indian tradition of thinking, to be animal by birth. Unless this animality that man acquires the moment he takes his birth is removed, an individual person is lost in the baseness of his nature and fails to become either a good man or a good citizen. Immersed in animality, he engages in actions that reinforce his bondage to the phenomenal world. As Manu (*Manusmriti* II.27-28) notes, " in the case of *dwijas,* the taints (or *doshas* or sins) are due to (father's) seed and the uterus (of the mother)." Or, as Atri notes, "a person is known as a Brahman by birth, he is said to be *dwija* (twice-born) on account of *samskaras*, he becomes a *vipra* by learning; he is called Shrotriya on account of all these three."[32] The implication of this comment by Atri is very clear. It is that, as long as a person does not undergo the investiture ceremony with a girdle of *munja* grass, that is, till the *upanayana* or sacred thread ceremony has taken place, he is treated as a *shudra* despite his birth in a high caste.[33] The removal of taints as well as the elimination, as far as possible, of the possibility of accumulating further taints is a necessary step not only towards the formation of the character of the individual but also towards leading life according to an ideal vision. Needless to say that both of these are organically linked. Without this vision, the formation of character is usually determined by the changing, ever-fickle fashion of opinion. In the sweeping current of changing streams of opinion culture loses its authority and becomes a matter of taste and entertainment. Since the ideal vision of life is rooted in the primordial insight into the structure of order, it is this primordial insight that constitutes the foundation of culture. Thus, the development and sustenance of culture in history depends on the extent to which culture takes its inspiration and is informed by religious thought and practices. Most of these practices, as Manu (II.27-28) points out, include *homas* performed during pregnancy and by *jatakarma* (ceremony on birth), *chaula* (tonsure) and by *upanayana*. Needless to say that these are some of the most important *samskaras* that form an integral part of the constellation of *samskaras* and the Hindus, especially those belonging to the higher castes, are required to habitually perform.[34]

It is clear from what Atri says about *samskaras*—no one by birth alone can attain the highest ideal stage of life; a person has to undergo a process of the training of character that terminates in that person becoming a Shrotriya, that is, a wise and noble person according to the light of the *Vedic* world-view. And the highest ideal of man that the Veda posits is the reaching to the stage of *sarvata* (wholeness). Man, according to what St. Augustine calls an exterior man, must live and act in this world, fulfil his own life needs and preserve the basic structure of his lived world without which his own survival and sustenance will certainly be in jeopardy. In addition, he has also his own interior world with its own peculiar needs which must be fulfilled if man is to be able to preserve the basic structure of the lived world and, at the same time, seek his own liberation from the entanglements of this world. It is in this context that the importance of *purushartha* can be appreciated. While the pursuit of *kama* and *artha* is aimed largely for ensuring provisioning for fulfilling ordinary life needs, the pursuit of *dharma*[35] refers to the need of regulating the pursuit of *kama* and *artha* in such a way that the good of others as well as one's own are equally and fairly served.

With the inclusion of *dharma* in the framework of *purushartha*, we move imperceptibly towards the interior of man, into his inner world where mind and will function to speak and, that is, the world of Mitra and *Varuna*, to use *Vedic* terms. To put it differently, it is the world where *Purusha* resides. The cultivation of *dharma* is possible only when man turns inwards, towards his own inner world and accepts the suzerainty of the indwelling *Purusha* and, as a consequence, becomes *swarat.* It is only on this basis that man is enabled to rein in his self-aggrandizing tendency, consciously work for reconciliation between self-interest and public good. All this instills in him the feeling of *lokasamgraha* the concrete external expression and consequence of the preservation of the lived world. Thus the *Vedic* scheme of the mode of man's thinking and acting, that is, the pattern of his living underlines the utmost need of integrating the external aspect or dimension with the internal aspect or dimension of man's existence. But this integration does not by any means mean the suppression of the claims of man's exterior and its needs; it means only that exterior of man must be placed under and subjugated to the suzerainty of the superior element available in his interior, that is, his soul as the sensorium of divine. It signifies that the hoped for integration of the exterior man with the interior world of man, the interior which consciously and actively acknowledges the presence of the divine in his being, is possible when the interior man is fully disciplined, well-ordered and integrated, in his own turn, with the world beyond (that is, *asau loka,* as *Chhandogya Upanishad* calls it) but which is also within him. The search for compatibility and integrity, that is, *sarvata*, is thus the basic concern of the *Vedic* world-view.

To achieve *sarvata* requires a transition from *abhijnana* to *prajnana.* While the former refers to the knowledge of *asya loka,* that is, the phenomenal world, the latter pertains to the world-transcendent entity. Both these knowledge systems are necessary for man to discharge the responsibilities of this world and the world beyond this world. Thus acquisition of the knowledge known as *vijnana* (that, is the knowledge relevant for this world only)[36] and *jnana* (knowledge of the *asau loka*) is the aim of learning according to the traditional Indian thinking. It is only on the basis of the learning of *vijnana* and *jnana* that man can achieve *sarvata.* The different stages of achieving *sarvata* are, as Atri suggests, *dwijata, vipratwa and* Shrotriya*twa.* Passing through all these stages of education and learning, and training, particularly of conduct, man attains the understanding of the true relationship of the self with the Self. This relationship is "a kind of synthesis (*skr. Samdhi, samadhi, samjnana*) by which our internal conflict is resolved...."[37] As a consequence of this, man becomes *swarat*; to put it differently, he becomes self-controlled and comes to be grounded in the nave of the Supreme Being. To be so grounded is something like the placement of an axle in a well-oiled axle-hole of a chariot in order to facilitate the smooth movement of the wheel. This, in the *Vedic* perspective, is real *sukha* (happiness, bliss).[38] Thus, to attain *sukha* is dependent and consequent upon man being grounded (*stha*) in his *swa* (that is, his own, self, not the empirical self but the *atman*). To become *swastha* means being supported (*pratishtha*) when the Supreme Being rides (*adhistha*) the chariot of man's body or being as a consequence of his faith (*astha*) in Him.

It is this transition from *vijnana* to *jnana* that holds the key to the formation of man in the *Vedic* perspective; central to this formation is the fundamental role of performing *samskaras.* The performance of *samskaras* is instrumental in making man aware of the need to establish a firm linkage of his finite existence with the absolute, the source of truth, meaning and value. The import of this formation is the gradual unfoldment of man's true character as a spiritual being according to the ideal vision of desirable life. This is equivalent to a work of painting that gradually unfolds itself on account of the interplay between several colours (with which it is drawn). Similarly, *brahmanya* (the true status of Brahman, (that is, he who knows Brahma) is brought out by the performance of *samskaras* according to prescribed rites.[39] Thus, the purpose of *samskaras*, as Kane notes, is the all-round development of a person. " The *samskaras* had been treated from the very ancient times as necessary for unfolding the latent capacities of man for development and as being the outward symbols or signs of the inner change which would fit human beings for corporate life and they also tended to confer a certain status on those who underwent them."[40]

The real significance of *samskaras*, as Rajabali Pandeya puts it, pertains to religious, physical, intellectual acts of purification and refinement or rites prescribed for these purposes. By virtue of undergoing these rites or acts, a person becomes a fully developed and mature member of society. *Samskaras* of Hindus incorporate all fundamental ideas, religious rites and rituals, their concomitant rules and procedures. The purpose (of *samskaras*) is not simply formal physical purification but the purification, refinement and perfection of the personality of a person.[41]

References

1. Hans Jonas, *The Gnostic Religion: The Message of the Alien God and the Beginning of Christianity* (Boston: Beacon Press,1963), p. 252.
2. For a very explicit statement on this, see David Hume, *Dialogues Concerning Natural Religion*, quoted in Carl L. Becker, *The Heavenly City of Eighteenth Century Philosophers* (New Haven: Yale University Press, 1960), p. 56.
3. Plato, Timeaus 29c d.
4. For a detailed discussion in this regard, see Ramashray Roy, *Beyond Ego's Domain: Being and Order in the Veda* (Delhi: Shipra Publications, 1999), chap. 3.
5. See Charles Taylor, *Hegel and Modern Society* (Cambridge: Cambridge University Press, 1976).
6. This is what *Vedic pratiyantam*, Buddhist paravritti, and Platonic, periagoge, all these terms imply.
7. Cicero, De Natura Deorum II.II.II, quoted in Jonas, op. cit., 245.
8. See *Shatapath Brahman* (Sh. Br.) 11.2.6.13-14; cf. *RV* X.124.6; Sh. B. 12.5.2.13; AB 11.4; Br. Up.VI.II.14; See also Ananda Coomaraswamy, "*Atma-yajna:* Self-Sacrifice," in *Selected Papers.*
9. Yupa (also called ashwatha, skambha), the cosmic tree symbolises the sapta loka at the apex of which stands Truth and at the bottom, the Earth. It also represents the mode of the descent of the divine into matter as well as the ascent of man to Sastyaloka.
10. As Baldeva Upadhyaya notes:

    Yajna signifies those actions that make the purification of the body, of the senses, of the ego, and of the mind possible. The fruit yielded by this is meant to benefit not the individual but others, which does not create new layers (on the pure soul) but removes those layers that we created earlier and which helps man to proceed on the path of well being and leads ultimately to final knowledge. *Vaidiks Sahitya aur Samskriti* (Varanasi: Sharada Sansthan, 1973), p. 493.

11. *Prokshanadijanya Samskaro Yajnangaapurodasheshwiti Dravyadharmah*, Vachaspatya Brihadabhidhan, 5, 5188.

12. Cf. *Raghuvamsha, 3.35: Nisargasamskaravineet ityasu nripena chakre yuvarajashabdabhak. And Kumarasambhava,1.28: Samskrtyevagira manishi taya saputascha.*

13. Cf. Vachaspatya *Brihadabhidan: snanachamanadijnyah samskara dehe udpadyamanani tadabhidhanani jive kalpayanti. And Manusmriti 2:26: karyat sharira-samskarah pavanah pretya cheha cha.*

14. Cf.Vachaspatya *Brihadabhidhana, op. cit: Brihyadeshcheha yajnangatapradanaya vaidikamargena prokshanadi.*

15. Eric Voegelin, *History of Political Ideas: Hellenism, Rome, and Early Christianity*, ed. Athanosis Moulakis (Columbia: University of Missouri Press, 1997, I, p.20.

16. *Chh. Up.* 8.12.1.

17. Cf. Sigmund Freud, "Our mind is no peacefully self-contained unity. It is rather to be compared to a modern state in which a mob, eager for enjoyment and destruction, has to be held down forcefully by a prudent superior class." Quoted in Philip Rieff, *Freud: The Mind of the Moralist* (New York: Anchor Books, 1961), p. 63.

18. As Br. Up. II.v.15 puts it, the Self is the ruler of all beings and the king of all beings. Central to all sentient beings and, especially to man, as Ait. Ar. III.2.1 puts it, is prana which is identified as breath, the central entity to which all the organs in man's body are bound and on which they converge. But there is no one prana in human body. As AV X.82.2 points out, there are implanted in human body seven paranas and, according to RV X.82.2, there is Vishwakarman beyond these seven pranas who binds them together with vatarajju (wind-cord). These seven pranas are identified as seven Rishis in SB and are themselves the creation of the One beyond them; They are the manifestation of the One beyond them (rishasya sapa sakam ye asya gopa mahato babhuvah, AV VIII.8.9).

19. RV I.164.20 identifies these atmas as two *suparnas, bhoktri suparna* (the agent, the enjoyer) and *sakshi suparna* (the witness).

20. Cf. AV X.8.32.

21. Coomaraswamy, "Windows of the Soul," in *What is Civilisation?* p. 53.

22. Cf. J. L. Mehta, *Philosophy and Religion: Essays in Interpretation* (New Delhi: ICPR, 1990), pp. 278-79.

23. RV X.124.6.; SB 12.5.2.13; AB II.4; Br. Up.VI.11.14.

24. Cf. JUB 1.14.1: "He should be one whose gods are far away. Verily, it is insofar as he approaches the gods with himself (*atmana devah upasate*) that becomes gods for him;" and Br. Up. 1.Iv.10: "So whosoever approaches a deity as being other, thinking 'He is one, I another' does not comprehend; he is a mere victim of them."

25. Upadhyay, op. cit. p. 493.

26. Jan Gonda, *The Vision of the Vedic Poets* (Delhi: Munshiram Manoharlal, 1984), p. 18.
27. Heinrich Zimmer, *Philosophies of India*, ed. Joseph Campbell (London: Rroutledge & Kegan Paul, 1952), p. 4.
28. Voegelin, *Order and History: Plato and Aristotle*, III, p. 2.
29. Upadhyay, op. cit.
30. *Samskaronama sa bhavati yasminjate padartho bhavati yogyah kasyachidarthasya.* Shabar on *Jaimini Sutra* III.1.3.
31. *Yogyata cha sarvata dwiprakara doshapanayanena gunantarapajanena cha bhavati, Tanravartika*, p. 1115 quoted in P. V. Kane, *History of Dharmashastra* (Poona: Bhandarkar Oriental Research Institute, 1974), II, p. 191.
32. *Janmana brahmano jneyat samskaraidwija uchyate; vidyaya yati vipratwam Shrotriyastribhireva cha.* Also quoted in Kane, op. cit. p. 189.
33. Harit in Vashshtha *Dharmasutra*, II.6; cf. *Manusmriti*, II.171-72.
34. Kane notes that "the exact significance of samskaras in the development of higher human personality was left rather vague in our authorities and their treatment of the purpose of samskaras is not very elaborate or exhaustive." Op. cit. p. 192. But is it necessary for these authorities to undertake an elaborate or exhaustive discussion of who man is and how an individual person can conform to the idea of the ideal notion of who man is? Moreover, the clues to who man is are very clearly given in the *Vedic* as well as subsequent literature.
35. Needless to say that *dharma* is the later version of the *Vedic* Rita.
36. For a very useful discussion on this subject, see Motilal Shastri, *Bharatiyya Drishti se 'Vijana" Shabda ka Samanwaya* (Jaipur: Rajasthan Patrika, Pvt. Ltd.).
37. Raimundo Panikkar, *The Vedic Experience: Mantramanjari* (Pondicherry: All India Books, 1983), p. 477.
38. The term 'sukha" is derived from conjunction of "su" meaning goodness, beauty, happiness and "kha" meaning the hole in the nave of the wheel in which the axle is inserted.
39. *Chitrakarma yathanekai rangairunmilyati shanih; Brahmanyamapii tadvasyatsamskarai vidhipurvakai.* Parasar VIII.19.
40. Kane, op. cit., p. 192.
41. Rajbali Pandeya, *Hindu Samskaras* (Varanasi: Chaukhamba Vidyabhawan, 1995), p. 19.

5

Dharma, Morality and Samskara

The sequence *Brahma–yajna–Vishwa* reveals more than the way the cosmos has been perceived to be created. It is a sequence that represents in symbolic form the content of what the sages, philosophers and mystics perceive from their "heart's eye" about the truth of reality. But what these sages, philosophers and mystics 'see' has two fundamental aspects. In the first place, it recounts through what Plato calls "a likely story" or what *Brihaddevata* (2.120) calls *"bhavavrittam"*[1] the way Brahma transformed himself into the phenomenal, perceptible world. The process of becoming of *Brahma* into *vishwa* makes explicit the essential relatedness between the fundamental components *Brahma, Yajna* and *Vishwa* and shows how different aspects of the visible world are but the different manifestations of one single reality. In essence, then, there is no substantive difference between what Brahma is and what he eventually becomes.

The process of becoming is essentially the process of creating *nama* (name) and *rupa* (form) that are not only so many perceptible signs of the absolute but also its signature. These names and forms constitute what both *Chhandogya* and B*riadaranyaka Upanishads* identify as *pura* (that is, the city) which the Unkown, the *Purusha,* makes its residence. As YV 31.19 puts it: Prajapati moves in every womb; although he is never born, he is born, again and again, in manifold forms. It is this primordial relationship between the Unborn and the born, between Brahma and *vishwa* that is the source of order in the cosmos. It is this order that the Veda identifies as *rita.* That is why *RV V.15.2* underlines the fact that,

Riten ritam dharunam dharayanta yajnasya shake parame vyoman;
Divo dharmndharune edusho nrinjatairajatam abhi ye nanakshu.

That is, they (continue the process of) transporting *rita* by *rita* for maintaining the strength of *yajna* in the highest empyrean. They bring together those who support *dharma* to sit at the *yajna* which is the stay of heaven.

Rita constitutes the sum-total of all those principles that regulate and control the functioning of every being in this world. It concerns, as Miller points out, " the dynamics of manifestation, the process of world unfoldment at all levels."[2] Rita constitutes the sole ground on which, to borrow the wording of *RVIII.54.8*, rest all moving and stationary beings whether animals, birds or creatures of every kind (*ejad dhruvam patyate vishwamekam charat patatri vishunam vijatam*). And what is distinctive about *rita* is that the course of thing, every body in this world, even that of the Sun, the *Ritasya pantha* is unalterable and cannot be impeded. As *Ait. Br.1.5.5.1* notes:

Ritameve parmeshthi ritam natyeti kinchana;
Rrite samudreahitam ritam bhumiriyamashrita.

Rita alone is *parameshthi*, there is nothing else than *rita*. Placed in the ocean of *rita*, earth is nourished and supported by *rita*.

Rita operates everywhere and in manifold ways, *Ritasya drilha dharunani santi puruni chandra vapushe* (firmly fixed is the foundation of *rita* shining in beauty, manifold are its beauteous forms, *RVV.23.9*). But its ordinances work differently in different spheres. In the human world, for example, while the form and nature of man, the process of his birth, growth, decay, all these are determined, the exercise of freedom by him is not. The call to freedom is certainly heeded and freedom exercised. But its exercise is not always governed by or conforms to *rita*. All structures that can potentially be utilised to moderate the excesses of freedom are, of course, there. This highlights the phenomenon of *bandhuta* (homology) between different spheres and aspects of the cosmos. But while form and nature are fully realised according to the principles of *rita* in the *adhidaivika* and *adhibhautik* spheres, only form and the necessary structure to support this form are determined and conditioned in the case of man. His nature acquires specific attributes and qualities in time and space. Thus, man's ultimate nature or destiny is given only as a possibility.

The actualisation of this possibility depends on the extent to which man succeeds in transcending his nature *qua* a natural being. If he remains content in treating himself purely as a biologically, psychologically and sociologically determined being, he tends to forget or ignore the claims of his spirit or the soul as the sensorium of divine. When man *qua* natural man ignores or neglects his soul, he loses his powers of discrimination, regulation and discipline. As a result, his appetites and desires attain dominance and emerge to fill the gap created by the withdrawal or the banishment of the soul from the seat of over-lordship of the senses. Integration of different capacities of the individual becomes difficult and the relationship between the individual and the cosmos is disrupted. The consequent disorder of the soul leads to what Plato calls *polypragmosyne,* the readiness to engage in multifarious activities which are not the person's proper business and *allotriopragmosyne* (meddlesomeness, officious interference).[3]

This inevitably leads to the merger, in the Freudian frame of reference, of the ego and *id* exemplifying Freud's saying that "where *id* was, there ego shall be." It does not mean that "the ego should replace the *id* but that the *id* should come to exist in the domain of the ego—that is, it should shed the illusion of integral, controlled selfhood and dissolve into those associative chains normally repressed into the unconscious."[4] This also means that the self emerges, as Rieff suggests, "as a subject of struggle between two objective forces—unregenerate instincts and overbearing culture. Between these two forces there may be compromises but no resolution. Since the individual can neither extirpate his instincts nor wholly reject the demands of society, his character expresses the way in which he organises and appeases the conflict between the two."[5] This struggle is real and escape from it is either surrender of the self to the *id* or to the super-ego. If it is the former, man is ruled by the unruly mob of appetites and desires; if, on the other hand, it is the latter, he is ruled by "oppressive" tradition, conventions or regnant fashion of opinions. The individual has no other choice in this situation than what is euphemistically called adaptation. In any case, he is not his own master; he is ruled either by his passions or impersonal social norms with an ingrained tendency to degenerate into corrupt practices—norms in whose making the individual has had no say.

This situation signifies the loss of freedom making man what *Chh. Up.* calls *anyarat.* "If they (*i.e.*) men are ruled by others and live in perishable worlds, they are not free to act as they wish in all worlds" (*Chh. Up.* VII.25.2). This suggests that integrated, controlled selfhood cannot be attained if the individual surrenders either to his *id* or the super-ego. In either case, he loses the capacity to self-rule and, as a consequence, comes into conflict with himself and with his external world. For integrated, controlled self-hood, it is necessary to install a superior ordering entity which can successfully quell the rebellion of appetites and desires. Without "murdering" the dominant attributes of man *qua* natural man, man can only live, he cannot lead his life. As such, it is necessary to discipline and regulate life in the light of an ideal vision of the pattern of living.

In order to overcome or transcend the natural state, man as a biologically, psychologically and sociologically determined entity is prone to fall into, it is necessary to contemplate and imitate the cosmic order, that is, *rita.* Contemplation and imitation of *rita* signify not only the acquisition of knowledge relevant for self-transcendence; it is also necessary for man to internalise the principles of *rita* that should govern the conduct of human affairs and shape his orientation and behavior in accordance with these principles. There are two distinct but inter-related aspects of this need of contemplating and imitating *rita.* In the first place, man and god and society and the world constitute a primordial community of being. The community with its quatenarian structure, as Voegelin observes, is and is not the datum of human experience. It is a datum of human experience in so far as it is known to man by virtue of his participation in the mystery of its being. It is not a datum of experience in so far as it is not given in the manner of an object of the external world but is knowable only from the perspective of participation in it.[6]

The first two elements of this quatenarian structure refer to the relationship between what *Chh. Up.* calls "*asya loka* (this world) and "*asau loka*" (the world beyond). These two *lokas* are symptomatic of the fundamental divide between the world of the mortals and that of the immortals. This does not by any means suggest that the two *lokas* are separate and autonomous and, therefore, unrelated. According to the discussion among three persons well-versed in *udgitha*[7], it is the *akasha* (sky) which is the *gati* of *asya loka* insofar as "all beings arise from *akasha* alone and are finally dissolved into it; because *akasha* alone is greater (*jyayan*) than all these and is the support (*parayan*) at all times (*Chh. Up.* 1.9.1).

But this is not the final answer. It is true that *Chh. Up.* 1.9.2. identifies *akasha* to be a better *udgitha.* However, it also identifies a*ntah aksini purusha* (that is, the person in the eye, *Ibid.*, 1.11.7), as *udgitha.* And as *Sh. Br.*14.4.1.25 underlines, *ut* stands for *prana* which animates everything in this world and *githa* stands for *vak.* It is apparent, then, that *akasha* itself is not the highest *udgitha.* There is something beyond it which, in the last analysis, is the ultimate, that is, *gati.* This *gati* is, of course, the Supreme Being. And the relationship between *asya loka* and *asau loka* can be made dynamic and beneficial only when the soul of the individual is attuned to his highest *gati,* the ground and support of the *asya loka* and every being in it. Thus to keep the relationship between the phenomenal world and the world beyond is one of the fundamental conditions of salubrious human existence.

In the second place, the bond of communitarian relationship between society and the world is exemplified by the claim of the former to be the representative of truth. This representation points to the fact that social order is grounded in, informed and animated by an interpretation of truth that is transcendental, trans-individual. It is also true that the institutional structure of society and its practices, all these are inspired by the interpretation of truth that society embraces. However, the character of society as the representative of the truth can be preserved only when individual members of society embrace that truth as constituting the anchor and the pivot of their life activities. This is possible only when individual members contemplate the order of the cosmos and imitate it in their own life. This contemplation and imitation proves to be fruitful not just by knowing what this order substantively is but by engaging into action that ensures the transition from knowing virtue to having virtue. Thus, what is necessary for living according to the principles of the cosmic order is not alone the knowledge of what virtue is, but also the performance of certain practices that draw their inspiration, structure and justification from these principles.

The quaternarian structure of the primordial community, thus, underlines the need to keep alive the process of exchange between men and gods, on the one hand, and the need for individuals to participate, through certain religious and spiritual practices, in the mystery of existence, on the other. The process of exchange between man and god is necessary to preserve cosmic metabolism in which, as *Taittiriya Samhita*, I.8.4.i, notes, is emphasised that "Give thou to me, I shall give to thee; Bestow upon me; I shall bestow upon thee; Accepting my offering, I shall accept thy offering". But the preservation and sustenance of this exchange process cannot be ensured unless man becomes god-like by overcoming/transcending his base nature. As *Aitereya* Brahman puts it: *Satyam samhita vai daiva anritasamhita manushya* (it is only the gods who are imbued with truth, not men,cf.*SB*, i.i.i.4).To turn away from *anrita* and begin the search for truth is to look inward; to the external light located in the cave of man's interior. This is possible when individuals perform *yajna*. As *Taittiriya Samhita*, V.5.21 notes, the God entered into man and made the mortal his house. However as he divided himself into many parts as beings, he was unable to emerge out of them whole and well integrated. He could become whole only if he could be reassembled and integrated. This required that gods and men make sacrifices, that is, perform *yajna*. The gods did the *yajna* and *Prajapati* began to regain his wholeness. Moreover, by performing *yajna* the gods went up to heaven. But they were afraid that, doing *yajna*, men and particularly

Rishis among them, too, would become like gods. They, therefore joined the heaven with a *yupa* (pillar) in order to confuse and, therefore, prevent men and *Rishis* from going to heaven. They buried the front end of the *yupa* in the earth. When men and *Rishis* wished to do *yajna*, they found the *yupa* only with the wrong end pointing towards the heaven. They, therefore, uprooted the *yupa* and buried it again with its head pointing towards the heaven. And then they could know the *yajna* and go to heaven (or become god-like) by performing it.[8] It does need to be pointed out that this *yupa* is nothing else than the cosmic tree or the *Ashwattha*, or *Sapta loka* representing at one and the same time the relatedness of this world with the world beyond and the need to keep alive this relationship through performing *yajna.*

Thus *yajna* is an essential part of the *Vedic* cosmogony; it signifies not only the process through which the cosmos is created but also the means of preserving and sustaining the cosmic order. But is the Veda simply a store-house of *karmakanda*, that is, merely a set of external practices, as Umesh Chandra Pandeya argues?[9] To treat the Veda simply as the store-house of *karmakanda* delineating the process of conducting certain religious practices is to rob both *yajna* and its source, the Veda, of their real significance. It must be emphasised that the *Vedic* literature makes a clear and precise distinction between the mere performance of *yajna* and *yajna* as a means of inner transformation, a necessary step towards self-transcendence. For example, *RV VIII.76.3* underlines the fact that none attains Him (Indra) by works of sacrifice. As such, what is important in the *Vedic* perspective is not the *yajna* enacted outwardly, but what is accomplished inwardly by the understanding sacrificer. The emphasis in Veda is on *adhyatmikka antaram agnihotra.* In it is no external *havya* (offering) is used insofar as *vihavya* (without any external oblation) is superior (*asti nu tasmadojiyo, yad vihavyanejire, RVVII.* 5.4). In this *antaram agnihotrai* the sacrificer, *RVIV*.6.1 declares, yokes himself, like an understanding horse (*swayam ayuji hayona vidwana; cf. Git* V.27). And when the sacrificer engages in *antaram agnihotra*, he becomes the ladle for the gods (*asyam yaschamasho devepanah*) who drink from it and revel (*tasmin madyantam, AVX. viii.3.35*).

It is in this context that the distinction that *Sh. Br.* makes between *satisada* and *satrasada* assumes importance. While *satisada* signifies one who is seated in the *yajna* in reality, that is, he performs the *yajna* by supporting it with his mind (*manasa adhavayati, Sh. Br. 11.2.4.8*) and he is, in essence, seated amongst the gods (*satisu devatasa sidantah*), the latter refers to a sacrificer who just sits at the session of the *yajna* only to offer external oblation to the gods. The *satisada* does not offer any external *havya* but, instead, himself becomes the oblation (cf. *RV X.124.6*; *Sh. Br. XII.5.2.13*; *Br. Up. VI.ii.14*). In contradistinction to the *satisada, satrasada* goes on performing *yajna* offering not himself but only external oblation to please gods so that he/she may get sons, riches, prowess, etc. This brings into play another *Vedic* distinction, that is, beween *atmayaji* and *devayaji*, the former referring to a sacrificer who offers himself as oblation and the latter only brings tributes to the gods (*Sh. Br. XI. 2.6.13-14*).[11] This distinction, Coomaraswamy suggests "is of active and passive viae, of 'salvation' from 'liberation.'[12]

It is, then, clear that for men to do as the gods did in order to become god-like, they have to imitate what *AB 30.1* calls *devashilpa* which sublimates man's desires and appetites. However, the natural man happens to be spiritually blind.[13] That is why he cannot make a distinction between the Sun whom everyone sees and the Sun which not all know with the mind (*pahyanti sarve chakshusa no manasa vida, AV X.8.14*). As a result, man's interior is pervaded by disorder produced by the rebellion of desires and appetites. This disorder spreads outward and disrupts order in society promoted and reinforced by what Aristotle calls *pleonexia* (self-aggrandisement). This disorder plays havoc with the quatenarian structure of the primordial community and breaks asunder the wholeness of man's existence reducing it to what Iris Murdoch calls a "broken totality."

It is true that *yajna*, understood in the sense of *antaram agnihotra* is the proper means of mending this broken totality. However, for two important reasons the recourse to *antaram agnihotra* becomes extremely difficult. In the first place, despite the realisation of the central importance in accomplishing self-transcendence, most individuals are incapable of performing *antaram agnihota* because of natural or existential constraints. In the second place, *yajna* is usually performed by individuals. However, its ramifications are not confined to individual lives alone; they spill over community life and relations. For one thing, it symbolises a pre-existing consensus about the ideal pattern of life that the community as a whole has embraced and seeks to realise in individual and communal life. For another, if it is the affirmation and renewal of the linkage between the finite and the absolute, it is also the celebration of the shareable commonality that sustains and reinforces the sense of community and its different props. And, lastly, for many, the path to self-transformation passes through the gateway of *karmakanda,* that is, external religious practices. It is the performance of *karmakanda* that, for many, constitutes the ground of consciousness of their being members of a larger order in which they participate in their own ways and according to one's innate capacities and, through this participation, they acquire and retain qualities that make them human beings in the true sense of the term.

It is against this background that we can appreciate the emphasis that traditional Indian thinking places on the essential connection among *dharma,* morality, and *samskaras.* This connection is seen to be very vital in view of the need to maintain a delicate but easily breakable link between the good of one person and the good of every person This link, as we have already seen, is broken when man comes under the sway of his passions and becomes the willing slave of many mad masters or becomes *kamachara.* The very fact that a person has become a willing slave of many mad masters signifies the fact that he does not recognise or if he recognises he does not pay any attention to any authority external to and beyond himself. He is free in the modern sense of the term to decide what he wants to do and how to do it.

When a person acts according to the modern conception of freedom, he tends to lose sight of the fact that whatever he proposes to do or actually does, has vital impact on what others contemplate or actually do. Losing sight of this vital fact, the individual person usually does what he considers to be in the best of his interest. This he is compelled to do because, in the first place, he does not usually have the information about what consequences his action is likely to produce for others and, in the second place, even if he has the requisite information of the likely consequences of his projected action, he has no knowledge of the differential impact of his action in different contexts. He is, as a result, induced, by the pressure of the need to satisfy his desire, to act as what him please. But once he engages in action he is likely to promote his own welfare ignoring the consideration of whether or not what he does is beneficial for others.

It is in this context that we can appreciate the need to resolve the possible tension between the good of one individual and the good of all individuals. And since the resolution of this tension requires the conscious acceptance of the fact that man is a member of a larger entity that emanates from and is supported by the divine ground of being—a ground that constitutes the source for man of truth, meaning and value—this acceptance must become an integral part of the life world of the people constituting a particular society. This acceptance signifies, first, the conscious acknowledgement of the fact that man becomes *swarat* only when he recognises that his body is the abode of *Purusha.* Since this conscious identity is usually broken under the pressure of the everydayness, it needs to be reactivated in this world by living according to the ideal of *varnashrama dharma,* that is, duties of man according to the four life stages that the Hindu tradition identifies and those that are prescribed by four *purusharthas.*

The *varna dharma* identifies four stages of life, the first of which is the stage of appropriate training for assuming the responsibilities imposed upon a person by his birth in this world, the second refers to the duties of a householder, the third to a state that is preparatory before one retires from an active householder and turns to work for his own liberation (that is *moksha*). Similarly, *pursharthas* refer to *kama* (desire), *artha* (means of satisfying desires), *dharma* (righteousness), *and moksha.* The *Vedic* world-view does not reject the claim of the phenomenal world, that is, everydayness and, therefore, deems it necessary to satisfy desires and mobilize resources necessary for the satisfaction of different desires but under the suzerainty of *dharma* so that the resolution of the tension between the good of one individual and the good of all individuals can become possible. The last *purushartha,* that is, *moksha,* is necessary for a person because he has also his spiritual life, pursuing which he can be liberated from the bondage of the phenomenal world and its claims. As such, both material and spiritual aspects of the existence of man have an equal weight and the responsibilities associated with each of these aspects must be discharged effectively and efficiently in order to establish order in one's own interior and in the world, particularly the social universe, outside him.

It is in this perspective that we can appreciate the significance of the relationship between human purposes, the right to achieve a particular purpose, and the spiritual quest, that is, liberation by being actively attuned to the indwelling *Purusha.* Needless to say that to live according to the tenets of the four *purusharthas* is to actively search for truth, meaning, and value in one's life. The concept of value in traditional Indian thinking is associated with the central concept of *prayojana,* that is, purpose. Its philosophical definition is "*yamadhikritya purushah pravartate.* It is necessary to explain the meaning of the terms *adhikritya* and *purusha.* The term *adhikritya* means *uttarottararamaniyavastuspriha,* that is, the desire of progressively pleasing things in an ascending scale of values.

"Progressively pleasing things" does not refer to things that please a person working under the influence of his ego; it must be interpreted from the perspective of what pleases a particular person as well as the need of a person to become imbued with right reason or *prama.* It therefore connotes *lokottarahldajanakjnanavishayah* (a knowledge that equips a person with the discriminating power for judging what is pleasing not only to himself but for all). In this perspective, *adhikara* means the pursuit of transcendental and pure and absolute knowledge productive of perpetually increasing beatitude in which the *purusha* is the replica in this world of the transcendental but manifest *Purusha.* In this beatitude, infinite truth, beauty and goodness are implicit.

It is apparent from the discussion above that the highest purpose in everybody's life, according to the traditional Indian thinking, is the achievement of liberation which cannot be insured if man remains immersed in materiality and restricts his life activities only to the pursuit of *kama* and *dharma*. Such an immersion is considered, in almost all religious traditions, as reinforcing karmic bonds and leads to the accumulation of more layers of ignorance about who man actually is. It is this accumulation of karmic bonds that reinforces the separation of the *purusha* in the phenomenal sense from the transcendental sense. What needs to be emphasised here is the fact that man is supposed to be standing in a relation of homology with the *Purusha* in the transcendental sense. This means that man is the exact replica of the maker of the cosmos albeit at a micro-level.

In order to appreciate this homological relationship between *purusha* in the phenomenal sense and in the transcendental sense, it is necessary, first to elucidate the significance of *Purusha* in the transcendental sense. As *AV xi.8.13* underlines: "Pourers-together namely are those who brought together the things; having poured together the whole mortal, the gods entered the man." Thus, the gods made the mortal their abode and then entered it" (*griham kritwa martya devah purushaavishan*, *AV 1.8.18*). The mortal abode is not without apertures. Man is supposed to represent *triloka*, that is three lokas and in each of these three *lokas* reside seven *Rishis*. But who bored out these apertures? *AV X.2.6*). And *RV II.15.3* identifies the power that bore these apertures as Indra who dug up the rivers with his *vajra* (*vajren khanyatrinnadinam*). As a result, *pranas* resound in every vein and every pore of man (*iyamasya dhamyate nadirayam girbhi pariskkritah* (*RV X.135.7*). It is thus clear that, as *Br. Up. IV.V.12* claims, everything in this cosmos is *Brahma's* breath or, to use another metaphor, sparks of the divine (*yathagne kshudra visphullinga vyucharanti, Br. Up. II.I. 20*; *Mund. Up. II.I.I*), or, as *Mund. Up. I.I.7* puts it, extension of the Supreme Being. It is also clear as Tait. Up. puts it: *sa yaschayam' purush. Yaschayaditya. Sa ekah* (He that is here in the human person, and He that is there in the Sun are one.

Given the identity between the person in the Sun and the human person, it follows that as long as this identity is not total, the human person will not be perfect; he will, as a consequence, lack harmony in his own interior and is likely to disturb balance and order in the social world. In the *Vedic* perspective, this lack of harmony due to *avidya* is related mainly to what Abhinava Gupta calls *buddhigata* referring to uncertain and erroneous judgement. In addition, the transformation of the Absolute into *vishwa* is also the process of the unlimited becoming progressively limited, the process of the *apeiron* being bound by *peras* as Plato calls it. In this process two things happen. There occurs, first, a split between subject and object (*dwedhapat*) and, second, the object takes hold of the person and increases the distance between the individual self and the Universal Self. The Infinite, which has five essences, such as, eternity (*nityatwa*), all permanence (*vyapakatwa*), plenitude (*purnatwa*), omniscience (*sarvajnata*), and omnipotence (*sarvakartritwa*), comes, in its procession, to impose upon itself five limitations or sheaths or *kosha.* Eternity is circumscribed by *kala* (time), all-permanence by determination (*niyati*), plenitude by desire (*raga*), omniscience by intellect (*buddhi*), and omnipotence by limited capacity.

The four sheaths are the source of errors, each of which represents a different possibility of error. The *annamaya kosha* engenders attachment and stimulates acquisitiveness and possessiveness. The *pranamaya kosha* is the source of the love for life (*jijivisha*), while *manomaya kosha* represents the psyche in its all complexity of volitions and ideas, the differentiation between the Self and the individual selves, the overflow of passions. And since mind is prone to the flux of pleasant and painful states of the mind, it is liable to error. And, lastly, the *vijnanamaya kosha,* too, is liable to error insofar as it has evolved from *natura naturans*; it can, and usually does, commit the error of treating the empirical self as the true self. As a result, it can and usually get immersed in materiality and suffers *dukha* (unhappiness). The linking of *prayojana* with worthiness *adhikara*) *and Purusha* derives its significance from this perspective in which is also grounded the concept of *samsakaras.*

The significance of *samskaras* is derived from this traditional Indian perspective on life and its different activities subsumed under the *varna* and *purushartha* schemes. Looking from this perspective, it is clear that the purpose of *samskaras* is not the performance of external religious practices, nor any ceremonial performance of these practices.[14] It is true that, as *Manusmriti* 2.66 puts it, *samskaras sharirasya* (that is, *samakaras* purify the body). But it must be emphasizd that the ramification of *samskaras* goes much beyond the mere purification of the body. The purification of the body, that is, draining the body of all its impurities and corrupting elements, is a necessary part of *yajna*. Without the performance of *samsakaras* in this sense, *yajna* must remain a lifeless ritual without any religious or spiritual significance. It is true that Harit makes a distinction between *daiva* and *brahma samsakaras* (*dwividhah samskaro bhavati, brahmo daivasya, garbhanadi smarto brahma*). While *yahna* is included in *daiva samskara*, other religious practices performed on different occasions of a person's life cycle are categorised as *brahma samskara*. It must, however, be emphasised that *yajna* as a part of *samaskara*, when performed in the right spirit, constitutes the most important means of internal transformation. But this transformation will lack meaning and relevance if it does not influence and gets reflected in personal lives and social relations.

Yajna must be defined in terms both of the process of internal transformation and the resultant sublimation of orientation to life and world, motivational pattern and behavioural propriety and finesse. The real purport of *yajna* is, therefore, a radical transformation and renovation of attitude so that the quatenarian structure of the primordial community of man and god and society and world can be preserved and safeguarded. It is on this basis alone that the resolution of the tension and conflict resulting from the antagonism between the personal and the collective, between the good of one individual and the good of all individuals, can be effected. For this, it is necessary for man to transcend his base nature and *yajna* happens to be the best means, the means *par excellence,* of making this transcendence possible. As Baldeva Upadhyaya observes:

> *Yajna* signifies that which is instrumental in the purification of the body; it is equally efficacious in purifying man's ego-sense and his mind. It is a purificatory action that

does not result in serving or promoting self-interest; its result also helps in achieving the good of others. It does not by any means create a fresh layer of karmic bondage but, instead, weakens and dissolves the old ones. (As a result of this), it paves the way for the real good of the individual, making it possible for him to acquire knowledge. Sacrifice and acquisition, both are integral aspects of action. To give up that which is insubstantial and unreal and embrace that which is substantial and real are acts that are supportive of *yajna*. Skill in action helps diminishing the impure and augmenting the pure.[15]

Needless to say that it is the extension of the *Vedic* idea of *yajna* that later culminates in *karmakanda*. Treating *karmakanda* as a field in itself separated from other fields that owe their origin to none else than the *Vedic* world-view, *karmakanda* appears to be focusing on certain external religious practices without any internal significance and, therefore, divorced from its engendering spiritual experience or significance. As has already been pointed out, to treat the Veda as simply a compendium of rites and rituals constituting the integral part of *yajna* interpreted merely as a generic name for so many external religious practices is not only to miss the real significance of *yajna* but also to rob the Veda of spiritual evocative power and its transformatory potential.

As has also been indicated earlier, the *Vedic* emphasis is not on *devayajna* but rather on the *atmayajna* referring to the need of self-transcendence that alone paves the way for the preservation of the quatenarian structure of the primordial community of man and god and society and world. Thus, what the Veda says is not to be interpreted in any literal sense; it should be interpreted in symbolic terms. This is quite clear because the language that the Veda employs, is not direct but indirect; it does not describe the reality meant to be observed, but evokes a certain mental state that is conducive to self-transcendence through self-transformation.

It is against this background that the emphasis laid by the Mimamsa School on *dharma* as whatever the Veda says is, to say the least, misleading. Given the fact that the Veda uses *aparoksha* (indirect language), the real purport of the Veda is hidden in myths, aphorisms, evocative prayers to different gods, etc. its import cannot be deciphered by literally translating the *Vedic Mantras* since, on the surface, the *Vedic Mantras*, as Bloomfield sees it, are simply utilitarian asking the gods to grant sons, riches and prowess, etc. and favour only the rich men who can gift thousands of cows and a large quantity of wealth to the Brahmans. As such, the real import of the *Vedic Mantras* eludes those who are not equipped either with the spiritual experience or appropriate scholarship to decipher their meaning.

It needs to be emphasised that there are only scattered references in the Veda to *samskaras.* Similarly, the Veda does not present a detailed and systematic discussion of *yajna* that we find, for example, in the Kalpa literature. The definition of Kalpa as *kalpyate samarthyate yagaprayogo'atra*, that is, the literature in which the uses and purposes of *yajna* find detailed discussion and description. As such, the Kalpa literature is the store-house of information about *yajna* and the way different types of *yajnas* must be performed. In other words, the Kalpa literature presents a detailed information on all *yajnas* that have been conceived by the Veda. This is a further confirmation of the fact that the Veda is not a compendium of *yajna* as a generic name for different external religious practices related to religious rites, ceremonies, and rituals. Detailed description of both *yajna* and *samsakaras* are totally absent in the Veda. As indicated earlier, references to *samskaras* are far and few between in the Veda. RVV.76.2 talks of *gharma* (a vessel for heating milk especially for Ashwins) that has been purified (*samskrit*) and invokes Ashwins to protect it.

If we extend the meaning of this *Mantra* to human body, it, too represents a vessel in which the process of *atmayajna* occurs. The body, too, needs to be purified. But this does not simply mean all those actions that are instrumental in making the body clean and purified of all its external impurities. It does not need to be emphasised that to clean the body of its external, material impurities forms only a part, albeit an important, part of the purificatrory process. Human body does not simply represent the external appearance or organs. Central to the conception of the human body is a holistic view that treats it as a composite of intelligence, energy and appetites; that is to say, it is composite of thinking, speaking and doing. To cleanse the body of its impurities, therefore, signifies purity in all these aspects. When conceived as such, the cleansing of the body signifies proper conduct at the personal, institutional and social levels. This, needless to say, is the field of *achara* (conduct) which forms an integral part of a person as a member of the primordial community.

The propriety of *achara* rests upon the extent to which a person adheres to moral considerations in his everyday social life. The source of morality is, of course, *dharma* signifying a trans-individual perspective on human life and its pragmatic and higher concerns. Needless to say that *dharma* connotes a set of abstract principles which receive concrete expression as *vyavahara* (practices) in different time and space. It is true that the source of *dharma* is what the Veda says, but not in the Mimamsa sense. The Veda offers only a dim insight into the structure of order. This dim insight into the structure of order does not by any means incorporate elaborate principles or a detailed blueprint of social organisation, its institutional arrangement, and practices, all of which has an important bearing on the orientation and conduct of persons located in different life situations. This insight does gain a glimpse of truth about order, to be sure. However, this glimpse neither gains all of the truth, nor is in a position to establish an ultimate order for man. The primordial insight into the truth of order is gradually elaborated in principles of social organisation and personal conduct. This elaboration is symptomatic of man's effort to fit himself and his spiritual and pragmatic concerns in the embracing order of heaven and earth as a means of finding meaning and value in his uncertain finite existence.

Dharma owes its origin to this dim primordial insight into the truth of order and represents an effort to imitate the principles that are seen to emanate from and exemplify the essential nature of truth. The Veda is, in a very important sense, a symbolic and mythical expression of the experience of transcendence. This experience yields only a very vague and ambiguous insight into the truth of order without offering any set of elaborate principles and rules pertaining to the social organisation and personal conduct. All these principles and rules are framed later in the *Smriti* literature; however, these principles and rules are embedded, informed by and inexorably tied up with the experience of the *Vedic* seer poets or *kavirmaneesis*. It is only in this sense that whatever the Veda says constitutes *dharma* must be understood.

The elaboration of these principles and rules is also symptomatic of the proliferation of the *Vedic* literature into *Shruti* and *Smriti* literature. The former represents an account in symbolic and mythic form of the experience of transcendence while the latter signifies the elaboration of the principles of *dharma* derived from the primordial insight of *Kavirmaneeshis* into the structure of order. *Shrutistu vedo vijneyo dharmashastram tu vai smriti* (*Manusmriti*, 2.10). Thus, *Smriti* literature draws its inspiration from and is embedded in the *Vedic* articulation of the experience of transcendence. The authenticity and legitimacy of *Smriti* literature derive from their being based on *Shruti*:

> *Purva vijnana vishayam vijnanam smriti ruchyate;*
> *Purva jnanad vina tasyat pramanyam Navadharyate.*

That *Smriti* literature draws its authenticity and legitimacy from the pre-existing knowledge, that is, the knowledge of the experience of transcendence as detailed in the *shruti* literature exemplifying the real significance of what is called Sutra. literature. *Sutra* means thread that joins it with the pre-existent system of knowledge, that is, the *Vedic* literature. The *Kalpasutra*, which details out the purpose and procedures of *yajna*, is further divided into four areas of specialisation. These are *Srautasutra*, *Grihyasutra*, *Dharmasutra* and *Shulbasutra*. What concerns us here is the nature of *Dharma-sutra* and *Grihyasutra* and their relationship.

The substantive content of *Dharmasutra* relates to devotion to God, good moral conduct, social and personal codes of conduct and responsibilities. In other words *Dharma Sutra* focuses on the linkage between the finite existence of man and the absolute source of meaning and value. In dealing with this linkage, *Dharmashastra* joins *vyavahara* (practices) with their underlying principles derived from the essential linkage between the finite and the absolute. As such, *Dharmashastra* covers the entire range of human life in all its stages and all its aspects.

It should be obvious, then, that *Dharmasutra* focuses on the wholeness of human existence and, in doing so, it gives a definite direction to man's life and prescribes a well defined pathway to follow this direction. Following this path, man can make himself respectable and find a place of respect in society. *Dharmasutra* does not remain content with underlining the need to live a morally satisfying life but also how the tenets of moral living can be translated into moral norms and modes of action and test moral principles on the touchstone of everydayness. As Umesh Chạndra Mishra observes, " Hindu *dharma* sees in man endless potentialities and capabilities. It therefore aims at regulating and disciplining individual existence"[16], making it possible for the individual to realise these potentialities. "It is true", Mishra argues, "that it takes into account even the smallest problems of life, gives its judgement, and guides the individual as he journeys in this world of here and now. However, in doing so, it does not curb individual freedom in any way ...*Swasya cha priyamatmanah.* ..."[17]

Lest it be interpreted to mean the willfulness of individual to follow his own whims and caprices, an impression that Mishra seems to create, the substantive thrust of the term *swasya cha parmatmanah* is to follow one's conscience purified by the soul's attunement to the divine ground of being. It is only the soul touched by the flash of eternity that can decide and act upon what is dear to it. Such a decision cannot in any way be said to be an exercise of freedom since it is governed by considerations of what is moral. Thus any decision and action based on it must fulfil, at one and the same time, two conditions: it must conform to the demands of morality and it should be supportive of the idea of *lokasamgraha* (sustenance of the lived world). It is here that we can see the play of unity of principles and actions congealing in *vyavahara*, that is, *achara.*

Achara, thus, implies conformity to certain standards that must govern personal and social action that ensures integrity in personal life and harmony in social relations. It is symptomatic of the necessary transition between "knowing virtue" to "having virtue". It is because of this that the Hindu view of life attributes so much importance to *achara*.[18] As *Vashishtha Dharmasutra*, 6.4 puts it, " A person lacking good moral conduct may be well-versed in *Vedic* or *shastric* knowledge. But for all that, he is like a blind person who cannot experience the pleasure of watching his beautiful wife. Needless to say that given the central importance of *achara* in the Hindu cultural perspective, it cannot be treated as incorporating a set of standards of personal conduct set by the person himself. It signifies a group attribute that has evolved out of a particular idea of man and its location and role in the phenomenal world–the idea that is expressive of the resolve of a particular human association to preserve and promote the integrity of the quatenarian structure of the primordial community of man and god and society and world.

It is by virtue of this that it is very difficult to separate the personal from the communal insofar as what is considered to be exclusively personal, too, has certain potentials of promoting or blocking the possibility of self-transcendence, of safeguarding or disrupting social harmony and concord, and of protecting, safeguarding or harming cosmic metabolism. It is because of the predominance of the pursuit of highly private concerns that tends to disrupt the wholeness of Hindu view on life and divide human conduct in water-tight compartments of personal and social. It is, therefore, not surprising that *Dharmasutra* and *Grihyasutra* overlap in their treatment of what is worth doing for a householder and that for a person. And in thus overlapping, the *Dharmasutra*, the backbone of *Samskaras*, the field assigned to *Grihyasutra*, has sought to weld together even the smallest events and diverse occasions of man's life cycle by making it necessary for every householder to perform certain religious rites and rituals throughout life as a matter of religious duty.

It is true that the performance of *samskaras* is incumbent upon every householder and a man becomes a householder only when he is married. And as such, only married couples are entitled to and are under the necessity of performing *samskaras.* It is because of this that the discipline dealing with *samskaras* is called *Grihyasutra.* It is at the time of marriage that *Agni* (the sacred fire) is installed in the house and all rites and rituals are performed in this *Agni.* And since these rites and rituals are performed in this sacred fire, they are also called *pakayajna.* Thus the performance of all *yajnas* in *Agni* installed in the house of a householder at the time of his marriage are *pakayajnas.* But *paka* does not signify the act of *cooking*; it means perfection in two different but interrelated senses. In the first place, since the performance of *yajna* follow certain set patterns, rules and procedures as laid down in the Sutra literature, it is perfect. In the second place, the performance of these *samskaras* aim at making a person perfect.

Given this dual nature of performance of *samskaras*, it is but natural that it joins the realm of gods and men. As a result of this dual nature, *samskaras* span over two different but not unrelated realms, that is, imperishable and perishable, unchanging and changing, permanent and transitory. And it is because of this double referents that *samskaras*, too, exhibit a dual nature. Whereas their performance follows certain fixed, immutable rules and procedures, they also allow for local variations. That is why their performance also allows for *grama vachanam cha kuryuh*, that the performance of *samskaras* also incorporates local traditions and ways of doing things.

References

1. *Brihaddevata*, I.120 defines *bhavavrittam* as *akhyan* (story) which gives an account of what was or was not before the creation and how this cosmos came to be. This story focuses on the genesis, existence, change, increase, decrease and annihilation. *Ibid.*, 2.121. See also, Lakshman Sarup, ed. *The Nighantu and the Nirukta* (Delhi: Motilal Banarasidas, 1984), I.I.
2. Jeanine Miller, *The Vision of Cosmic Order in the Vedas* (London: Routledge & Kegan Paul,1985), p. 38.
3. *The Republic*, 434 b-c,444 b.
4. L.A.Sass, "The Self and its Vicissitudes: An Archaeological Study of the Psycho-Analytic Avantgarde", *Social Research*, 55 (1988).

5. Freud quoted in Philip Rieff, *Freud : The Mind of the Moralist* (New York: Anchor Books,1961), p.29.
6. Eric Voegelin, *Israel and Revolution: Order and History*, Vol. III (Baton Rouge: Louisiana State University Press, 1986), p. 1.
7. *Udgitha* is commonly understood as the chanting of Saman verses. But this conceals its real purport.
8. *Aitereya Brahman*, II-I.
9. *Baudhayana Dharmasutra*, ed. Umesh Chandra Pandeya (Varanasi: Chaukhamba Sanskrit Sansthan, Vs.2055), p.1.
10. For a very useful discussion, see A.K. Coomaraswami, "Atma Yajna: Self Sacrifice," in *Selected Papers*, p. 108.
11. Cf. *Jaiminiya Upanishad Brahman* (JUB), I.14.I: " He should not be one whose gods are far away. Verily, it is insofar as he approaches the gods with himself (*atmanadeva upasate*) that becomes god for him. And *Br.Up.I.IV.10*: "So whoever approaches the deity as being other, thinking he is one, and I another, does not comprehend; he is a mere victim of them".
12. Coomaraswami, *Selected Papers*, p. 132.
13. Coomaraswami, "Windows of the Soul" in *What is Civilisation?* (Delhi, Oxford University Press,1989), p. 53.
14. Rajabali Pandeya, *Hindu Samskara*, *op. cit.* and Baladeva Upadhyaya,*Vaidika Sahitya aur Samskriti*, p. 493.
15. *Baudhayana Dharmashastra*, p. 19
16. *Ibid.*
17. Cf. *Vashistha Dharmasutra*, 6.1
18. *Acharah Paramodharmah sarveshamiti nischayah;*
    Hinacharaparitatma Pretya cheta cha nashyati.

6

Marriage as Samskara

It is well known that marriage constitutes an important as well as an integral part of the *samskaras* of the Hindus. This is so for several reasons. In the first place, no religious ceremony, such as *homa* (offerings to the gods through the medium of *Agni*), that is, *yajna* in the true sense of the term, can be undertaken by a Hindu who has remained unmarried. A person who remains unmarried is declared to be unfit for performing *yajna*; he is dubbed as *ayajniya,* that is, a person who is not permitted to perform *yajna* (*ayajniyo va esha yo'patnik, TB 2.2.2.6*). The importance of marriage lies in the fact that a person who remains unmarried is considered to be incomplete; only when he gets married, he is supposed to be a complete being, a worthy candidate for performing all religious rites. As such, he becomes complete only when he is joined together by his consort that is his counterpart, the female principle. It is no wonder, then, that one of the most important godheads in Indian mythology is *Ardhanarishwar,* a being who is half male and half female, that is, the symbol of conjoint parenthood. *TB 2.9.4.7* puts it: *atho ardho va esha atmanah yat patni* (an unmarried person is only half complete, his wife is the other half).

There is another reason for the importance that is attached to the institution of marriage in Hindu society. This has to do with the *ashrama vyavastha* (the system of life stages). The system of life stages is the recognition that the world as it is, is; it can neither be denied nor ignored. To deny or ignore it amounts, at the one and the same time, to denying or ignoring the very existence of God whose emanation the world happens to be. Nor can the world be treated as something that is profane and that corrupts man or makes him incapable of getting himself or, to be precise, his soul attuned to the divine ground of being. There is, of course, the view associated largely with Pythagoras who treats both this world and man's body corrupt and, by the same token, corrupting agents. This world as well as the body is the prison-house of the soul, the soul that, in contrast to both the world and the human body, is the essential part of the God and his sensorium. Being imprisoned in the corrupt and corrupting body and the world, the soul is made an unwilling resident of a domain that is not suitable for those works that are aimed at freeing the soul from its bondage. If the soul is to be freed of its thralldom to the body or the world, the claim of the body or the world for that matter must be forcefully resisted, even rejected.

Needless to say that the body or the world is, on this view, a corrupting agent, an unnecessary evil. As such, each of the two constitutes an unnecessary restraint on and an obstacle to any meaningful spiritual quest. Once both the world and the human body are considered to be corrupt and, therefore polluting and corrupting, this view leads inexorably to the conclusion that the world is devoid of the presence of the divine ground of being and, therefore, lacks divine order. This does not, however, mean that the world totally lacks order; it does have an order, but it is an order that resists God who, in turn, condemns and, therefore resists the world as being corrupt. Needless to say that, on this view, the world must be left alone and, if possible, it should altogether be left. In contradistinction to this view, the *Vedic* world-view, as already pointed out, treats both the body and the world as part of the divine, a *vivarta* of the One Beyond who becomes the *vishwa* in the process of his becoming. As such, both the body and the world, too, are sacred, not profane. They are, therefore, the proper medium and appropriate means through which one can very well seek attunement of one's soul to the divine ground of being. If this is true, then, it is also true that the claims of the body or the world can neither be taken lightly nor can they be dismissed as something that are corrupt and corrupting and, therefore, not worthy of man's serious attention, particularly in matters spiritual. It cannot be denied that to be engrossed in the process of satisfying the demands of the body or the world to the neglect or exclusion of the claim of the soul makes a person *kamachara,* as Ch. U. puts it, and turns him into a spiritually blind person. And a spiritually blind person harbours a "sick" soul; he becomes possessed by insatiable desires and appetites. Driven by his desires and appetites, he makes the world into a hunting ground for finding the wherewithal of satisfying his insatiable desires and appetites. Thus the world, when reduced to the status of a hunting ground becomes a poor place; when dirempted from its transcendental ground, it is reduced to the degrading status of an instrument to be used, even abused, for realising the self-defined purposes of self-aggrendising persons.

It is in this context that we can appreciate the need for establishing a balance between the need to satisfy bodily or worldly demands and the claim of the soul. Without establishing such a balance the individual loses balance and harmony in his interior, comes in conflict with his fellowmen and goes out of tune with the source of his being. It is to prevent this from happening that the *Vedic* world-view insists on the need to establish a balance in man's interior and promote harmony between him and his world. But such a balance in man's interior, as has already been pointed out, cannot be established as long as man treats his different faculties—soul, intelligence, energy and appetites—as co-equal and, therefore, autonomous. Once they are treated as co-equals, only compromise among these autonomous and co-equal faculties is possible, whenever they happen to be opposed to each other. But this compromise, when somehow arrived at, is always subject to disruption at any moment because no controlling superior element is available within the interior of man that can intervene and force them to come to some compromise and keep peace—a compromise that is satisfactory to all and the peace that proves durable. As such, it has to be recognised, first, that there is the need of such a superior element in man's interior and, second, that this superior element is none else than the soul itself. It is, therefore, necessary that the soul must be installed and established as the ruling element in man's interior that can then establish order within and harmony without.

Needless to point out that it is the establishment of the soul as the ruling element in the interior of man that constitutes the source of human excellence. And by its very nature such an ideal of human excellence fuses and promotes interaction between aesthetic, moral and religious elements. It is such an ideal of human excellence that the *Vedic* world-view celebrates and makes it incumbent on every person to aspire for and actively strives to realise it in his/her own life. The active pursuit of this ideal steers man's destiny in the sea of phenomenal world marked by chaos and unrest of troubled life and restores the balance in man's life by inspiring him to attune his soul to the highest reality that happens to be the substratum of the phenomenal world and that often seems to be shrouded in the mist of ignorance and the resultant cupidity. The system of life stages prevalent among the Hindus provides a structural prop for safeguarding the consciously active pursuit of the ideal of human excellence vouchsafed by the *Vedic* world-view. It constitutes a structure that allows every person to actively establish the balance between the claims of his body and the good of his soul, if it has not been established before or, alternatively, restore it if it has been disrupted by the swirls of change in the lived world.

The *ashramavyavstha*[1] represents a system which combines in it the possibility of the pursuit of the concerns of both the world here and now and the world beyond. Note, for example, the fact that the first two stages of man's life, that is, *Brahmacharya* (a part of life devoted to learning, preparatory to the bearing of the responsibilities of a householder) and *Grihasthashrama* (the life of the householder) culminate in the third, that is, *Banaprastha* (that part of life which is devoted to preparation for renouncement) prior to the last stage of life, that is, *Samnyasa* (renunciation) in which a person breaks all his ties with his near and dear ones, turns away from the world of bondage and all that it implies and turns around to seek his own freedom from the unending cycles of births and deaths. It is that part of life stage in which a person undertakes a serious spiritual quest. This division of the whole span of a person's life into four different stages is important insofar as it allows a person to pursue all the *purusharthas* (life objects or purposes worthy of pursuit). The four *purusharthas,* that is, *kama, artha, dharma, and moksha*, blend in themselves this worldly and other-worldly concerns in a nice balance indicating at once two things. In the first place, it is recognised that desires of all sorts that go into the determination of different life purposes must be fulfilled if man is to attain happiness and completeness. In the second place, the satisfaction of these desires, if they are to yield the greatest good of the individual and ensure social concord at the same time, must be subjected to the suzerainty of *dharma.* Once a person has performed all his worldly responsibilities, he must, then, turn to seek the well being of his own inner self.

Thus it is quite clear that the *Vedic* world-view recognises the concerns of this world to be as important and vital as those that are associated with the world beyond. Once these two concerns are treated as central to man's existence, it becomes necessary to do everything to safeguard the integrity of the lived world and to contribute to its continued existence. As such, it is incumbent on every person to perform his worldly duties with diligence and devotion. To contribute to the continued existence of the lived world implies, in the most general term, the continuance of the human race. This is possible only when the institution of marriage is established and it is seen to it that it functions well. To get married is to enter a new life, a life of duties and responsibilities that pertain, first to the *asau loka,* then to the society at large, then to the members of the household, and then to the person himself who marries. It is no wonder, then, that *Shabdakalpadruma* defines *vivaha* (marriage) as *vivaha vishishtam vahanam,* that is, something that implies the bearing of responsibilities in a particular way. It is true, as *MS* 3.20 notes, *vivaha bharya praptihetuh* (marriage is contracted in order to get a wife). However, the very act of marrying involves a shift in a person's orientation, that is,, it involves a shift from a person's focus on "me" to "mine" symbolising the formation of a family and the need of its continuance over time. The very shift from "me' to "mine" is indicative of the addition to a man's life of two important dimensions, that of time and space. That is to say, the person, when he gets married begins to think in terms of future generations and he becomes instrumental not only in expanding the size of his family but also in ensuring the continuity of the race he belongs to. Thus, when married, the individual is forced to shift the focus of his attention and life concerns from his well being to the well-being and welfare of others close to him and closely related to him by virtue of being an essential component of the net-work of relationships. The life of the householder is, therefore, the life of practicing the ideal of love of others instead of self-love.

Lastly, it is, therefore, quite clear that the real import of marriage is not the search for a life partner for sexual pleasure alone but sexual pleasure aimed at the continuation of the race one belongs to. But the continuation of the race itself involves, on the one hand, the repayment of certain debts a person incurs simply by the act of taking birth and getting help from some important sources for performing his worldly duties and, on the other, the continuance of the race at a higher level of existence. Insofar as the repayment of these debts is concerned, the tradition of Hindu thinking identifies three kinds of *rina* (debt) that every person contracts by virtue of being born in this world. As *TS 6.3.10.5* notes:

> *jayamanoha vai Brahmanastribhirri navan jayate brahmacharyena rishiyo yajnena devabhyah prajaya pitribhyah*

(When born, a person incurs three debts which he can repay through *Brahmacharya* (the practice of celibacy), to Rishis, through *yajna* to the gods, and through begetting children to his father.

It is quite clear why the institution of marriage occupies a place of such central importance in the life pattern of the Hindus. The importance of marriage lies not only in the fact that marriage permits a person to perform religious rites, that is, *yajna*, which constitute the means of discharging the debts one owes to the gods but also because it is essential for repaying one's debt to his father.

The repayment of the debt to the father is simply a means of ensuring the continuity of the race and needless to say that marriage is instrumental in it. But what is also important in this regard is that the continuity of the race in itself is not that significant as its continuance at a higher level of existence. The need of the existence of the race at a higher level of existence means the performance of all the *samskaras* that constitute for a Hindu a vital means of purification, spiritual elevation and spiritual liberation. The performance of most of these *samskaras* takes place in the life of the householder It is not, therefore, surprising that *grhasthashrama* (the life stage of a householder) occupies the place of pride in the Hindu social system. According to Manu, all other *ashramas* are dependent on *grihasthashrama* for the simple reason that it helps other *ashrams* with sustenance and knowledge.[2] It is clear, then that the *grihasthashrama* is considered to be not only the centre-piece of the *ashramavyavastha;* it also signifies that a weak person is not capable of bearing the heavy responsibilities of the life of a householder.[3]

It is, therefore, not surprising that, given the importance of the *grihasthashrama* and the key role in it of marriage, an unmarried person has been debarred from performing *yajna* and declared *ayajniya.* Quoting an unknown author, Apararka draws in his commentary on *Yagyavalkya Smriti* our attention to the fact that the wife is the supreme most important factor in the realisation of both *artha* and *kama.* An unmarried person, no matter which caste he belongs to, is not worthy of performing any religious act.[4] In view of the central importance of marriage for the Hindus, it is marriage that is considered in Mithila to be the foremost of all *samskaras;* it is something like *primus inter pares.* The significance of all the *samskaras* is dependent on the marriage *samskara.* And since marriage constitutes a key *samskara,* it is performed as religious rite and it therefore needs to be sanctified by Brahmans and gods. Thus, marriage as an important part of the *yajna* needs to be sanctified and witnessed by *Agni*, gods, *Purohits* and family relations and friend and well-wishers. Marriage can take only after *samavartana samskara*, that is, the rite on returning home from the Guru's *Ashrama.* As *MS* 3.2 prescribes, "(A student) who has studied in due order the three Vedas, or two, or even one only, without breaking (the rules of) studentship, shall enter the order of the householder." But he can do so, as *MS* 3.4 underlines, only after he takes his bath and performs *samavartan samskara* with the permission of his teacher. What is also interesting to note in this connection is the fact that no marriage is considered legitimate unless it has been sanctified by certain religious rites and rituals. As *YS* 1.76 notes: *Nodakena bina chayam kanyayah patiruchyate; panigrahanasamskarat patitwan saptame pade.* It is thus clear that no act of marriage, no matter whichever way it has been performed, can be considered legitimate if it has not been sanctified by certain religious rites.

Given the fact that marriage has multidimensional ramifications —religious, social and personal—the act of marriage needs to be a well-modulated function in such a way that it does not infringe certain boundaries set by the *Shastras*, cultural traditions, and well established local social conventions. Needless to say that, given its multifaceted significance, the reduction to the point of almost zero of personal choice in selecting a life partner becomes inevitable. This is so for the simple reason that the exercise of personal choice in the selection of a life partner is bound to take its erratic course independent of all religious, social and familial norms. And violation of norms is considered, by traditional Indian opinion, to be the certain cause of anarchy and chaos in the social order reflected in the disruption of *varnashramadharma.* As such, marriages are governed largely, even exclusively in a large number of cases, by religious tradition and social conventions. It must be emphasised here that social conventions and practices, too, are largely governed by the rules, regulations, and processes that are sanctified by and are in keeping with the *Shastric* tradition and religious texts.

It does not, however, signify by any means that locally prevalent social conventions and practices conform totally to *Shastric* injunctions. To expect the locally prevalent social conventions to fully conform to *Shastric* injunctions is neither desirable nor practical. This is so for the simple reason that any abstract idea that is supposed to be above the variations of time and space, undergoes the process of change the moment it enters the stream of time and assumes different forms in different space and time. This is true of *dharma* which gets differentiated into diverse *vyavahaara* under varied temporal and spatial influences. This is also true of *Shastric* injunctions about marriage that assume different forms apart from being encumbered by local customs and local understandings of *Shastric* injunctions. What needs to be pointed out is that even *Shastras* recognise and lend validity and legitimacy to it. However, these practices and usages must not go against the spirit of the spiritual world-view that undergirds, influences and animates religious and social practices and customs.

Historically eight different kinds of marriages[5] are said to have been prevalent or, alternatively, considered to be ideally possible. Of these eight types, no one form exists in its original or pure form and intent. The passage of time has slowly wrought transformations in all forms of marriages. Some of them have altogether disappeared while others have undergone radical sea change and have appeared in entirely new forms. For example, the *Paishachic* marriage was seldom in vogue and squarely condemned by all the writers of religious texts. The *Rakshasi* marriage, though infrequently practised and said to be a legitimate form of marriage, was prevalent especially among the Kshatriyas.[6] *Gandharva* marriage, once very much in vogue, has almost disappeared; it is only now under the stress of modernisation that it is again making its appearance in the form of love marriages. The *Asuri* marriage is prevalent even today but largely among the people who stand very low on social hierarchy. *Prajapatya* marriage was entered into on the request of the male seeking a life-mate and was sanctified so that the newly married couple may perform their social and religious duties. This form of marriage has, perhaps, never been in vogue. The *Arsha* form of marriage, even if it was prevalent in the olden times, has disappeared altogether subsequently. *Daiva* form of marriage, too, has totally disappeared even while it may have been practised once upon a time. The *Brahma* form of marriage, supposed to be the purest form, may have been widely prevalent as is, perhaps, exemplified by the marriage of *Surya* (R*V X.85*).

The prevalent form of marriage today is a modified form of *Brahma* marriage in the sense that the father of the marriageable girl or any other relative for that matter, if the father is deceased or incapable for any reason, finds a suitable life partner for her and makes a *dana* (gift in the religious sense of the term) to the bridegroom. Of course, the custom of paying dowry, sometimes very huge ones, has extremely corrupted the purest form of this type of marriage and has, at one and the same time, proved to be a social bane.[7] Whatever may have been the changes that have in time overtaken different forms of marriages, the *pratimana* (paradigm) of all marriages among the Hindus has its roots in the *Vedic* cosmogony, or *bhavavrittam* as *Brihaddevata* calls it. It is this *bhavavrittam* which also finds its expression in Platonic "likely story" of the creation. This is a story that recounts the way the One Unknown may possibly have become many in the process of its transformation. That is to say, this is a process through which the transcendent entity called the Unknown or Brahma in the *Vedic* parlance assumes form and becomes, as a result, embodied (or what Plato calls *enhylon eidos*). In other words, the *Vedic* cosmogony is the likely story of the way the entity that is wholly abstract or formless or exists simply as an Idea assumes a material form and becomes many. And when the One transforms itself into numerous *nama* (name) and *rupa* (form), we have the resultant cosmos.

The process of coming into being of the cosmos is, of course, not something that can be apprehended as one does an object in the phenomenal world. It is a process that only a *gambhirachetas* (*RV VIII.8.2*), that is, a person endowed with profound knowledge of that which is completely ineffable, can discern and describe, that too very vaguely through the medium of myths and symbols. The *Vedic* poets endowed with a super-sensuous vision created hymns that contain "knowledge about the process of creation or self-manifestation by which the Divine has become this all, and also the knowledge of the Divine as the inner unity of all that is there."[8] And what the *gambhirachetas Vedic* seer-poets see is the absolute truth: *ekam sadviprah bahudha vadanti* (there is only one truth although the wise speak of it in many ways, *RV 1.164.46*). But this seeing is not the ordinary seeing which is done with the help of the physical eyes; it is done through what Jan Gonda calls "heart's eye;" this is equivalent to *bodhi* (direct experience, enlightenment) rather than *buddhi* (thinking in concepts). The truth that *bodhi* yields is not like the knowledge of an object that can be apprehended through concepts and possessed like a thing. Also, it is not something that can be cognitively analysed and categorised. It is a truth that can be gained only through experience engendered through participation in the larger reality, a reality larger than the limited contingent existence of a person or a race; it can be realised through a consciousness that is only illumined through the attunement of the soul to the truth of being as well as the momentary flash of eternity.

The experience of the Beyond can certainly be expressed in words, whether spoken or written. However, the reality behind these words still remains nameless; it is impersonal and unembodied. "He who experiences it as concretely present remains the God beyond his presence."[9] As such, the language used to describe the God beyond his presence is "fraught with the problem of symbolising the experience of a not-experienciable divine reality."[10] It is true that the cosmos is what the Veda identifies as the *praket* (symbol) of what is *apraket* (signless). However, as a symbol, it tends to bring a reality of a specific sort to the fore instead of the reality it is supposed to display or disclose. As a result, the visible world fails to convey fully the nature and identity of its own maker. If the maker cannot be revealed by what he makes, the process of the making of the world is all the more a mystery. As Dirghatamas puts it, *ya I chakar na so asya veda ya i dadarsha hiruginnu tasmat* (he who has made it does not know it and he who has beheld it has it also verily hidden, *RV I. 164. 32*).[11] In the lack of exact knowledge about the maker or about the process of the making of this world, one can only speculate about both. One can only tell a story, the most likely story, which is as close to the reality it purports to depict as possible.

If one furnishes account no less convincing than any other, we must be content, remembering that I who speak and you my judges are only human, and consequently it is fitting that we should, in all these matters, accept the likely story and look for nothing further."[12]

Needless to say that, like any other culture, Indian culture, too, has a likely story of the creation process through which the cosmos came into being. It is this likely story that defines the *Vedic* cosmogony that constitutes the nurturing and sustaining ground of Indian culture as well as the paradigm of marriage among the

Hindus in the phenomenal world. The hero of this likely story is, of course, the Absolute himself who transforms himself through a well-defined process and becomes what we know as the *vishwa*, the cosmos. The transformation of the One into many takes place through the ever-pervasive and ever-occurring process of *yajna.* Before the initiation of the cosmic *yajna*, also known as the *Purushamedha Yajna,* the One, *Tadekam,* was modeless in his omnipresence, not yet selfed (*atmanvi*),[13] as Ananda Coomaraswamy puts it; it is undifferentiated, yet unmanifest. Before the One begins to grow, transmutate, and take different shapes, it is neither the creator nor the God the *vishwa* comes to know about. It is only with the help of primordial self-sacrifice (*i.e. Purushamedha*, *RV X.90*) that he not only becomes aware of himself but also becomes the world, that is, he becomes a creator.

Once the cosmic *yajna* begins, the transformation of the One into many is described in the *Vedic* likely story in many different ways. On of the ways of transformation of the One into many is identified as the transformation of *Swayambhoo* into the cosmos through his gradual descent from an abstract idea into concrete form assuming the form of a five-tiered cosmos. These tiers, are known, in the *Vedic* parlance, as *Mandalas*, They are; *Swayambhoo*, Parameshthi, *Surya* or Indra, Chandra, and *Prithivi.* What is interesting to note in this regard is the fact that there are two distinct stages in the procession of the One before it becomes the *vishwa* or many. The first state, called the *purvarddha,* is the one in which the One undergoes a series of non-material transformations till the appearance of the first material body, that is, the Sun. After that further material changes take place till the *Prithivi* takes a concrete shape. Another interesting fact about the transformation of the One into many is the alternation of two opposite but complementary principles into which the Absolute splits in the process of transformation, that is, *Agni* and *Soma.* If *Swayambhoo* represents the principle of *Agni*, Parameshthi stands for *Soma.* Likewise if the Sun represents *Agni*, Chandra is the symbol of *Soma.* And, lastly, *Prithivi* is nothing else but a very large material mass containing what is called *martagni* or "dead" *Agni.*

In the *mandala* scheme of the cosmos, Parameshthi is called *ritasadan*, the abode of Rita (*RV VII.36.1*); it is an inexhaustible ocean of *apah,* the substratum, as *RVX.125.7* underlines, of infinite possibilities of *rupa* and *nama.* It is this *apah* that is considered to be *divyanam* (water for gods) according to *RVIX.10.5*) and described as *vishwasya sthatur jagato janitri* (the parent of all that moves or does not move in the universe, *RVVI.50.7*), *ambah*, mother, *TB 1.23.16*; *apo asmanmatarah* (*apah* is our mother, *RVX.17.10*) and *vishwanyanyo bhuwan jayan, Soma* who has generated everything in this world (*RVII. 40.5*). Thus, Parameshthi, as the abode of *apah* or *Soma,* contains in itself immense possibilities or causes of the myriad *nama* and *rupa.* That is why it is called the ocean of causes. It is Parameshthi, the ocean of Rita, that is identified by *YV11.20* as the *yoni* (womb) of *Agni* (cf. *Apam pristhamasi yoniragne,* the surface of *apah* is the womb of *Agni* (*YV11.29; 13.2*). It is this ocean of *apah* that, as *YV 17.30* puts it, received the primeval germ wherein the gods were gathered all together. The relationship between *apah* and *Agni* is thus very intimate. It is *apah* that, as already pointed out, contains within it innumerable possibilities of forms and their eventual appearance in concrete shapes. *Soma* is identified by *RVX.5.1* as capable of giving limitless births, *bhurijanma.* But its potentiality as *bhurujanma* is not realised till it produces its own opposite but complementary principle. This principle is nothing else but *Agni.* Once *Agni* is born, the concomitant principles, *Agni* and *Soma,* become the source of what is known in the *Vedic* perspective as *devasrishti* (birth of gods) and *bhutasrishti* (generation of corporeal beings).

It is, thus, clear that *apah* represents the mother principle (cf. *SB 6.1.9; 10.1.1.4*). That is why *RVVIII.96.1* declares *apah* to be Indra's mother and *RVX. 91.6* declares that *apo agnim janayanta matarah* (mother *apah* gave birth to *Agni*). However, the relation between *Agni* and *apah* is not fully explained by mother and son relationship. This relation is, as a matter of fact, multi-faceted; it is a relationship which *SB2.1.14* describes as that of *yosha* (female)-*vrisha* (male) underlining the fact that they mate or enter into syzygy (*mithuna*). It is this syzygy that is a necessary condition of the creation process. As it says, Water (*apah*) moreover, is female (*yosha*) and *Agni* is *vrisha* (male); so that he thereby supplies the latter with productive male. And since this world (*idam sarvam*) is pervaded (or obtained, *apta*) by water, he sets up the fire, after he has obtained it by means of it. That is why he brings water.[14]

The husband and wife relation between *Agni* and *Soma* is again underlined in *RV IV.58.8-9* and *RV IX2.3* equates *Soma* as *yosha* who bedecked with jewels and well-decorated, goes to meet he husband, that is, *Agni*. It is also interesting to note that *Agni-Sopma* relationship has been conceived of as a relationship between *Annada* (eater of food) and *Anna* (food). For example, *SB 6.6.3.3* identifies the sun (*Aditya*) as the eater and *Soma* as the food. Thus *Soma* as *Anna* is the sustainer and energiser of *Agni*; without the sustenance that *Soma* provides to *Agni* it will fail to take a material form or become a *pinda*, that is, mass. That is why *Soma* is called *Agni*'s body (*agnestanurasi*, *YV5.1*). All this goes to show that the relationship that is existent between *Agni* and *Soma* is characterised by opposition and complementarity. And all such relationships are depicted in the Veda as sexual relationships, generally as syzygy, *mithuna*.[15]

Needlessly to say that, metaphorically speaking, it is the marriage between *Agni* and *Soma* that is the point of origin of *bhutasrishti*. That is to say, with the birth of *Agni*, the process of creation enters the second stage, that is, *uttrararddha*, the stage when the non-material Being gets progressively enwrapped in material covering and appears as a *pinda*, that is, mass. It is this primordial syzygy between *Agni* and *Soma* that is the *arche* or *prima causa*, of all marriages that occur in the world, at least in the Hindu world. And all these marriages are so many examples of the *Vedic* saying that men do as the gods once did. By following the example of gods, men seek to relate themselves, through the act of marriage, to the world beyond, to the world of gods and remind themselves of the source from which they have sprung and express symbolically their intention to ever renew the relationship between themselves and the gods. It is entirely a different matter that this primal syzygy has, for various reasons we need go into here, been drained of its spiritual and religious content along with the complete eclipse of the engendering spiritual experience behind this religious practice. With the loss of this engendering spiritual experience, all mimetic including that of marriage have been to symbols shorn of all its deeper, spiritual significance. Nonetheless, it still constitutes a constant reminder of the existence of the quatenarian communitarian principle that operates between man and God and between society and the world.

That the symbol of the primordial syzygy between *Agni* and *Soma* still retains its perennial significance is exemplified by the practice prevalent among the Brahmans, especially the Shrotriyas of Mithila. When the bridegroom, after the marriage ceremony has been completed, takes his wife to his own house away from her father's house, one of the corners of the *chadar* hanging loose around his neck is tied up with one of the corners of the wife's *uttariya* or Sari. This in itself is the symbol of the eternal unity between the husband and the wife that has been celebrated through the act of marriage. However, what is of greater importance here is the fact that on one of the corners of the *chadar* of the husband are imprinted two figures, one of *Agni* and the other of the moon (or *Soma*). Below these figures happens to be the imprint of the left hand of the wife. The aggregate of all of these symbolically represents the primordial syzygy between *Agni* and *Soma*, whose one instance, the marriage of the boy and the girl happens to exemplify. Along with this, the imprint of the left hand of the girl symbolises her consent to the marriage as well as the intent to live up to the spirit of the eternal syzygy of the two gods in married life.

Another way in which this primordial syzygy is referred to and described is the marriage of *Surya* (*RV X.85*) which constitutes, for the Hindus even today, after the lapse of millennia, the paradigm of all marriages among the mortals as well as the source of the *Mantras* with the help of which the marriages of the mortals are sanctified. Needless to point to the fact that *Surya* herself is an *amartya* (immortal) who is given in marriage to another *amartya,* that is, *Ashwinis.* Insofar as the marriage of *Surya* exemplifies the act of marriage between two *amartyas*, it is apparent that this particular act of marriage has by no means a reference to something, marriage in this case, that takes place between two mortals. As such, *Surya*'s marriage has no physical basis or significance; it is a symbolic act which has meaning insofar as it refers, on the one hand, to some functions on the cosmic level, particularly in the cosmic *yajna*, pointing to the coming together of some crucial elements necessary for the continuance of the cosmic *yajna* or the process of the transformation of the One Unknown into *vishwa,* signifying the process of creation. On the other hand, the *Surya* marriage constitutes a paradigm for all earthly marriages for the Hindus as *praxis* in the true sense of the term.[16] As divine figures, *Surya* is no less a divine personage than the daughter of the Sun or *Surya* himself and *Ashwinis* represent *dwidaivatwa*, that is, a pair of twin divinities. They are said to appear in the sky before the advent of the dawn in a golden carriage driven by horses. *Ashwinis* also symbolise a *nakshatra* (a star) which presides over two other *nakshatras.*[17] *Ashwinis* are also identified by *SB 4.1.5.16* as *Dyau* (the Sun) and *Prithivi* (the earth) who have obtained possession of everything; they are said to be adorned with the garland of *pushkar,* that is, lotus flowers; they are called *Agni,* that is the lotus of this earth, and the Sun, particularly that of yonder sky. It is also interesting to note that *Dyau* and *Prithivi* are called the wheels of the chariot *Ashwinis* ride while travelling in the firmament. The third wheel of *Ashwinis*' chariot (*Ashwinis* are said to ride a three-wheeled chariot) is the Absolute himself.

It is, therefore, obvious from all these that the act of marriage between *Surya* and *Ashwinis* has only a symbolic significance although its counterpart in the phenomenal world is played and replayed innumerable times in the acts of marriage among the Hindus. It is also necessary to re-examine briefly the question of who actually *Surya* was married to. This is necessary in view of the fact some texts allude to this marriage as having taken place between *Surya* and *Soma.* Note, for example that, as *AB* 4.7 points out, Prajapati resolved to give *Surya*, who he has begotten form *Savita*, to *Soma* in marriage. He invited all the gods. He prepared a weapon made up of one thousand *richas*, that is, hymns, as sacred objects to be placed before the bridegroom. But every one of the gods wanted to marry *Surya.* In order to get a solution of this difficult situation, it was decided to hold a race in which the gods will have to take part. And whoever won the race would, then, be entitled to have *Surya* as his wife. In the race that ensued, *Agni* and *Ashwinis* jointly won the race because all other gods, who had taken a lead agreed to the request of *Agni* and *Ashwinis.* The view that *Surya* was married to *Soma* is based upon this.[18]

However, there is enough evidence in the Veda itself that confirms that *Surya* was actually married to *Ashwinis.* Take, for example, *AV I.82.2* which refers to *Bhaga* advising to bring a wife by the road *Ashwinis* carried *Surya* (on his chariot). Again, *RV I. 116. 17* refers to *Surya* ascending the chariot of *Ashwinis* (cf. *RV I.184.3* and *RV IV.43.6*). All this is further confirmed by the fact that Prajapati did make up his mind to offer *Surya* to *Soma* in marriage. However, each of the gods too waned to get *Surya* as wife. *Ashwinis* won and, as a reward, they were wedded to *Surya.* What is also noteworthy in this connection is the fact that Wilson translates *RV X.85.9* thus: *Soma* was desirous of a bride; the two *Ashwinis* were the groomsmen when *Savitri* gave *Surya* who was ripe for a husband, (to *Soma* endowed) with intelligence.[19] However, what this *Mantra* signifies is that *Soma* expressed his desire to marry *Surya*, but when *Ashwinis* won the race, *Surya* was married to them.

We need not now stop here to further offer evidence in support of the marriage of *Surya* with *Ashwinis.* The reference produced above amply prove that *Surya* was, in fact, married to *Ashwinis.* We must return to probing deeper into the esoteric significance of the marriage of *Surya* with *Ashwinis* and its meaning for marriage among the mortals. As has already been pointed out, *Ashwinis* represent *Dyau* and *Prithivi*; *Prithivi* in its own turn is called *ghritavati* or *aswavati* and *aswavati* is one of the names of *Soma.* It is also interesting to note in this connection that the pair of *Dyau* and *Prithivi* is also known as *ahoratri* or *Samvatsar.*[20] Add to it the fact that Prajapati is also known as *Samvatsar,* as is made clear in *SB 11.1.6.13* which underlines the fact that Prajapati, by creating *Samvatsar,* in fact, created a counterpart of himself. In becoming *Samvatsar*, Prajapati completes his transformation into *vishwa.* And the *vishwa* that he created was created, as has already been pointed out, in two distinct stages, *purvarddha* and *uttararddha. Ashwinis* appear during the first stage of the creation while *Surya* appear, as the first symbol of *pinda,* that is, mass, in the second stage of the creation.

The beginning of the second stage of creation heralds, as already indicated, the beginning of *bhutasrishti,* that is, procreation. The process of procreation assumes the transformation of the Absolute which takes place in five different stages. *Swayambhoo* first processes into *Avyaya,* then, subsequently into *Akshara, Kshara, Jiva,* and *vitta.*[20] What is of importance here is to note that, with the appearance of *Akshara,* the *graha Surya* and *nakstra Ashwinis* also appear. The simultaneous appearance of all these three elements crucial to the process of creation is indicative of the beginning of *bhutasrishti.* In the process of *bhutasrishti* the syzygy between *Surya* and *Ashwini* is of crucial importance. This is further confirmed by the fact that, in the Vedic likely story of the process of creation, the *asat,* that is, that which has neither a form nor a center, signifying a pure formless energy, gets transformed into *sat,* that is, something that has both form and a center, that is, a mass. It is in this perspective that we can understand the real import of *RV X.85.18* which reads as follows:

> *Purvaparam charato mayayaitoshishu krilat opariyato adhwara*
> *vishwananyo bhuvanbhichasta ritumranyo vidadhamjayate punah.*

The two (the sun and moon) wandering in thought one after the other, youthful, sportive, approach the sacrifice.

The sacrifice here is not the sacrifice of the *Karmakanda*, but the cosmic sacrifice exemplified by *Purushamedha* signifying the transformation of the *Purusha* into the cosmos. It is this sacrifice that the Sun and the Moon are said to approach because, without syzygy between them, the process of *bhutasrishti* will never begin. The indication is available in the following rik that is, *RV X.85.13*:

> *Suryah vaahatuhpragat savita yamavarijat;*
> *Aghasu hanyante yavo'junyoh parhyute.*

As Wilson translates it, *Surya*'s bridal procession that *Savitri* despatched has advanced; the oxen are whipped along in the *Magha* (constellation); she is borne (to her husband's house) in the *Arjuni* (constellation). This literal translation successfully drains this rik of all its symbolic significance. What, in fact, it signifies is that the bridal procession does start in the *Magha* constellation but reaches its destination in the *Arjuni* constellation. So far Wilson is doing fine. But what, in fact he does miss is that in this procession what substantively happens refers to the fact that the divine light shining in the first stage of the creation gave way to the darkness of the second stage of the creation, the stage which signifies the progressive embodiment of the un-embodied, that is the Absolute. It refers substantively to the fact that as long as the divine light is unpolluted and uncorrupted by any material incursion, it is pure and effulgent. But when it is progressively covered by materiality in the process of transformation, its brightness gets dimmed and may finally be totally engulfed in complete darkness (of ignorance). As has already been pointed out, the Sun is the first material embodiment and stands in the middle of the process of creation. The material embodiment exemplified by the Sun is denoted by the third *vivarta* of *Swayambhoo*, that is *akshara* signifying the greater differentiation in the process of creation. The accompanying *graha* and *nakshatra* are respectively the sun and *Ashwinis*. This again confirms the beginning of the process of the material part of the creation.

These two (the Sun and the Moon) wandering in thought one after the other, youthful, sportive, approach the sacrifice; one of them looks over the world and the other regulating the seasons is born again and again. The obvious reference here is, again, to the syzygy between *Agni* and *Soma* as the beginning of the process of creation. The moon is also the point of origin for counting the seasons and undergoes the stages of increase and wane. This is exactly the case with *Surya* too as the riks in *RVX.85* underline. That the marriage of *Surya* has special significance in the *Vedic* cosmogony cannot be over-stressed and doubted. It is her marriage that allows the Sun to look over all the worlds insofar as without her marriage there would not be all the worlds to look over. Her marriage is testimony to the coming together of two opposite but complementary principles, a necessary condition for the process of creation to move ahead. And since marriages are contracted in the phenomenal world primarily for begetting sons or daughters as a precondition of the continuance of the race and at the same time a step towards the repayment of *pitririna* (the debt to one's father), marriages in the phenomenal world must be patterned after the divine paradigm and informed by spiritual significance contained in the marriage of *Surya* and *Ashwinis* as a contributory element in the process of creation.[21] It is no wonder, then, that the hymns of *Surya*'s marriage are so profusely used in marriages among the mortals, especially those mortals who are Hindus. Besides, different stages and components hinted in *Surya*'s marriage are also followed in the marriages contracted by mortals.

In the strict sense of the term, the *Rigvedic sukta* referring to *Surya*'s marriage does not offer any details or delineates the steps that are followed in the marriages among the Hindus. The elaborate rites and rituals that we find in different *Grihyasutras* are not even obliquely referred to in *RV X.85*. In the main, what this *Sukta* describes are the bridal suit of *Surya*, the kind of chariot *Ashwinis* have to take her home with them, the prayer to release her from the gods to be offered to her husband, prayer for safety in her travel to her husband's house, etc. As such, the *Surya* Sukta, as already indicated, refers only symbolically to the act of marriage as a divine instance of coming together of two opposite but complementary principles for the express purpose of continuing the race. And since marriage has multiple significance, it is but natural that it should be regulated by and conducted in accordance with certain religious principles and procedures. The regulation and conduct of marriages, particularly among the caste groups located at the upper echelons of the caste hierarchy, are governed in Mithila according to *Paraskar and Gobhil Grihyasutras.* What follows below is based on the *Paraskar Grihya Sutra.*

According to this *Sutra*, marriages are to be performed only during the *shukla* (bright) fortnight after the Sun has travelled north (*uttarayana*). In other words, marriages are to be performed during the onset of certain *nakshatras* (constellations). Marriages performed in these *nakshatras* are considered auspicious. These *nakshatrs* are: *Uttara Falguni*, *Hasta*, *Chitra*, *Uttarashadha*, *Shravan*, *Dhanishtha*, *Uttarabhadrapada*, *Revati*, and *Ashwini*. Similar to *mundana, Yajnopavita and Simantonnayana,* marriages must take place in a specially constructed temporary or permanent structure (*mandapa*) in the open outside the house. The process of marriage begins with the search for a suitable life partner for the girl. It is seldom that the boy or his relatives conducts the search for a suitable life partner for the boy. And since religious considerations and social considerations have gradually eroded over the years, it is the social and familial considerations involved with social prestige and rank in society that have assumed foremost importance in contracting marriages. But whatever the manner in which a bridegroom has been found for a girl, the marriage ceremony follows largely the procedures laid down by the *Paraskar Grihyasutra.* When the marriage has been fixed and the auspicious day and time determined for the marriage, the bridegroom along with his kinsmen, friends, neighbours and relatives makes a trek to the bride's place (usually in the day time in the case of the Shrotriyas) to get the marriage solemnised. The first act in the marriage ceremony is *bhusamskara* (purification of the place where the marriage is to take place). It is this purified (*samskrita*) place where the sacred *Agni* for *homa* is to be kindled. Needless to say that *Agni* is considered to be the mouth of the gods that receives all the offerings meant for the gods. *Paraskar* (1.4.3) prescribes five ways in which *bhusakskara* must be done for the installation of the sacred *Agni*, which is called *Grihyagni.*

What should also be noted in this connection is that all types of *yajna—huta, ahuta, prahuta, and prashita*—are performed in this *Agni* (cf. *MS 3.36*), although the kindling of *Agni* is recommended through *arani manthan*, that is, the production of *Agni* through the rubbing of two pieces of sticks, it is now rarely done; it has been discarded in favour of much easier methods of producing *Agni.* After the *Grihyagni* has been installed, the ceremony of marriage begins. It begins with the offering of the bridal dress to the bride by the bridegroom. While offering the bridal dress, the bridegroom offers a prayer to Tantu Devi to bless the bride with a blameless life.[21] This is followed by making the bride and the bridegroom stand face-to-face by the bride's father. This is annointed by prayer for strengthening the resolve of the bride and the bridegroom to live united for the entire life (*RV X.85.47*). The father then begins the process of *kanyadana* (the act of the gifting of the girl to the boy selected for her). When the *kanyadana* is duly performed, the married couple comes out of the *mandap* and the father of the bride makes them, that is, the newly married girl and the boy face each other and the bridegroom recites the *Mantra* that expresses the wish that the bride may be well-behaved, may not become hostile to her husband, be kind to the cattle-wealth and men, in general, and be respectful to the gods. The *Mantra* that is recited are from *RV X.85*, riks *40* and *41*. These riks mean that *Soma* as the first to obtain *Surya*; he gave her to *Gandharva* who, in turn, gave her to *Agni* and *Agni* has given her to the boy.[22] After this the couple makes *pradakshina*, that is, the girl and the boy go round the *homagni*, the sacrificial fire, during which the bridegroom expresses his wish to sexually enjoy the girl for the purposes of reproduction and wealth.

This is followed by *homa* in which fourteen offerings are made to different gods, such as, Prajapati, Indra, *Agni*, and *Soma*.[23] After this the recitation of *mahavyahriti*, that is, the names of the first three *lokas, bhuh, bhuvah and swah,* is recited. This is followed by *sarvaprayashchit,* another offering to Prajapati[24] and, then, the *swishtakrita*.[25] Another important step in the marriage ceremony is what is called *Lajahoma,* that is, the scattering of puffed paddy, by the bride. The brother of the bride, that is the *syala,* the brother-in-law of the bridegroom, puts in a leaf puffed paddy and places the puffed paddy in the hand of the bride who then makes three offerings while standing all the while reciting a *Mantra* requesting *Aryaman* to detach her from her father's house and attach her to her husband's.[26] The rite of *lajahoma* is performed thrice while reciting *Mantras;* however, the fourth offering is made silently. For the first three offerings of *Laja,* the bridegroom holds the right hand of the bride expressing his wish in the *Mantra* meaning that they both, the husband and the wife, may enjoy long life and well being. In addition, he also recites the famous *Mantra* pertaining to the syzygy of the gods; this *Mantra* declares that I am *Visnhu*, you are *Lakshmi*; I am *Trideva* and you are *Devi*; and I am *Sama* and you are *Richa*. This signifies the eternal unity of the husband and the wife. Then the bridegroom expresses his wish that they may enjoy long life and a hundred sons. This part of the ritual is concluded by *Shilarohana* (climbing upon a stone) symbolising a rock-like love and devotion on the part of the bride for her husband.

Yet another ritual involved in the marriage ceremony is *Saptapadi*, literally, seven steps, which the bride and the bridegroom take from the marriage place to the north of the *mandap*. At each step, the bridegroom recites a *Mantra* which ends with *vishnustwa nayatu,* which means may Vishnu inspire you for *anna* (food that sustains) in the first step. In the subsequent steps the second is meant for energy, the third for wealth, the fourth for happiness, the fifth for cattle wealth, the sixth for good weather (favourable to agriculture), and the seventh for friendship. The significance of the *Saptapadi* is very clear. As has already been pointed out, marriage is primarily contracted for generating *praja,* that is sons and daughters; they cannot be sustained without the necessary wherewithal subsumed under the generic name of *vitta,* that is, resources of different kinds. But it is *anna* that is the source of energy necessary for reproduction and mobilising necessary resources for the sustenance of the *praja*. Needless to say that both of these are necessary for the life of the householder. And since there are other concomitant resources, such as the cattle wealth, good weather for producing necessary food, and friendship with his wife in discharging the duties of a householder, the bridegroom prays for all these. To have all these is a pre-requisite of a happy married life as well as a well-run household. After *Saptapadi* the couple leaves the *mandap* for the bridegroom's house. But before leaving the marriage place they have a look on a pitcherful of water with which a person happens to be standing to the north of the *mandap*. The water is then sprinkled over the couple praying *Apah* to make the bride healthy. It is then the time for the bride to look at the Sun and the star, *Dhruva*, in the night time praying to be firm in her love for her husband like the star *Dhruva*. When the husband returns home with his bride, the husband does *nityahoma* everyday. The last rite in the marriage ceremony is the *chaturthi,* that is, with an interregnum of four days. That is, it is only on the fourth day that the marriage is consummated after performing certain rites, mostly according to *gramavachanam*, that is, local rites and rituals or folk rituals. On the fourth day late in the night, the marriage *Agni* is kindled on the right of which the image of Brahma (an important functionary in any *yana*) as well as a water-filled pitcher is placed. A special *charu* (usually a kind of rice pudding) is prepared for making offerings to gods, particularly for *Agni* and *Soma.* It does not need to be repeated here that it is the syzygy between the two divinities, that is, *Agni* and *Soma*, that is the origin of the creation, or the *idam sarvam,* as we know it. It is also needless to say that the newly married couple is also soon going to be engaged in the act of creation or rather procreation, that is, the generation of *praja.* The next five offerings consisting of *ghee* (clarified butter) are made to *Vayu*, the Sun, the Moon and the *Gandharva.* The portion of *ghee* that remains after each offering is deposited in the pitcher. When the offerings are made, the *ghee*-mingled water from the pitcher is sprinkled over the bride with the prayer that whatever harmful elements (harmful to the husband, to the cattle wealth, to the fame of the house, etc.) may be there, must be destroyed. After that, the remainder of the *charu* is given to the wife by the husband to eat. The bride is, in actual practice, fed by her husband. All the while the husband expresses his resolve that they are now one, they have one mind, and one purpose.

It is only after all this that the marriage is considered to be religiously sanctified and the couple can now engage in the act of procreation. If perchance the bridegroom happens to die before the rites of *chaturthi* have not been completed, the girl is considered to be unmarried.

References

1. cf. MS 4.1-2
2. MS 3.77-78
3. MS 3.79

4. *patnidharmarthakaman karnam pravarmsmritam;*
   Apatniko naro bhupa karmayogyo na jayate;
   Brhamanh kshatriyo vapi vaishyah shudro api va narah.
5. These are: *pisacha, Rakshasa, Gandharva, Asur, Prajapatya, Arsha, Daiva* and *Brahma.*
6. cf. MS 3.24; also RV 1.1.112; 1.117.2; X. 39.7
7. However, the Shrotiyas of Mithila are so far free of this vice.
8. A. Ramamurty, *The Central Philosophy of the Rigveda* (Delhi: Ajanta Publications, 1991), p. 63.
9. Eric Voegelin, *Order and History V: In Search of Order*, p. 68.
10. Loc. cit.
11. Cf. RV X.129.7.
12. Plato, *Timaeaes,* 29 C-D.
13. Ananda Coomaraswamy, *A New Approach to the Vedas* (Delhi: Aparna Publications, 1985), p. 58; cf. RV I. 164. 4.
14. As Coomaraswamy writes, "...if conjoint principles are considered in their reciprocity, it is the manifested God that is masculine and unmanifested Godhead that is the feminine power, as being the inexhaustible reservoir of all possibilities, including that of manifestation....Into the womb of the infinite *Soma* puts the embryo (RVX.74.5), "Divine Biunity," *Major Essays: Metaphysics*, ed. Roger Lipsey (Princeton: Princeton University Press, 1972), Vol. 1., pp. 232-33.
15. On this, see, S. A. Dange, *Sexual Synbolism from the Vedic Rituals* (Delhi: Ajanta Publications, 1979).
16. Aristotelian *praxis* is equivalent to Indian *Shastra* meaning *shansanam and shasanam.*
17. On this see, *Vachaspatyam* and *Shabda Kalpadruma.*
18. Sayan has erroneously concluded on the basis of AB 4.7 that *Surya* was married to *Soma.* What is, however, indicated in AB 4.7 is that Prajapati made his mind to offer his daughter to *Soma* in marriage.
19. The relevant *Mantra* has used the term "vadhuyu" which simply means a person desirous of a wife and the term *vara* means bridegroom. See RVI.83.2; V.60.4; IX.101.14; AV2.36.1,5-6; 11.8.1; AB 4.7.1.
20. *Samvatsar* is a conjoint of sam+vas+sar, that is the state of equilibrium, *sthiti* (existence), and motion respectively. See Motilal Shastri, *Ishwar Krishna Rahasya* (Jaipur: Rajasthan Patrika, Ltd., ?), p. 80; See also AV 11. 4.21: *Ekam padam notkhidati saliladdhamsa uchharan,* the Swan does not extract one foot from the sea.... Samvatsar thus signifies that which moves, but does not leave its place.
21. It is interesting to note that this act of offering the bridal dress has, again, a reference to the process of creation, particularly to *yajna.* Note, for example, that AV 13.1.6 refers to the fact that when Rohit created heaven and earth, Parameshthi stretched the *tantu* (thread). It is this stretching of thread which sustains the cosmic *yajna.* It is also interesting to add here that even in

garbhadhana, specially the act of copulation for engendering *praja,* a definite reference to the process of creation at the cosmic level is mimetically acted.

22. It does not by any stretch of imagination means that *Surya* was married four times. The word "*pati*" does not only mean husband; it also means overlord who takes care of those under his protection. This becomes clear from the fact that, according to one interpretation, this *Mantra* means that in the first stage of her childhood the girl is calm (*Soma*), in the second, she is aware of the household work (*Gandharva*), in the third stage, she begins to be invaded by the heat of sexuality, that is, she becomes aware of herself as a person who has sexual urges (*Agni*), and the fourth stage of her girlhood, she is ready to beget a husband.
23. It needs to be emphasised that there is an inner logic to the sequence followed in offering *ahutis.* Note, for example, that Prajapati is the creator of the universe, while Indra is the kindler who replenishes the strength of Prajapati who has become exhausted in the process of creation. The process of creation begins with the syzygy between *Agni* and *Soma* and the result is the *triloka,* that is, *bhuh* (*Prithivi*), *bhuwah* (Antariksha, the sky), and *swah* (the Sun).
24. Insofar as *Prayashchita* is concerned, every person is considered to commit seven sins which he must wipe out by the rite of *prayashchit* everyday.
25. *Swishtakrita* is performed to pray to the gods for well being.
26. A reference to *Aryaman* here takes note of the fact that, according to AV14.1.17, *Aryaman* is *pativedanam,* that is, the finder of husband.

7

Marriage—The Question of Genealogical Suitability

There goes a saying that marriages are made in the heaven. This saying, it must be presumed, applies both to what is usually known as arranged marriages and love marriages that are prevalent in a large part of the world and is now increasingly making in-roads into the traditional Indian socio-cultural scene. This saying applies to love marriage in two important senses. In the first place, the act of falling in love with someone is not the act of volition or rational choice. In the second place, since the act of falling in love necessarily involves two persons; as such, the other person, too, must reciprocate. But it is not certain that the other person, whom one loves, too, will fall in love with that person.

It is also not certain that the other person whom one has come to love will reciprocate in the manner the person who loves wishes that person to respond to his love. More importantly, even if two persons love each other intensely, it is not certain that they will continue to love each other or will eventually enter into a marital compact to live together and engage into the act of procreation as a necessary condition of the continuity of the race. As such, even love marriages involve a great amount of uncertainty caused by the intervention of several factors, both seen and unseen. And the unseen factors, though not incorporated in the Aristotelian schema of causes, form an integral part of traditional Indian thinking and are characterised as *prarabdha* or *daiva* or the intervention of the heaven in human affairs.

In the case of arranged marriages, the number of unseen factors increases tremendously. These unseen factors are associated with the process of change that has affected the India society, in general, and society and culture in Mithila (in North Bihar), in particular, since the fourteenth century. The source of this change, in the first place, was the perception of threat emanating from the Muslim invasion followed by a long period of Muslim rule in India and, in the second place, by the long and fateful British rule in India. The perception of threat to society and culture, particularly in Mithila, in the fourteenth century forced the people, belonging particularly to the upper echelons of society, to turn inward if they were to save their society to undergo the process of undesirable change and protect their culture from getting completely eroded by the progressive penetration of the Muslim rule and the hostile and frequently demeaning attitude and behaviour of the Muslim rulers towards the Hindus.[1] The Brahmans of Mithila devised certain ways and means in the fourteenth century to protect and preserve their social and cultural heritage one of which was to fortify their bastion of kulachara (that is, the socio-cultural patterns of behaviour sanctioned by the shastriya tradition and customs) by certain innovations in their work-ways in keeping with their cultural traditions.[2]

But the accent on following *kulachara*, (that is, the behavioural patterns of families graded on the scale of caste differences and ritual status traditionally enjoyed by different families) meant, in the first place, holding on very strongly to the tradition hierarchy of caste and status and, in the second place, let this hierarchy play a major part in influencing social life and relationships, in general, and marriage relations, in particular. In a highly differentiated social organisation, this meant the hardening of social arteries and ossification of traditions and customs grounded in this tradition. This meant that marriages were contracted not on the basis of individual choice, cutting at the root of love marriages, but according to the tenets of kulachara, that is, within permissible groups that also if certain other conditions were fulfilled. This meant a very strict observance of conditions prescribed by the

Dharmashastras and the customs followed by a particular group of families placed in the caste and status hierarchy. Needless to say that this precluded individual choice in the matter of choosing a life partner. Such a choice was never considered in such a society to be the matter of individual likes and dislikes; it was rather influenced by the considerations of status and social compatibility.

But, then, alien influences under the dispensations of the British Rule in India began to impinge on the settling of marriage contracts in the society in Mithila as well as in other places. The need for the boys to get higher education for ensuring status mobility and for getting access to better job opportunities had as well some very important impact on the settlement of marriage contracts. In the first place, dowry began to climb higher and higher, except in the case of a few caste groups and, in the second place, love marriages even in socially and culturally closed caste groups began to take place. As a result of the progressively growing importance of dowry, the selection of suitable girls for boys holding or expecting better jobs was freed from the excessive constraints placed on marriage by *shastric* injunctions or custom. However, the fact remains that the restraint of *sagotra* (that is, marriage within a lineage descending from the same *adipurusha*, the original person from which a particular lineage links itself) marriage still applies in all the upper castes.

What is interesting to observe is the fact that whether it is arranged marriages or, for that matter, a love marriage, marriages among the upper Hindu caste groups have to be sanctified by performing marriage *samskara.* And, as we have already seen, all earthly marriages among the upper caste Hindus are modelled upon the heavenly *pratimana* (that is, model or standard or, better still, paradigm). This *pratimana*, as we have already pointed out refers to the process of creation. Before the process of creation started, there was only one entity in existence, a situation, which in the *Vedic* perspective, is symbolised by *pralaya,* that is, a situation when nothing existed; there was neither *asat* nor, for that matter, *sat.* As is evident form the famous *Nasadiya Sukta* of the *Rigveda* (*RV X. 129*), before the world came into being, there was neither *asat* nor *sat*, nor anything else.... In this state of "thing-less-ness", commonly interpreted as the void, there arose in the heart of the Absolute the desire, as the first occurrence of something before the process of creation started. It is this desire that, as *RV X. 129.4* underlines, links together the existing with the non-existing.

The advent of desire has the consequence of splitting the one existent entity into two opposite but complementary principles or entities. The conjoint parent of the pre-creation stage, the parent who existed as one in the state of void, or as *ardhanarishwar,* representing the fusion of two contrary principles or entities, now splits in two different parents, the male and the female principles. Underlying this *Vedic* perspective is the idea that when the creator is disturbed by the desire to have some companion, that is, the desire to create *praja* (beings) he, impelled by his own desire, assumed the form of two separate but complementary entities. It is this splitting up of the One into two opposite but complementary entities that is characterised in *Brihadaranyak Upanishad* as the process of *dwedhapat.*[3] The diremption from the One of the contrary but complementary principle would not have been possible if the One were not the living conjoint, the unity of the cohabitant parents (*RV I.140.3; III.7.1*).

This separation of the cohabitant parents into two opposite but complementary entities is not a sufficient condition for the process of creation to start and continue. It is a necessary but not a sufficient condition. What is also necessary is the fact that the separated opposite principles or entities must now join together to work for the creation to start and continue. This joining together of the opposite but complementary entities is conceived, in the *Vedic* perspective, as syzygy or *mithuna* which, interestingly enough is characterised in the *Rigveda* itself as *Brahma kilvisha* (the sin of Brahma because he married his own daughter and produced a son). This syzygy results in the birth of the son, (*Indragni*) of light (*jyotis*), of the Sun (the first material transformation of the non-material Absolute), "*Savitur* the creator, who wears the visible forms of all things" (*Vishwa rupani prati munchate Kavih, RV V.81.2*) Thus the separation of the conjoint principle is also the beginning of the process of remotion or becoming. "By the separation of the prior, the latter came forth" (*RV X.27.23*). It is thus clear that the conjunction of *manas* (Intelligence, or Platonic *Nous*), or the form of the Absolute before the process of creation started, or *Manyu* with *Vak* (matter in one sense of the term)[4] constitutes what Meister Eckhart calls, "the act of fecundation inherent in eternity."[5] It is by virtue of this fecundation that *asat* becomes *sat*, that is, what was *ab initio* centreless and formless now assumes concrete forms with individual centers.

It is true that the transformation or *vivarta* of the One into many is symbolised in terms of the marriage or syzygy between two opposite but complementary principles. However, what is involved here is the process of *yajna* at the cosmic level signifying the fact that the interaction between two different entities produces a third element, in this case, the birth of the son in the form of the Sun, the first material manifestation of the Absolute made possible through the process of *yajna*. As such, it is needless to say that the process of the transformation of the One into many, or, to put it differently, the emergence of a third element as a result of the coming together of two entities, is *yajna*. This *yajna* takes place on a continuous basis at three different levels of existence: *adhidaivika* (at the levels of the devas), *adhyatmika* (at the level of the human psyche), and *adhibhautika* (at the level of the physical existence). It is as a result of this continuous process of *yajna* at different levels that *praja* is ever begotten and *vitta* (essential resources for the survival and well-being of the created beings).

Needless to say that this same analogy of syzygy or marriage is transferred to marriages that take place in the phenomenal world. This transference of analogy of marriage between immortals to mortals underlines the importance of marriage, whether arranged or as a result of love between two persons, for the continuance of the process of creation begun by the Absolute itself. This transference of the analogy from the world of the gods to the world of the mortals suggests, at one and the same time, two things. In the first place, it suggests that the principal objective of marriage is procreation so that the continuance of the human race is assured so that the threat to God's creation on annihilation is removed, not the satisfaction of lust. In the second place, the marriage, in this perspective, is like the *yajna* signifying the process of creation by the God. And if it is *yajna,* it must be made sacred through the performance of religious rites and rituals so that marriages in the phenomenal world, too, retain their sacred character. That is why the act of marriage is considered to be an instance of *samskara* insofar as the act of marriage is necessary for the continuation of the human race itself. It is, therefore, not surprising that the act of marriage is made sacred by resorting to certain rites and rituals as prescribed by *Grihyasutras.*

But the need to make the act of marriage sacred does not mean that marriage is simply a matter that is governed only by religious prescription. Even the *Grihyasutras*, as we have already seen, permit the inclusion of local customs and usages which are excluded from the marriage ceremony. As we shall see shortly, numerous local customs and usages have traditionally formed an integral part of the marriage ceremony. And since local customs and usages tend to vary radically from one place to another and from one time segment to another, there is always the probability that large variations from one place to another and, by the same token, from one caste group to another, will occur. It is, therefore, of great interest to find out in what ways, if any, different caste groups differ insofar as marriage rites and rituals and local rituals and usages are concerned. It is with this purpose in mind that three different caste groups in the geographical and cultural unit called Mithila were included for study to uncover these differences.

Mithila has for long been a land known for its very important contributions to the history of ideas in India as well as to the patterns of socio-cultural life and relations unique to Indian civilisation. It has also been famous for being the stronghold of Indian traditions and customs institutionalised in the mist of history. These traditions and customs continue to mould, inform, and legitimise social practices in Indian society even today. The uninterrupted continuance of traditions and customs on a very long span of time points to a widely shared world-view and persistence over a long haul of history of the structure of socio-cultural life and relations based on this world-view. Perhaps, it is this continuity of traditional world-view that not only allows the numerous caste groups that inhabit the land of Mithila to follow unswervingly the religious rites and rituals in all walks of life prescribed by the *Dharmashastra* written long ago but also to have peaceful relationship among themselves with a fairly low level of conflict potential (in comparison to other parts of Bihar).

The caste groups residing in this area are numerous describing a very wide spectrum of socio-cultural formations. For the sake of convenience, however, these caste groups can be divided into three broad groupings, that is:

(a) the upper castes comprising Brahmans, Bhumihar Brahmans; Kshatriyas or Rajputs, and Kayasthas;

(b) Intermediate castes composed of Yadavas, Koeris, Kurmis, and intermediate caste groups traditionally considered to be clean castes; and

(c) lower castes and jatis and Muslims, all considered unclean for ritual purposes.

Each of these groups has its own well-defined customs and traditions that, despite the continuous thrusts of attack by the process of secularisation and modernisation, continue even now to shape and form their thought-ways and work-ways in social organisation and group life and relations.

These traditions and customs that a particular caste-group lives by animate their social life in two distinct but interconnected manners. While, in the first place, they ascribe and define the identity typical to each of these caste groups, they, also, in the second place, relate these groups to the source, the *arche*, of the tradition which binds in unity all these distinct groups and weave them together into an organic whole. However, in this process, while the upper echelon of the social hierarchy is fully governed by traditional norms, mores and socio-religious practices, the lower echelons of society in Mithila, as elsewhere also, enjoy enough freedom to fashion, develop and perfect diverse ways of relating themselves to the *arche* principle. The rituals and practices of different castes, therefore, work as the indicators of both the degree of caste differentiation and cultural consanguinity.

The level of differentiation in the rituals and practices of one cluster or group of castes is, most of the times, lesser than that compared to the other clusters or groups of castes. This, at one and the same time, works as an instrument of preserving group identity as well as protecting against radical variation from the bond of organicity and singularity of Indian culture. The present study is an attempt to explore and understand the degree to which differences and differentiation have taken place in the self-understanding of the nature of traditional Indian religious and cultural patterns. In order to do that, the study of *samsakara* offers a unique opportunity since they constitute the external signs of internal religious beliefs and cultural life of a community. Since the study of all the *samskaras* is out of the question, the focus in this study is on the exploration of the *samskara* of marriage as it is lived and practised in three upper caste groups in Mithila. These caste groups are: Shrotriya Brahmans, Bhumihara Brahmans, and Rajputs residing in Mithila. The exclusive concern with these caste groups insofar as the question of exploring the marriage *samskara* is involved, is due to the fact that it is these caste groups that are very particular about observing *samskaras,* in general, and marriage *samskara,* in particular. While all these three caste groups draw the necessary cues for observing religious rituals and practices from the same source, variations occur, perhaps, because of the historical continuity of Mithila's typical *Vedic* consciousness. The level of such consciousness admittedly varies among these three castes. And, according to the degree their self-understanding of religious principles and practices also varies their caste status in the social hierarchy.

The Shrotriyas are considered to be the purest practitioners as well as the most faithful repository of Brahmanic (*i.e.* the *Vedic*) world view and life style. As such, they are placed, in Mithila, on the uppermost echelon of the caste hierarchy. Although they constitute a splinter group of the traditional Maithil Brahmans, they are ascribed the highest rating insofar as the understanding and practice of the *Vedic* world-view and the prescribed *yajnika* life style are concerned. This demarcation came into exisence in the early part of the 14th century when the Maithil society was under the worst ever threat of Muslim invasions followed by a largescale persecution of the Hindus in this area. The group since known as the Shrotriyas proved perhaps the toughest to bend and break under the pressure of alien persecution. They still continue to live in the land of Mithila with their conspicuous thought-ways and work-ways.

The domicile of the Shrotriyas is, now, confined to the parts of the districts of Darbhanga, Madhubani, Purnea, Katihar, and Saharsa in the state of Bihar. Their population is not more than twenty thousand in all. Divided into several moolagramas (root villages) and *gotras* (a shared common lineal descent originating from a common *adipurusha*, the largest number of Shrotriyas resides in the districts of Madhubani and Darbhanga. Known for their stoicism in everyday life, this group of Maithil Brahmans still considers scholarship as the cherished orientation and vocation in social life. As such, this group seems to provide a reference point of rituals and social practices for other caste-groups residing in this area to follow and practice. However, in case of those caste-groups that migrated to Mithila much later, this characterisation has a lesser hold and, therefore, lesser relevance. That is to say, the caste groups that arrived in Mithila much later than, for example, the Brahmans, in general, and the Shrotriya Brahmans, in particular, have carried with them some of their rituals and practices typical to the land of their original domicile.

The Bhumihar Brahmans of this region, for example, trace their ancestry back to the 16th century when they are said to have migrated from Magadha region for taking benefits of better service and trade opportunities that were available under the dominance of other ruling caste-groups. They count their *moolagrama* (root villages) which, they say, are located in areas beyond the borders of Mithila, *e.g.* Kusauthia, Pilkhiaita, etc. It is, however, interesting to note that, for their ritual practices, they depend upon Maithil pandits who are locally available and not on those residing in

Magadh area. In the course of several centuries that Bhumihar Brahmans have lived in Mithila, they have adopted the language and food habits of the residents of Mithila, though not the dress and manners of the Shrotriya and non-Shrotriya Maithil Brahmans. Bhumihars are widely spread in Mithila and, by visual estimation, their population is generally estimated to be about two hundred thousands in this area.

If migration in later times, carrying the fragments of rituals and practices of their root villages and the adoption of language and food habits of Mithila and distinction in dress manners are taken as relevant indicators, the Rajputs residing in Mithila, too, have a story not much dissimilar to that of the Bhumihar Brahmans. However, the one remarkable difference between them is that while the Bhumiharas consider themselves as Brahmans, the Rajputs trace their ancestry to the legendary Rajput warriors. They are also similar insofar as neither of these two groups has developed, organised and institutionalised genealogical records. In addition, they also follow the non-Maithil astrological calendar or the system of calculating auspicious days and moments for the observance of religious rites, rituals, and *vratas* as well as for determining auspicious days and moments for initiating new pragmatic activities and secular practices including that of marriage *samskara.*

The Rajputs of Mithila, who trace (mostly without any evidence on record) their roots back to Rajputana, are believed to have migrated to the territory of Mithila and Nepal during 13th and 14th centuries. There are, however, some families that claim their ancestry to Karnat lineage, a community that is supposed to have come from Dharwad, at present a part of the Maharashtra state, to Mithila as invaders and became the rulers of Mithila during the 11th-14th centuries, although this contention has not yet been corroborated by any written or any other firm evidence. The caste sub-divisions of the Rajputs in Mithila are reported to be spanning over the Rathaurs, Chauhans, Chandels and Karmabars. The total population of the Rajputs in Mithila, according to visual estimation as well as the reports received from the respondents themselves, does not exceed one hundred and twenty-five thousands. The

Rajputs, occupying now various professions in different parts of Mithila, seem to have adopted most of the traits of Maithil culture insofar as their routine life and conduct and observance of *samskaras* are concerned. Like the Bhumihars of Mithila, the Rajputs, too, depend on Maithil Brahman pandits for the conduct of their s*amskaras.* Given a few important differences in details, however, the philosophy of life and rituals of the three caste groups residing in Mithila, namely, the Shrotriyas, the Bhumihar Brahmans and the Rajputs are similar insofar as all these three groups derive the legitimacy of their *samskaras* from the overarching principles originating in the *Vedic* world-view. The exploration of the *samskara* of marriage as performed in these three caste groups reveals the details of their caste-wise understanding of the philosophy of marriage, the rituals and other social practices as practised in real life.

Marriage is considered as one of the most important *samskaras* in Mithila, as elsewhere in the Indian subcontinent. The reason for this is not far to seek. Marriage constitutes the essential and prior condition of procreation. And since the act of procreation is considered to be a sacred act, it must follow the pattern of its divine *pratimana.* It is for this reason that the act of marriage must be made sacred by lending to it a divine quality and, therefore, sanctified by the performance of certain religious rites and rituals that must form an integral part of culture. In addition, since the sacred fire in the house of a householder cannot be lit before he is married and since no other *samskaras* can be performed by any householder in a house if it lacks the sacred fire, the marriage *samsakara* is considered to be the first of the samskaras. In Mithila, therefore, the marriage *samskara* is considered to be the first of the ten *samskaras.* All the three caste groups covered by this study, viz., the Shrotriyas, the Bhumihara Brahmans and the Rajputs, share the idea of the primacy of the marriage *samskara* and its priority over all other *samskaras.*

The requisite data necessary for the exploration of the ways and means of the observance of the marriage *samskara* by all the three caste groups were collected by observation in real life situations followed by intensive interviews of the persons, both male and female, who have actively been engaged in the overseeing of the performance of the marriage *samskara.* Both actual observation and intensive interviews following the performance of the marriage ceremony in each of the three caste groups suggest that the analysis of the information obtained can best be carried on if it is organised by the steps that follow in a sequence beginning form the settlement of marriage contract and continued till the end of the fourth day (*chaturthi*) when the marriage is actually consummated. These sequential steps are: (1) a-*swajana,* that is, ascertaining the minimum permissible genealogical distance between the proposed bride and the groom; (2) geographical considerations in terms of contiguity and availability of suitable life partner; (3) the observance of religious rites and rituals in the course of the performance of the marriage *samskara,* both sanctified by the *Grihyasutras* or Shastriya and those practised locally or the *laukika vyavahara.* This chapter as well as the next describes the ways and means of performing the marriage ceremony both at the bride's place and that of the bridegroom. Also, proper attention is paid to reflecting about the level of discursive consciousness in each of the three caste groups regarding the significance of marriage rituals, the phenomenon of female dominance in the performance of different rites and rituals connected with marriage, the role of money in arranging marriage contracts and the impact of modernisation on the institution of marriage.

After there has been some discussion between two families about entering into a marital relationship either directly by the head of the family or its representative and both the families have agreed to make a particular marriage proposal a reality, the first step towards formalising the agreement in what is known in Mithila as the *a-swajana nirnaya.* It signifies the process of ascertaining the necessary genealogical distance between the bride and the groom. The practice followed by the Shrotriyas of *a-swajana nirnaya*, though very much typical to the Shrotriyas, is followed by all the Maithil Brahmans of Mithila. However, in other caste groups under study, the factors entering into as well as the mode of *aswajana nirnaya* are different. The mode which the Shrotriyas follow is the most transparent and disciplined insofar as the Panjikara (scholar-keeper of genealogical records) has to orally recite the tables checking all the sixteen *kulas* of the proposed bride and the groom in the presence of the prominent members of both the families. Since this work is done at a public place, in addition to the members of the families, there may be present at the place, where the *aswajana nirnaya* is being given by the Panjikara, numerous onlookers, too, who witness the *nirnaya,* even though passively. The parameters of *aswajana nirnaya* among the Shrotriyas include several important considerations. The first of these considerations is that the bride and the groom should not belong to the same *gotra.* The second consideration concerns the fact the bride's father should not have an equal number of *Pravaras* as that of the groom's father. The third consideration has to do with the fact that the prospective bride should not be located at the sixth level of descent from any of the groom's ancestors in his paternal line. This means that the bride should be genealogically located in the seventh generation (or onwards) counted from any of the groom's paternal ancestors (*pitripaksha*). The fourth consideration demands that the bride should be located at least on the fifth generation from any of the groom's maternal ancestors (*matripaksha*). The fifth consideration requires that the bride should not be the offspring (*santana*) of the groom's mother's stepbrother. The sixth consideration emphasises that the bride should not, in any way, be the *santana* (descendant) of the groom's grandfather (maternal or paternal). And, the last consideration refers to the need that the bride should, in no way, be the s*apindya* of the groom's mother.

Once all of these criteria relating to the genealogical situation concerning the proposed marriage are satisfied, the two, that is, the bride and the bridegroom, are declared *a-swajana, i.e.* 'not akin'. It is only after this stage of genealogical determination of *a-swajana* is completed that a proposal of marriage can be considered legitimate among the Shrotriyas. For such an intricate process of genealogical determination, the Shrotriyas have necessarily to depend on their genealogical records that they have been compiling since the 10th century and which was socially organised in the 13th century by Harisingh Deva, the Karnat king of Mithila. Since then these records are being kept and updated by a specialised scholar group, called the Panjikaras. It is with the help of these Panjikaras that the *a-swajana nirnaya* is concluded.

While the consideration of matrimonial proposals in Shrotriya caste group primarily requires the categorical fulfilment of the criteria of *a-swajana nirnaya*, the Bhumiharas and Rajputs residing in this area have different denominators for deciding the match regarding genealogical distance between the bride and the groom. The latter two caste groups seem to pick up a few points from the general inventory of the criteria of *a-swajana* the Shrotriyas, and follow and work out a plan of decision-making on that basis. This seems to happen because the a-*swajana nirnaya* of the Shrotriyas is chiefly governed by the *Grihyasutras* of *Paraskara*, *Govila* and *Aswalayana* and the *Smriti* of *Yajnavalkya*. Since none of the latter caste groups denies the tenets of these Sutras and *Smritis* (may be because of the role of Maithil pandits in the performance of their *samskaras*), they seem to emulate the religious position taken by the Shrotriyas. They, as such, appear to consider the Shrotriya's shastriya practices as their reference point for most of the shastriya purposes. This, however, does not mean that the variations in their mode of rituals and other practices can, in any way, be undermined. Some of the points of distinction occur because of the fact that neither the Rajputs nor the Bhumiharas settled in this region have an institutionalised organisation, as do the Shrotriyas, on a continuous basis of genealogical records. The Bhumiharas and the Rajputs are, therefore, governed by certain other considerations also that are peculiar to themselves.

The Rajputs rely on the distinction of *gotra*. In the area covered by this investigation more than ten *gotras* of Rajputs were reported to exist. The nomenclature of the *gotras* are the same as that of the Brahmans, like Shandilya, Batsa, Kashyapa, etc. The Rajputs consider the phenomenon of *gotravarjya* (elimination of the similarity of *gotra*) as the sole denominator of legitimate marriage. Besides, there is the practice of not marrying one's son with a bride belonging to the village where one's daughter has been married. This factor is reported to have fallen in disuse for about a decade now and the Rajputs of this area freely settle matrimonial relations in any village. They do not also seem to practice *moolavarjya* (elimination on the basis of root village). This, however, is not the case with the Bhumiharas. The Bhumiharas practice both *gotravarjya* and *moolavarjya* in the settlement of marriage negotiations. And insofar as *gotravarjya* is concerned, the Bhumiharas claim to be much purer in practice than even the Shrotriyas. For example, they report that at least five gotras have to be eliminated before the genealogical legitimacy can be established in a particular proposal of marriage. This is to say, the bride must not belong to (a) the groom's (father's) gotra; (b) to his maternal grandfather's gotra; (c) to his father's maternal grandfather's gotra; (d) to his grandfather's maternal grandfather's gotra; and (e) to his grandmother's maternal grandfather's gotra. For the bride, however, it is sufficient to determine whether the groom belongs to her father's gotra or not. This system of *gotravarjya,* the respondents observed, was gradually being compromised and nowadays only the first three levels of injunction in *gotravarjya* is in vogue. There are six gotras of Bhumiharas, namely, Kashyapa, Parashara, Shandilya, Bharadwaj, Vatsa and Kaushika, that are found in the area under study. Besides, the phenomenon of *moolavarjya,* Bhumiharas report, saves them from the chances of cousin marriage. They, therefore, eliminate the *moolagrama* (root village) of the groom's father and also that of the groom's maternal grandfather. While finding a suitable bride or bridegroom, the family members may have to go beyond the territory of Mithila. They do not mind this and often explore the regions south of the Ganges to the distant districts of the central Bihar. This is also the case with the Rajputs settled in this region. They, too, have no inhibitions in moving beyond the territory of Mithila for matrimonial contracts.

The need to eliminate illegitimate marriage relationship between two persons relating both to *moolavarjya* and *gotravarjya* considerations brings into play the geographical factor because of the availability of suitable matches. In case of these two caste groups, namely, the Rajputs and the Bhumihara Brahmans, neither their adopted Maithil customs nor their adopted Maithili language or habits seems to preclude their movement beyond the territory of

Mithila for matrimonial purposes. As a consequence of going far and wide in the search of suitable match for marriageable girls, these caste-groups tend to allow the incursion of non-local alien considerations and practices insofar as the content as well as the performance of marriage rituals are concerned. With the result, the related symbols, floor paintings, frescoes, texts and tunes of the native folk songs also reflect some vital changes. The inevitable result that follows is the lack of consistency as well as the lowering down of the level of discursive consciousness insofar as the performance of *samskaras,* in general, and marriage *samskara,* in particular, is involved.

It is this factor that brings about the most pronounced distinction between these two caste groups, on the one hand, and the Shrotriyas, on the other. The Shrotriyas are an endogamous community and matrimonial relationship is confined to about twenty-five villages spread over the districts of Darbhanga, Madhubani, Purnea, Saharsa and Katihar. The Shrotriyas work out their matrimonial selections within their cultural territory and remain extremely conscious of vernacular, food, dress, rituals, ritualistic symbols, floor paintings, wall paintings, text and tune of their folk songs, their traditional norms of routine and ceremonial etiquette, etc. This parameter of preference demands that the norm of endogamy must be maintained above all other considerations, if any. On the other hand, the absence of such a cultural parameter of preference in the other two caste-groups, viz., the Rajputs and the Bhumiharas, allows them to give expression to their preference in terms of economic strata, political status, power, dowry and educational eligibility for earning a living, either pursuing a trade or by service.

Added to these is their search for fáirness and moral character of family the boy belongs to. Needless to mention that the search for something more than a happy life (in modern terms) renders culture-specific factors, like the *laukika* rituals, vernacular, symbols and songs, as of only secondary importance. The territorial extent of possible matrimonial ties works as a very strong precipitating factor for undermining the native significance and character of the *samskara* of marriage in these two caste groups. In the process of inter-cultural mobility that marks matrimonial settlements in these two caste-groups if anything suffers most, it is the *laukika* rituals which generally remain undefined by the *Shastras* and protected only by the caring concern of the womenfolk of Mithila. In this context, the most remarkable inclusions (distortions?) have been found in the textual content and the notation of folk music, form and design of floor and wall paintings and the ways of performing non-shastriya rituals. By understanding these variations as the effect of inter-cultural matrimonial mobility in these two caste groups, one can easily infer the reasons that allow the Shrotriyas to retain and protect their distinct cultural identity in terms of tradition, the symbols, their meanings, purposes and intended effects.

This attribute of the Shrotriya community ascribes to it the role of the 'repository of Maithil culture'. It is because of such a cultural preoccupation of the Shrotriyas that the traditional ritualistic folk songs are still preserved (with their text and tune) and sung by the womenfolk with a very high degree of purity even after the lapse of about half a millennium of their being first written. Similar is the case with ritualistic floor paintings (known as *aripan*). While floor paintings used by the non-Shrotriya caste-groups show numerous modern inclusions, the Shrotriya *aripan* is still free from cross-cultural or, for that matter, market incursions. This factor is also pronounced insofar as the bridal/nuptial (face and dress) make up is concerned. Among the Rajputs and the Bhumiharas, the bride's facial and dress make up is, nowadays, done by the professional beauticians while the traditional Shrotriya style of make up is still in vogue. Shrotriya wall or floor paintings and make up styles were documented in the 1960's by one Shrotriya artist, the late Lakshminatha Jha. Before his work, none had attempted to record or preserve these materials. If one takes a look at these documented paintings for comparison with what is being done at present, one finds that there is no variation even after five decades of this compilation. Most of the Shrotriya respondents (females) above the age group of thirty years have shown uniform mode of preparing classified ritualistic paintings. Some of them have also explained the meaning of the symbols used in such paintings. On the other hand, ritualistic floor and wall paintings in Rajput and Bhumihara Brahman caste-groups appear to be rather simplistic constructions depicting, most of the times, constructions like *swastika* or *sarbatobhadra* which has little or no symbolic significance insofar as the Maithil *laukika* rituals are concerned.

Needless to say that these floor and wall paintings do not match either in style or in content with their Shrotriya counterparts. The Rajput and Bhumihara style of wall and floor paintings as well as ritualistic (folk) songs do have some extra-regional bearing. This difference is marked mostly in the realm of non-shastriya and *laukika* rituals. The shastriya rituals that are conducted by Maithil Brahman pandits do not show much difference either in the principles or in the processes of marriage *samskara.* It is, again, interesting to note that, while in a Shrotriya marriage there are numerous pandits to check the *Mantras* and the process directed by the performing pandit, members of the Rajput and Bhumihara caste groups are found to have little concern with what the Brahman pandits recite or perform, except for the sequence of important rituals.

Furthermore, in the Shrotriya marriage the ritual of *kanyadana* (gifting away the daughter to her groom) is performed by a senior male member of the family. It is because, they inform, some of the rituals preceding *kanyadana* are purely *Vedic* in nature and can be performed by persons who are 'initiates' and wear sacred thread. Therefore, only a male member of the family performs *kanyadana.* In non-Shrotriya caste groups under study there is no such rule for *kanyadana.* Both male and female members of the family can perform *kanyadana.* This point of difference between the Shrotriya and the other two caste groups, however, cannot be attributed to geographical factor alone because the non-Shrotriya groups of Maithil Brahmans, too, follow the practice of allowing female members of the family to perform *kanyadana.* The actual understanding of divergence or convergence in the mode of practice and conceptual status of the *samskara* of marriage in these three caste-groups can be had by a comparative description of rituals.

It is quite clear from the discussion above that one of the most important steps in the performance of the marriage *samskara* in Mithila is the very complicated process of what has been characterised above as *a-swajana nirnaya*, that is, the determination of the appropriate distance measured in terms of basically two considerations. The first of these considerations has to do with the fact that the girl and the boy who are under active consideration for a possible marriage alliance must not have descended from the same *adi purusha,* that is, the person from whom the members of a particular lineage group consider to have originally descended. As a member of such lineage group, the members of that particular group consider themselves to share the same *mula*, that is, origin. But the substantive meaning of *mula* or the question of origin cannot be restricted to the consideration of the *adi purusha* from whom a particular group of persons belonging to the same caste have descended. All such persons are said to share the same *gotra.* It also means that such a group must have originally the same because of their descent from the same *adi purusha.* Thus the substantive meaning of the term needs to be interpreted in two different ways. One way of interpreting the meaning of *mula* is to take note of the *adi purusha* from whom the members of a particular caste or sub-caste group trace their descent and the other way is to take note of the place where the members of a particular caste or sub-caste has been traditionally living or, alternatively, from where they migrated at some point of time to other places.

The need to take into account the factors of both *mula* and *gotra* in any marriage proposal has its root in the important consideration of avoiding the lapse of the caste group into a situation characterised by the predominance of weak, unhealthy and intellectually dull off-springs that in-breeding is likely to promote. It is basically the consideration of avoiding in-breeding that endows the factors of *mulavarjya and gotravarjya* with so much importance while deciding the propriety and social legitimacy of any proposed marriage alliance. However, for various reasons it is not always possible to completely avoid marriage alliances between persons belonging to the same *mula* either in the sense of sharing the same place of original inhabitation or the descent of the same *adi purusha.*

This is so for the reason that, even if a person shares the original place of origin, he may have a different *gotra* from others located in the same geographical space. Since there may be persons belonging to different *gotras* but sharing the same *mula,* it is quite permissible to have marriage alliance between persons of the same *mula* but having different *gotras.*

In contradistinction to this, there might exist a situation, that, for various reasons, may compel people to arrange marriages in a very small circle of people. For one thing, the total number of a particular caste group in a particular locality might be quite small. It is also possible that, given this small population of a particular caste may have different sub-castes with different *gotras.* But the very fact that the population of that particular caste group, even though constituted by different *gotras,* is, in fact, very small means a very dense network of marriage relationships making it very difficult to decide the permissible limits within which marriage alliances can legitimately be formed. In such a situation, it is not unusual for a family whose members have developed over the years a multiple relationships with the members of another family in the neighbourhood. For instance, a person may have a multiplex relationship with the member of another family but having a different *gotra.*

The case of the Shrotriyas is very typical in this regard. Note, for example, that their total number in the districts of Darbhanga and Madhubani does not probably exceed more that ten thousands. If they belonged to the same *mula* and *gotra,* marriage among them would be very difficult to arrange unless they went out of their immediate geographical confines and seek life partners in distant lands, a difficulty not many are either willing or capable of facing. They therefore undertake to have marriage alliances within the confines of a small geographical space. This small geographical confine is known among the people as the *panchakroshi,* that is to say, a geographical area having a diameter of roughly fifteen kilometres. It is within this geographical area that about ninety percent of marriage alliances among the Shrotriyas take place.

It is for this reason that most marriage alliances among the Shrotriyas place individual Shrotriyas in a network of multiplex relationships. For example, a particular individual, when married in a particular family tied-up in the same kind of multiplex relationship, may find himself as described in many different ways in addition to being the husband of the daughter of a particular person. He may, for example, be the son-in-law of a particular person, but, seen from another angle, he may also have the relationship with his father-in-law of a distant brother or an uncle and something else as well. It is this density of relationship incorporating every Shrotriya family as well as individual persons in the fold of a network of multiplex relationship that is a compelling fact of social existence of the Shrotriyas that forces them to be very, very meticulous in determining the permissible limits of genealogical distance between the girl and the boy for entering into a marriage alliance. It is, therefore, not surprising that the Shrotriyas take so much pains in making *a-swajana nirnaya* before formally approving a proposal of marriage alliance between two families. For this purpose, as we have already seen, they examine and explore meticulously genealogical distance going back to seven degrees of descent on both sides of the girl and the boy as well as on both sides of the parents of the girl and the boy.

The question can, however, be raised as to why this exploration should be limited only to seven degrees of descent on both sides. The limit of seven degrees of descent has the *Vedic* sanction in the sense that, according to the *Vedic* theory, a person inherits certain genetic attributes, properties, and qualities not only from his father but also from the father of the father till it reaches the seventh generation of one's ancestors or *pitris*. According to the calculations of the *Vedic* philosophical position, the son borrows from his father a certain amount of genetic properties which get exhausted once the seventh preceding generation is reached. Following this principle, a principle which is supported also by the scientific genetic theory DNA transfer from one generation to another by mother and father till one reaches the sixth or seventh preceding generation, every Hindu family must act accordingly in the settlement of marriage negotiations.

Insofar as the Shrotriyas are concerned, their sociological situation defined by their small number confined in a small geographical area compel them to religiously follow the injunction of avoiding a marriage alliance if it falls within seven generations of both sides, that is, both the girl and the boy. Given the additional factor of being bound together in a complex and multiplex network of relationship, the Shrotriyas are compelled to be very meticulous in *a-swajana nirnaya.* In contrast to the Shrotriyas, the case of the Bhumihara Brahmans and the Rajputs is somewhat different for two very important reasons. In the first place, both these caste groups have at their disposable a larger spatial domain from which to choose suitable boys for their daughters of marriageable age. In the second place, these two caste groups are more exposed to the influences of modernisation than what is the case with the Shrotriyas. Even when the Shrotriya families have advanced far on the scale of modernisation, they still continue to give their allegiance rather faithfully to the injunctions and prohibitions deriving both from Shastriya and *laukika* traditions affecting marriage decisions.

The reason for this is not far to seek. The Shrotriyas still have a very strong sense of self-identity based on their ritual rank among the Brahmans in the social order in Mithila. They would rather defend it by every means at their disposal for preserving their self-identity that faces the threat of collapse if the members of the Shrotriya caste group are allowed to marry outside the Shrotriya fold. It is in this sense that the small Brahman community of the Shrotriyas faces a very real dilemma in their contemporary existence. While the influence of modernisation is progressively becoming intense and compelling, and many individual members of the Shrotriya community have adopted modern ways of thought-ways and work-ways, they still have in their minds the overbearing presence of the community ethos as the invisible onlooker and the intolerant judge of whatever they do or wish to do. And what is very interesting is that very few of the Shrotriyas will openly defy the sanctions their community may like to impose on those who openly violate its long accepted rules of socio-religious conduct.

In effect, then, the Shrotriyas constitute a very small and almost a closed social formation that enjoys the status, both social and ritual, which they even today enjoy because of their separation from not only from the rest of the society but also from other Brahmans. Once this separation is somehow broken the fear of being drowned in the sea of the common mass of the people would become real for them. It is fear besides the need to prevent social sanctions from their caste brethren that induce them to conform so unswervingly to the age-old religious prescriptions insofar as the question of entering into a marriage alliance is concerned. In contradistinction to this, both the Rajputs and the Bhumihars are not faced by such a fear of either endangering the self-identity of their caste or, for that matter, invoking strong caste sanctions if they deviated from or broke certain religious prescriptions governing the settlements of marriage contracts.

What also needs to be noted here is the fact that the act of *a-swajana nirnaya* does not by any means constitute the first step in any settlement of marriage contract in the true sense of the term. Prior to this is the onerous task of finding a suitable groom for girls of marriageable age. The identification of a suitable match for a Shrotriya girl is somewhat easier than is the case with either the Bhumihara Brahman or the Rajputs. Shrotriyas, being a small community confined to a small geographical space as well as being well knit into a network of multiplex relationship, find it easier to identify suitable matches. Moreover, it is this cast group that is still free of the bane of dowry. In addition, what is distinctive about the Shrotriyas is the almost total absence of the considerations associated with the differences of wealth and other material indicators of status. This is not the case with the Bhumihara Brahmans or the Rajputs for whom these status-related considerations carry much weight. Also, the prevalence of paying steep dowries for marrying off daughters of marriageable girls that has progressively spread its tentacles also makes it very difficult for them to easily settle upon a marriage alliance.

It is only after these initial difficulties have been taken care of that the act of *a-swajana nirnaya* can take place. If the *a-swajan nirnaya* declares the proposed marriage between the girl and the boy, the date of marriage is fixed by mutual consent giving preference to the convenience of the family of the bridegroom. And then different rites and rituals connected with marriage begin to be performed. Rituals are the integral parts of *samskaras* and are essential insofar as they mark the beginning and end of any important occasion in life, be it the birth of a child or marriage or any other occasion essentially secular in nature but in the need of being made sacred. The rituals constitute the external enactment of some spiritually significant process undertaking in man's interior and, therefore, objectively observable. And since the performance of *samskasras* are meant to lend a spiritual content to a secular activity, the performance of rituals are governed by certain rules, regulations and processes prescribed by the *karmakanda* part of *Dharmashastra.* It is through the performance of these rituals that the intended transformation of a natural man into a social man capable of viewing society as a cosmion is possible and, therefore, attempted. There are also those rituals that the *Shastras* deliberately leave to local customs and traditions by saying that the Shastriya rituals must leave room for the performance of certain rituals that have the sanction of local traditions and customs. And in many cases, womenfolk are the real custodians of the knowledge of such tradition and customs and, therefore, they become the executors of these rituals. The rituals which are defined and prescribed by the *Shastras* are known as Shastriya rituals while the rituals associated with local tradition and customs are called *laukika vyavaharas*. It is, however, to be noted that most of the *laukika vyavaharas* draw their significance from and are based and derive their legitimacy from the fundamental tenets of the relevant *Shastras*. It is discussing these aspects of the marriage *samskara* that we turn to in the next chapter.

References

1. See, for example, Hetukar Jha, *Man in Indian Tradition: Vidyapati's Discourse on Purusa* (New Delhi: Aryan Books International, 2002), pp. 13-28. Writing his *Purusa Pariksha* in the first of the fourteenth century, Vidyapati took into account the fact that the Hindus and the Muslims were living side by side and noted its consequences. According to him, the religion of one became the object of ridicule for the other. The Turk forced anyone on the road to become his *beggar,* that is, a labourer without being paid any remuneration. Even a Brahman boy was forcibly taken out of his house to carry cow's hide

on his head. ...Temples were destroyed for the construction of mosques. The term Hindu was used as a term of abuse and insult. The situation was so bad that even a Turk of inferior rank could torture any Hindu if he became angry for whatsoever reason. And Vidyapati concluded that the way the Turks moved indicated that they wanted to terminate the very existence of the Hindus. Mahakavi Vidyapatikrita Kirtilata, trans. By V. S. Agrawala from Avahatta into Hindi (Jhansi: Sahitya Sadan, 1962).

2. The introduction of the system for the maintenance of genealogical charts of Brahman and Kayastha families in Mithila in the fourteenth century and the resultant *Panji* system is just one instance. The introduction of the *Panji* system was aimed at maintaining the purity of familial descent from the threat of corrupting because of inter-caste marriage and to prevent *sagotra* marriage.
3. Br. Up. I.4.3.
4. See Ramashray Roy, *Beyond Ego's Domain: Being and Order in the Veda* (Delhi: Shipra Publications, 1999), p. 107.
5. *Ibid*, p. 74.

8

Marriage Rituals—*Shastriya* and *Laukika*

The *samskara* of marriage incorporates rituals that are prescribed by the *Grihyasutras* as well as those that are sanctioned by locally prevalent traditions and customs. These two categories of rites and rituals are observed by all the three caste groups under discussion. While the Shastriya rituals are conducted by Brahman pandits in all these three groups, the *Laukika vyavaharas* are the exclusive concern of and, therefore, are the part of the exclusive domain of the womenfolk in all the three caste groups. The *Laukika* and Shastriya rituals and practices taken together complete the process of marriage in all the three caste groups.

In order to fully comprehend the significance of Shastriya rituals and *vyavaharas,* it is necessary to classify them with a view to highlighting their meaning and sequence in practice. At the outset, there are rituals that begin with the completion of marriage negotiations. The performance of these rituals begins with the communication of the news of the completion of the process of marriage settlement, that is, the completion of the process of *a-swajana nirnaya* to the families of both the bride and the groom. When this news is conveyed to both the sides, the performance of certain rituals begins. The set of these rituals closes with the departure of the groom from his place for marriage, on the one hand, and the preparation for *kanyadana* at the bride's place, on the other. For the sake of convenience, the rituals falling under this category are described, in this study, as type I. Another set of rituals begins with the arrival of the groom at the bride's place. Once the groom's convoy (called in Mithila the *barat*) enters the boundary of the village of the bride, this set of rituals begins to be performed. The series of rituals under this category ends with the rituals of *sinduradana*, veiling of the bride (*Ghoghat*) and *ashirvada* (blessings) with rice and *Durva* grass by the elders of both the groups. These rituals, again for the sake of convenience, are called in this study rituals of type II. Set III of rituals begins after the bride and the groom take their meals on the first day of the marriage. The rituals of this type continue for two successive days.

And then, there are rituals that are categorised as type IV; they take place on the fourth day of the marriage and end during the night of the same day. With the end of type IV rituals, the process of marriage is considered as finally solemnised. There are, after this, rituals which take place in the course of the departure of the bride for her husband's place. Since the departure of the bride from her father's place of residence and her arrival at the place of residence of her husband are two distinct but interrelated events, rituals related to these are typified as V and VI. Type V rituals are performed at the time of the bride's departure and type VI of rituals takes place on the arrival of the bride at her husband's place. And with the completion of the type VI rituals, the bride is physically and symbolically assimilated, integrated in the family of her husband.

It becomes relevant to note, at the very outset, that the sequence of rituals described above is modified and managed nowadays in a manner that suits the convenience of the bride's and the groom's family in terms of time requirements. And, secondly, in these sets of rituals, both the shastriya and *laukika* rituals are so inextricably interwoven that it becomes not only difficult but also almost impossible to evaluate these two parts in terms of the gradation of their religious significance. As such, deviancies, whether weak or strong, from the performance of rites and rituals either prescribed by the *Shastras* or sanctioned by local tradition and in vogue for a long time in particular localities constitute an important cue or pointer to understanding their proximity with the standards set long ago for these communities to observe.

Insofar as the first factor, that is, the time requirement, is concerned, the time spent at the bride's paternal place for the performance of different rites and rituals involved in the marriage *samskara* has been reduced, in most cases, for various socio-economic reasons, to just one day. This has gradually happened particularly in the course of the last four decades. The earlier practice was to finish the range of rituals over a long period of time. The phenomenon of the reduction of the length of time required for performing the rites and rituals covered by the marriage *samsakara* is characteristic now of all the three caste groups under discussion. In olden days, the groom used to stay for four days at the bride's place. The groom (in the Shrotriya caste group) was supposed to leave for his place on an astrologically suitable day without taking the bride along. The groom was supposed to return for taking away the bride after some time, usually within a year, or two or four years. Now this schedule of marriage has so changed that all the rites and rituals of this category are to be performed within four days. What is also interesting to note is the fact that most often only one day out of four days is spent at the bride's parent's place. The result is that, on the one hand, all the rituals have to be performed within a shorter span of time and, on the other, some of the rituals that were supposed to be performed at the bride's paternal place, are now either omitted or performed at the groom's place.

All the three caste groups, while justifying this reduction in the time scale spent on the performance of marriage *samskara,* argue on the same line. In doing so they refer to the fact that marriages now take place much later even after girls have crossed the age of puberty. This delay is caused because of the time consumed receiving a formal education in colleges and universities since the education of girls has become a necessity. Moreover, exigencies growing out of the increasing proportion of nuclear mode of family life, brought into operation because of the need to leave ancestral places of residence in order to exploit job and other opportunities in far-off places do on not make it any easier to find suitable boys for girls of marriageable age. The process of searching for a suitable bridegroom lengthens as a result. However, this shift does not alter the composite character of the rituals in any essential, substantive way; that is, it does not have the effect of eliminating any item of rites and rituals prescribed by Shastriya injunctions and *laukika* tradition. The traditional requirement of spending a particular length of time in performing marriage *samskara*, over the duration of four days has, of course, undergone the process of change. However, even while the duration of time has been reduced, the sequence of the rites and rituals to be performed is still the same despite there being a change in the locale. This, as already indicated, is true of all the three caste groups under study and all these caste groups have organised the performance of marriage *samskara* accordingly. The rituals are now planned and performed in such a way that only a minimal or no dislocation is caused because of the resetting of time schedule.

The shastriya rituals are drawn, as discussed earlier, from the *Grihyasutras*, the *Smritis* and the Vedas; it is for this reason that the *Mantras* that are recited in the course of the performance of different rites and rituals during the marriage ceremony in all the three communities is Sanskrit. These rituals are conducted by such scholars of Sanskrit who are particularly proficient in the performance of *karmakanda*. In contradistinction to shastriya rites and rituals, there are such rituals that are not specified or prescribed by Sutras or *Smritis* but the *Dharmashastra* ascribes equal importance and value to certain rites and rituals based not directly on them; they are sanctioned by locals customs and their justification is derived indirectly from the *Shastras*. These are the *Laukika vyavaharas* which the womenfolk preserve and perform during the performance of the marriage *samskara*. The language used in performing these rituals is most often native or, for certain rituals, Sabar (the language of *Tantra*). Male members of the community, even those who are learned in *shastras*, do not understand the text, the sequence or the significance of these *Laukika Mantras*. These *Mantras* are known to elder women of the community and are passed on to newer generations at an appropriate time. Those who know these *Mantras* do not speak or explain it to male members as a matter of custom. These rituals form a larger proportion of marriage ceremony as compared to the Shastriya ones.

Since the *laukika Mantras* draw their legitimisation from the *Shastras*, it seems as if the *Shastras* themselves confer the right and the responsibility of becoming and, more importantly, remaining the custodian of the knowledge as well as the secret contained in most of the *laukika* practices on the womenfolk. It is also important to note that these practices are supposed to contain certain symbolic meanings that are considered to have salience by virtue of their being grounded in the *Vedic* world-view. It is left entirely to the womenfolk to perform these rituals included in *laukika vyavaharas.* The realm of *laukika vyavaharas* is such that the male members are strictly forbidden to meddle with. No adult male member, except the groom, is allowed to be present while these rituals are being performed. Sometimes it creates a very funny situation when, because of astrological compulsions of adhering strictly to time schedule found to be auspicious, male members make repeated requests for expediting the process of the performance of the *laukika vyavaharas* only to be ignored by the womenfolk. This importance of the role of women in the observance of *laukika vyavaharas* is recognised and adhered to in all the three caste groups. All the rituals, whether Shastriya or *Laukika,* are practised by all these groups. However, to identify to the degree to which each of these caste groups adheres to perfectly or deviates from the set pattern of the performance as sanctioned by the *Shastras* or by local tradition, it is necessary to undertake a detailed description of both Shastriya and *Laukika* rituals.

Information available for such a description was collected in the course of the fieldwork. This information was checked for authenticity with the help of published studies relating to folk customs and traditions. However, except for the Shrotriya caste group, for which there were several published books, no published material was available for ascertaining which practices have been traditionally prevalent among the Rajputs and the Bhumihara Brahmans.

Insofar as the rites and rituals of Category 1 are concerned, they begin to be performed once the decision about the suitability of marriage is taken, the performance of different rites and rituals, both shastriya and *laulika,* begin to be performed both at the place of the bride and the bridegroom. In the case of the Shrotriyas, the marriage decision, as already pointed out, is called *a-swajana* decision. This decision is formalised in the form of what is called *siddhanta,* a written document recording the genealogical justifications for declaring a particular proposed marriage alliance as valid and therefore legitimate and signed, at least, by the Panjikara. The recording of the suitability of the marriage alliance in the form of *siddhanta* is not in vogue among either the Bhumihara Brahmans or the Rajputs. The former decide about a suitable match on the basis of both the considerations of *mulavarjya* (the elimination of root village) and *gotravarjya* (elimination of *gotra*). In the case of the Rajputs no Shastriya ritual was reported to be performed; matchmaking takes place by *moolavarjya* and *gotravarjya* in the manner discussed earlier.

In terms of *laukika r*ituals under this category, they take place both at the bridegroom's and the bride's village homes. These rituals that take place at the groom's place include the shaving of the groom's head by the barber, an activity undertaken before the performance of any religious rite since it is considered to be an initial step in the purification of the body of the performer of the *yajna.* This is followed by what in Mithila is known as *Kumaram,* that is, the worship of *Grama Devata* (village deity) after a dip in the village tank. The *Kumaram* is followed, in turn, by parching dry paddy seeds, known as *Lava Bhujab,* for use in the marriage rituals. This is usually done by the sister of the groom along with her husband. But before the groom can leave for the bride's place, a Brahmana from the bride's side must come to seek the permission of the groom and his elders before the act of marriage can take place. This is known as *ajna leba,* that is, seeking the permission of the bridegroom and his elders to make necessary preparations for the ensuing marriage.

Before the groom leaves his own place, a rectangular space on the north-eastern side of the western house with banana trees as pillars and yellow cloth as walls is earmarked; this is called *Naga.* A *Siki patia* (a straw matting) is placed inside this enclosure along with a *purhar* (that is, a painted earthen pitcher) and a *patil* (a painted earthen pot with a small *diya* (lamp inside). In addition, on the western wall of the western house is fixed up a *Doka kauri,* a special type of snail shell and sea-shell, with the paste of cow-dung underneath it. This enclosed space is made secure, that is free of any evil influence, by burning a compound of herbs while chanting *laukika Mantra*s. This is called *Nihuchhab.* It is after all these preliminary steps have been taken that the groom is ready to leave his village. But before he actually does leave his village, his mother spreads one corner of her sari over the head of the groom as an act symbolising that the groom is under the protection of his mother. The last ritual before the groom actually leaves for the bride's place is that of *Durvakshat*a. This means that the elders (both males and females) bless the groom with grass and rice. In this ritual, the males chant *V*edic *Mantra*, while the females sing marriage songs.

While all these rituals are being performed at the groom's place, the family members of the bride, too, remain busy performing certain rituals at their own place. Just as the *Kumaram* is performed at the groom's place, so, too, it is performed at the bride's place. It consists of the worship of *Gramadevata* after a holy dip in the village tank followed by the ritual of marrying a Mango tree with *Mahua* tree and the worship of *Kuladevata* (family deity), the worship with *laukika Mantra*s of Surya (the Sun god), Chandrama (the moon), Nava (Navanath?), Navagraha (the nine planets), Gauri (the consort of *Shiva*), *Sathi* (*Khasthika*). After all these takes place the ritual of what is called *Siuthi Notaba,* a facilitating ritual in which the bride's hair is split and divided in the middle and purified for the forthcoming ritual of putting vermilion by the groom. Along with all this, the marriage altar (that is, the preparation of the sacred vedi, on the north-eastern side of the courtyard is prepared. Only after all these preparatory steps have been initiated or completed, the act of *Ajna leba,* that is, seeking permission from the bridegroom and his elders takes place, for which a Brahman has to be sent to the groom's place. This is followed by what is called in Mithila as *Jamaya liyaoba.* For this, usually the brother or the cousin of the bride has to go to the groom's place to escort him down to the bride's place.

In the case of the Bhumihara Brahmans, the first *laukika* ritual is the Faladana or Tilak at the groom's place. This means that the male members of the bride's family and other near relatives and friends of the family go to the groom's place and solemnise the marriage alliance by the exchange of paddy seeds along with other items of gifts including money and clothes. This constitutes the first formal step taken to formalise the proposed marriage alliance among both the Bhumihars and the Rajputs. Sometimes, especially in the case of Rajputs, the *Tilak* ceremony can be preceded by *saguna.* Once the ritual of *saguna* and/or *tilaka* has been completed indicating the formalisation of the marriage contract, the performance of certain rituals at the bride's place are, then, initiated. These rites are *kumarama*, that is, the worship of *Gramadevata* after bathing in the village pond with the assistance of seven married (lady) assistants, *Mandap banai,* the making of the marriage altar in the case both of the Bhumihara Brahmans and the Rajputs. What is typical to the Bhumiharas are *Jhutikabandhan, Othangar,* and *Matrikapujan.* The ritual of *jhutikaband* is similar to *Siuthi Notaba* and signifies the split in the middle of the bride's hair for the purpose of purifying it for the placement of vermilion by the groom. *Othangar* signifies the thrashing of paddy seeds in traditional thrasher (*ukhal*) by the bride along with seven other married ladies barring widows. The *matrikapuja* is done by the person who is to perform *kanyadana* (gifting of the girl in marriage) in which lord Shiva is worshipped. In the case of the Rajputs, the rituals of *Ghritadhari* and *Nachchu* are also performed at the bride's place. The former signifies the pouring of ghee on a particular carving on the western wall of a house in the west while the latter refers to a ritual performed especially by a barber.

Insofar as the rituals falling under Category II are concerned, they begin, in the case of the Shrotriyas, with the offering of a prayer, called, *Abhyudayik*, that is, the evocation of and offerings to the ancestors (*pitra,* departed souls); it is followed by *Matrika pujan* that is, evocation of the deities enshrined in *matrika varnas* which, in the *Vedic* perspective signifies the worship of the primal mother of all beings and who eventually empowers the *Mantras* to become effective. Only after the *matrikapujan* has been completed does the ritual of what is known as *Asthongar* takes place. This ritual is performed in order to obtain rice after it have been made sacred.

For this, the groom is stringed along with seven married Brahmans and they together thrash paddy seeds in *ukhal* while chanting *Purushasukta* from the *Rigveda.* This ritual takes place on the south-western corner of the courtyard.

It is only after the ritual of *asthongar* has been completed that the most important ritual of the establishment of sacred fire in the house, the most essential item in the performance of any *yajna* can take place. This ritual is *Agnisthapan* in which the groom lights the sacred fire on the altar (*vedi*) that is situated on the north-eastern corner of the courtyard. The ritual of *agnisthapan* is followed by *samkalpa* (the will to do something) in this case to gift a girl in marriage (that is, *kanyadana*) to the bridegroom already selected for this purpose. For this, the groom has to sit before the *acharya* (the man who performs the *yajna* of *kanyadana* while the *acharya* takes the *samkalpa* (sacred decision) for gifting the girl to the groom, that is, *kanyadana.* The process of the gifting away of the girl in marriage, ritual called *Gotradhyaya* is performed. In performing this ritual, ancestral genealogical identity of the bride and the groom is narrated by chanting aloud attributes of the preceding generations on both the sides. This is done with a view to publicly declare the suitability of the proposed gifting of the *kanyadana.* This is done while the acharya offers *panchabhusana* (five types of ornaments), *Shayya* (bedding), and *arhana* (household utensils) to the groom with the avowed purpose of making the married life for the girl and the boy, that is, the life of the householder, easy so that the married couple can easily bear the responsibilities of a *grihastha,* the second of the life stages according to the Hindu tradition, and undertake the task of procreation under the blessings of Prajapati.

The *dana* (gift) of a girl, unlike other *danas* that are done with *tila* and *kusha* in one's hands, is done with rice in the hands of the *acharya* which signifies that, except for the express purpose specified for the *dana* of *kanya* (daughter), all other associating factors will remain intact and operative in the context of her paternal lineage. Once the gift of the girl is successfully completed, the *acharya* offers some gold (17 *anna*) as the *dakshina* of the *kanyadana* to the groom. Having received the *dakshina* for the gift of *kanya*, the groom takes her to the altar for initiating the process of marriage. The actual act of the gifting away of the bride takes place on the *Mandapa,* an especially built covered or even uncovered earmarked area for the *yajna* of marriage to take place. The act of *kanyadana* proceeds in a sequence beginning from *samkalpa* and going through the processes of *sindurdana, Prajapati havan, Laja havan, Saptapada,* and *Achhadana*, all performed according to the process prescribed in the *Grihyasutra.* Once these steps have been completed, the elders from both the families and other elderly persons attending the performance of *kanyadana*, bless the couple with rice and grass by chanting *Vedic Mantra*; they also offer *artha* (money) on this occasion as a token of their blessing.

The *laukika* rituals under this category that are performed by the Shrotriyas begin with what is called *Sankara:* Needless to say that this refers to the idols of *Shiva* and *Annapurna* which the groom's party has to bring along with them to the bride's place. These idols are the first things to enter the bride's courtyard and are put at the south-west corner. But before the groom reaches the boundary of the bride's village, the first person to bless him is the washerwoman (*dhobin*) who touches a portion of curd with her lips and toes and gives it to the bride to eat. When the groom arrives at the bride's house, he is first greeted with betel nuts and sacred thread and is shown a bamboo platter where there are two statues– one of a *Bak* (crane) and the other of a man known as *Thak* (cheat/*thag*). *Bak* symbolises concentrating faculty of the groom (his power of concentration as a householder) the other emphasises the fact that he must be aware about the wicked ways of the cheat who he may come across. This is called the ritual of *Gooa, Janau and Thak-Bak.*

Next follows the ritual of *Parikshani* in which a senior lady of the bride's group catches hold of the groom's nostrils (stops his breath) and moves him three times around the *mandap* which takes about 7 to 10 minutes. This is done in order to test the groom's capability of *pranayama* or strength in holding his breath. After thus satisfying themselves of the strength of the groom, the women take the groom to the northern part of the house where the bride waits for him after performing the worship of Gauri (the consort of Lord Shiva). The groom is, then, asked to look at the frescoes depicted on the walls of the northern house where images of Nayana Yogini—the legendary Yogini who had the power to attract even the most celibate yogis—have been drawn. This is done with an intention that the groom must always remain under the spell of the beauty and manners of the bride. The groom and the bride are, then, asked to bow to Sri--the symbol of well-being and *Samba* – the symbol of fraternal love. This is known as the ritual of *Nayana Yogini* and *Sri Samba.* The next step in this process is Kanya *parichaya*, that is, the groom is, then, supposed to identify his bride from two veiled (sitting) persons. This is the test of his ability of making appropriately succinct inference. After this, the groom holds the bride by her hands and brings her to the *mandapa* where the acharya performs the rites of *samkalpa* and *kanyàdana.* This is followed by shastriya rituals. Once the shastriya rituals have been gone through, *humaon* takes place. This means that womenfolk put paddy seeds, curd and banana on a beautifully crafted bamboo platter (called *chumaonak dala*) and move it above the heads of the newly wed couple not only to bless them but also to ward off evil forces. The newly wed couple is, then, asked to eat (only as a formality) from one platter having *chura* (thrashed rice/*chirva*) and *dahi* (curd).

Similar to the Shrotriyas, the Bhumihar Brahmans, too, begin the shastriya rituals with *Shri Puja,* that is, the worship of the presiding deity of the family for the avowed purpose of securing the blessings of the family deity for the well being and good fortune of the girl for getting a good husband. After this, the rituals of *Matrikapujan,* the offering of new cloths and bed to the groom, *kanyadana, dakshina, agnisthapana,* and other different rituals connected with the act of marriage follow in quick succession. Once these rituals have been completed, the bridegroom takes the bride to the vedi of marriage and all other shastriya rituals are performed as in the case of the Shrotriyas. Needless to say that insofar as the performance of the rites and rituals prescribed by the *Grihyasutras* are concerned, there is no variation from one caste group to another. What is, however, evident from the observation of the performance of different rites and rituals on the occasion of marriage in different caste groups is that there is, on the one hand, the difference in nomenclature and on the other, some difference in emphasis on the importance of a particular ritual.

It is in the domain of *Laukika vyavahara* that some vital differences can really be seen among different caste groups. Note, for example, that in the case of the Bhumihar Brahmans, the *laukika vyavaharas* included in Category II begins after the marriage party arrives at the doorstep of the bride's house. The first ritual that is performed is called *dwara lagai,* that is, the greeting of the marriage party by those persons who are family members of the bride, relations and villagers. Immediately after, the groom is escorted at an appropriate time to inner quarters of the bride's house. One of the reportedly modern practices that has recently made its way in the traditional stronghold of *laukika vyavaharas* is the exchange of garland by the bride and the groom. This is followed by the placing before the *Kuladevi* in the bride's house of what is known as *sagunadala* (a deep bamboo platter containing articles necessary for marriage as well as some cloths) brought by the marriage party.

Once the *sagunadala* has been placed before the *Kuladevi*, a maid-servant goes to the groom's party with a pitcher full of water and some mango leaves atop it in which the groom's party puts some money as a token of auspicious omen. This is called *Shankara mangai.* Soon after the ritual of *Kapara pahirab,* that is, the putting on by the bride the clothes brought by the groom's party takes place. After this, the brother of the bride puts a piece of elongated cloth (*gamachha*) around the groom's neck and brings him to the courtyard, an act called *angana anab.* The pandit (usually a Maithil Brahman) performs the ritual (called *larka chumaib*) of moving a bamboo platter with paddy and other things over the head of the groom. The groom is, then, greeted by womenfolk with *besan* (gram powder), *deepa* (earthen lamp, *diya*), *dahi* (curd), *kajal* and honey. This is called the ritual of *Parikshani.* Then there is the ritual of *Maraba bulai* in which the brother of the bride puts a piece of cloth (*gamachha*) around the neck of the groom and pulls him around the *mandapa* thrice. In this ritual the barber moves along with the two with a pot full of water. Then follows the act of *kanya nirikshana* (that is, seeing the bride) in which the groom has to identify his bride among other veiled girls. After that certain Shastriya rituals, already discussed, follow.

In case of the Rajputs, the *laukika* rituals begin with the greeting by a barber of the groom with a *Dahi kalash* and a pitcher full of water in order to ensure the completion of the marriage without any disturbance. Then *Parikshan* of the groom takes place in which the barber welcomes the groom with betel leaves and a *deepa* (an earthen lamp). The groom is, then, sent back to his camp who waits there until someone goes to bring him for other rituals. In the meantime the ritual of *Kanya Nirikshana* takes place in which the elder members from the groom's side are invited to see the bride. The groom is, then escorted by the bride's men from his camp to the bride's house. At the doorsteps of the bride's house, senior ladies greet the groom and the brother of the bride puts a towel (*gamachha*) around the neck of the groom and takes him three times around the *mandapa.* After this, the wife of the bride's brother puts some *kush* (sacred grass) and *Urad* (a type of pulse seeds) in an earthen pitcher and asks the groom to identify what it is. After all this, Shastriya rituals take place.

The groom then comes over to the *mandapa* and changes his clothes and moves to a house on the northern part of the house where the bride is waiting to be taken to the *vedi* of marriage. But before she is taken to the *vedi,* the groom is asked to identify his bride who is sitting in a cluster of three well covered girls. After the groom has identified his bride correctly or not, he takes the bride to the *vedi,* where the ritual of marriage takes place. After the completion of the rites and rituals of *kanyadana,* elders present there bless the newly wed couple. Once the giving of *ashirvada* is completed, the two *samadhis,* that is the respective fathers of the bride and the groom, embrace each other and the father of the girl presents to the father of the groom new clothes. After this the newly wed couple go to bow before the *Kuladevi.*

The Category III of shastriya rituals are few and far between for all the caste groups. Take, for example, the case of the Shrotriyas. After the rituals of marriage (i.e. *kanyadana*) have been performed, no shastriya ritual is performed except for instructing the newly wed couple to practice celibacy till the end of the fourth day of the marriage when certain *shatriya* rituals will be performed. In addition, the newly wed couple is not given any food that contains salt. But when it comes to the Bhumihara Brahmans and the Rajputs, no such instructions are, strictly given whether in the matter of refrain from having sex or eating saltless food. Insofar as *laukika vyavaharas* are concerned, there is great amount of variation from one caste group to another.

Insofar as the Shrotriyas are concerned, the *laukika* rituals of Category III that are performed on the second and the third day after the marriage ceremony begin, again, with *Gauri Puja.* Every morning the newly wed couple worships Gauri--the consort of Lord *Shiva.* In addition, every evening, too, the couple has to perform *Gauri Puja.* However, after the evening *puja* there takes place the ritual of *Janaua chori* in which the sacred thread of the groom and his ancestors is declared to have been stolen by some of the bride's female relatives. The performance of this ritual is accompanied by the chanting of some *Mantra*s. This is followed by what is known as *Mutthi chhorayab* and *Mahuak.* Every evening the groom has to open the tightly closed fist of the bride (without, of course, hurting her) and, then, the couple has to eat (as a formality) out of the same platter.

Once the rituals mentioned above have been performed, after the aforesaid rituals, the bamboo platter, called *chumaonak dala,* is moved, every evening, over the heads of the newly wed couple (in sitting posture); and after this the elders of the family (both males and females) bless the couple with throwing rice and grass over their heads. Every evening, too, the groom has to go to the northern house where the bride is already waiting for him. The couple, then, has to sleep together but in the presence of numerous womenfolk who observe the gesture and posture of the bride and the groom in order to ascertain that they have followed the norms of celibacy. In the course of his entry to the northern house, the groom has to uncover a pot with a small lamp inside it; this has to be done without making any sound otherwise, the groom has to suffer the torture of abuses hurled against his ancestors.

Coming to the Bhumiharas, one of the very important rituals under Category III is that of *Ghaskatti.* It is a ritual that signifies that the groom would not hesitate in doing the meanest of the mean work as a householder in order to support his family. What is necessary to note in this connection is the fact that the collection of fodder for the cattle wealth of a family engaged in agriculture is an important function though society looks askance at it because of status considerations. By inference, the significance of the cutting of grass as a part of marriage ritual lies in the fact that it underlines the importance of doing even the meanest of works, that is, meanest when looked at from the perspective of social status considerations, for the sustenance of the family in the life of the householder. After this, the groom and the bride both together put eatables in each other's platter; this is called *Mahuak.* This is followed by a feast that is given in the honour of the groom's party by the bride's side. This is called *Bhatkhai* or *Maryad* After this feast, the bride's side begs to be excused for any shortcomings that the bride's family may have committed in offering appropriate hospitality in keeping with the dignity of the groom's family. After all these rituals, the *Vidai,* that is departure of the bride to her husband's place/village takes place.

On the second and the third day of the marriage ceremony, the Rajputs perform different *laukika* rituals that begin from what is called *Khir khiyaon.* What happens on this occasion is that the newly wed couple is brought to the *mandap* and *khir* (a preparation of pudding made of milk and rice) is served for their food. This is followed by what is known as *Ladubechi,* that is, a ritual where some things are sold and purchased in between the groom and the bride's men, particularly her brother. This signifies that trade, for the well being of the family, must be done by the couple. A closely related ritual to *Ladubechi is Dhana purayab* signifying that the newly married couple must see to it that the stock of grains must not be allowed to deplete dangerously so that the family does not have to purchase it from the market

Similar to the Bhumiharas, the Rajputs, too, observe the ritual of *Maryad.* After the *maryada*, the newly wed couple unbinds the knots that were put before on the mandap. This is called *Maraba Bandhan Kholai.* This is followed by *Ghunghat.* For this purpose, the bride has to wear the *saree* brought specially for this ritual by the groom's father. On this occasion, the groom's father touches the head of the bride thrice with the gift (s*are*e) and, then leaves it to be put on by her. Then follows the ritual of *Chumaon* in which a bamboo platter with paddy, grass, curd and banana is moved over the heads of the sitting couple. The bride is, then, seen off to her husband's place along with the groom.

Then follows a series of rituals which we have placed under Category IV, incorporating a number of rituals both Shastriya and *Laukika.* We begin, first with the Shrotriyas. The first of the *Sahstriya* rituals Shrotriyas perform is the *Matrika Puja* as described earlier. This is followed by a ritual called the *Chaturthi Marriage.* This is a ritual that is performed to finally solemnise the marriage and without which the marriage is considered to be incomplete. In performing this ritual, the sacred fire is again lit for two types of *Havana,* that is, *Prajapati Havana* and *Laja Havana. After these havanas,* again, the ritual of *sinduradana* is performed seven times followed by a*shirvada* to the newly wed couple.

Then follows a series of *laukika* rituals beginning from the bathing the couple in the south-western corner of the courtyard, covered by *aripan* (floor painting done by rice paste). One of the agricultural appliance, called *palo* used to level a ploughed field, is put there in a horizontal position and the bride and the groom are made to sit on that and are bathed with water filled in a pitcher on the day of the groom's departure for marriage. This is followed by what is known as *Pik pisaon* in which the groom is given betal containing certain herbs which are supposed to keep the groom attracted to the bride. Then takes place what is called *Kumhar katti.* In this the groom is asked to chop into two by one stroke of the sword a white gourde (*kumhara/petha*). Then takes place the ritual of *Rai Bhela* in which a number of herbs is tied in the shawl/*chadar* of the groom in order to ward off evil spirits. At an auspicious moment, then, the bride and the groom are allowed to speak to each other for the first time. This is called *Muhabajji.* The groom brings some ornament known as *Thari-Pan* for the bride on this occasion. After this, the elders of the family honour the groom by offering him betel in large eating platters (*thali*–not of steel).

Once these rituals have been performed, the newly wed couple is brought to the northern house, called *Kohabar,* where the couple first performs *Gauri Puja.* This is followed by *Janaua chori* and *Mutthi chhorayab and Mahuak* already described earlier. Afterwards the bride takes some mustard oil in her hands and massages the legs of the groom, a ritual called *Tel laggi* signifying the notion that the wife will serve her husband faithfully. Just like the Rajputs, the Shrotriyas, too, perform the ritual of *Ladubechi.* It is followed by a *tantrika* ritual called *Durga-bidhi* with a view to keeping the couple unified and protected for ever, followed by yet another *tantrik* ritual called *Dasauth.* This ritual is also meant to protect the newly wed couple by chanting Sabar *Mantras* ten times while scattering (over the couple) different kinds of herbs and other things. This is avowedly done to ensure that the couple becomes well integrated psychologically and develops compatibility. After all these rituals have been performed the groom, the bride's brother and the bride sit in one file to take their meal (it is only a formality). This ritual is called *Saujanya* and then and only then the groom and the bride are given salted food and fish.

In the case of the Bhumiharas, the Shastriya rituals covered under Category IV begins with *Matrika Puja* followed by *Charturthi* marriage in which are performed the rituals of (a) *lajahavana;* (b) *sindurdana* (three times instead of seven times as is the case with the Shrotriyas); and (c) *acchadana.* The bride is, then, made to touch a herb (*karami*) and fish. She is also required to break open a sealed rice store (earthen storage drum, called *kothi*). Insofar as the performance of *Laukika* rituals are concerned, they are performed after the bride arrives at her husband's home. She must, however, abstain from taking any food before she arrives at her husband's home. Another series of Shastriya rituals are performed when the bride arrives at her husband's place. The bride is made to touch a platter full of *khira* (milk & rice preparation) on her arrival. She is, then, made to step over paddy seeds and grass put on a bamboo platter. After that, the bride and the groom are made to sit and the ladies move around a bamboo platter with paddy seeds, grass, curd and banana, over their heads. The bride is, then, made to distribute a special type of sweets called *ahibaka phar.*

In the case of the Rajputs, no Shastriya *rituals* were reported to have been performed insofar as Category IV is concerned. However, certain *Laukika* rituals do take place.

The last of the series of rituals performed to complete the process of marriage are those which we put under Categories V and VI. What needs to be emphasised here is that these rituals are performed only by the Shrotriyas. Insofar as Shastriya rituals are concerned, only the ritual of *Durvakshata,* that is, an act of blessing the newly wed couple by the elderly members of the groom's family, both male and female is followed, while the male members alone chant certain *Vedic Mantras.* Then follows a series of *Laukika* rituals beginning from what is called *Gharabhari* in which the groom puts a handful of paddy seeds in the *khoicha* (that is, the end part of the front of the saree called *anchal* which, for this purpose is made into the form of a receptacle) of the bride's mother saying, ' I have filled your house and now I am going to fill my parent's house'. After this, the ritual of *Panikatti* is performed in which the bride and the groom go to the village pond and offer prayer to *Varuna* (the presiding deity of water) and try to separate water by cutting it with a sword. When this does not succeed, that is, the water of the pond is not separated, they pray to *Varuna* to make their conjugal life as inseparable as the water. This is followed by another ritual symbolising the inseparability of the husband and wife. This ritual is *Jao ropab,* that is, the planting of a Java seed made of iron on the shore of the pond and again pray that they may not be separated as the java seed of iron.

When these rituals have been completed, the Shastriya rituals follow at the groom's place. The moment the bride's carriage enters the courtyard of the groom's house, a fisherman throws his fishing net on the carriage and covers it. After that, the bride alights from the carriage and sets her foot on a new piece of unrolled white cloth where a number of small lamps made of rice paste are lighted in ascending sequence; mango leaves are, then, placed one after another lamp and the bride ascends the steps by putting her feet, one after the other, on the lamps covered by mango leaves and then reaches the western house. The groom's mother makes the bride sit on her lap and feeds her boiled rice with milk. The bride, then, settles in the north-eastern corner of the western house which is already earmarked for her and stays there for four days. On the fourth day, in the evening, this ritual of what is known as *Bharaphori* takes place. In this ritual, the bride collects some cow-dung and house-dust in an earthen pot and puts it on her head. The younger brother of the bride is, then, asked to come; then the *deor* (the younger brother of the husband) comes with an ornamental cane and hits (only formally) the bride. The bride throws the dirt-filled pot to the ground and sits there. The younger brother of the groom persuades her to stand up but in vain. The groom, then, comes to take her by her hand, gives her some ornament and walks away with her. Then follows the important ritual of *Chini-Manchha*: That is, the same evening the bride serves in dinner fish curry and sugar to the members of the groom's family without the groom sitting with his family members. With this ritual, the process of marriage closes.

The rituals described above do not define, in any hard and fast way, the differentiation of the rituals, either time-wise or sequence-wise. Most of the times, even in the Shrotriya caste group (which serves, by and large, as a reference group for the standard of ritualistic purity), when the bride is taken to her husband's place on the day of the marriage itself, the rituals that are supposed to take place at the bride's paternal home, are performed at the groom's house. This often makes the intent of a particular ritual lose its significance. However, it is the Shrotriya caste-group which has been found to have evolved/developed alternative routes to address this problem of rituals. For instance, if a certain ritual, which generally takes place at the bride's paternal house, has to be performed at the groom's house, some lady, who is equally related to both the bride's and the groom's family, performs this ritual. This becomes possible because of the practice of endogamy in a caste-group whose population does not exceed twenty-five thousand. This is not the case with other caste groups under study and, as a result, most of the rituals, which have been recast in new time/place sequence, seem to have lost their substantive intent. Another perceptible difference in the understanding and practice of rituals between the Shrotriya caste group, on the one hand, and the Rajputs and Bhumihara Brahmans, on the other, is that the Shrotriya group is found to practice both Shastriya and *Laukika* rituals with greater Shastriya/*Tantrik* proximity than is the case with other two caste groups. The major indicator of this symptom is the level of substantive understanding of the meaning and process of both *Laukika* and Shastriya rituals which is admittedly higher among the members of the Shrotriya caste group than in those belonging to either the Rajput or the Bhumihar caste groups. Given the similarity in the nomenclature and content of rituals, it is only the Shrotriya caste group which seems to practice rituals in a manner that intends to consciously relate the details of the *samskara* with higher order principles which provide both the basis and purpose to all the *samskaras.* And, if all the rituals related to the *samskara* of marriage are scrutinised, one finds that the role of the women appears to be the most fundamental and catalytic in the completion of this *samskara.* The frescoes, floor paintings, *sabar Mantras*, ritualistic songs, their tune and text and sequence of different processes, besides their natural discriminatory instinct to elucidate, explain and elicit and reform the tendency of their male counterparts to abridge, even shorten by eliminating certain items from the long list of rituals concerning the marriage *isamakara* makes them the real actors in the performance of the *samskara* of marriage according to Shastriya and *Laukika* traditions.

Dharmashastra, in Mithila, ascribes equal importance to *Laukika* rituals as compared to the Shastriya ones. And it also considers the *Laukika* rituals as the exclusive domain of the womenfolk who prove to be their real guardian. Given the fact that the content of the *laukika* rituals is much larger than the Shastriya ones, the role of women becomes indispensable, nay, exceedingly dominant and central. They enjoy exclusive monopoly in performing these rituals which they meticulously learn in the course of real life situations related with the performance of rites and rituals on many sacred occasions under the tutelage of elderly ladies. Male members, even in enlightened families, are not aware of what the females do in the course of performing these rituals. The performance of *Laukika* rituals, therefore, reflect not only the gender dominance of womenfolk but also their indispensable role in the preservation of the organic character of Hindu society and social life and relations based on the principles of the *Vedic* world view by adhering very faithfully to the practices based on and derived from these principles.

None of the three caste groups under study follows the custom of match making in the marriage mart, called *Sabha* (a large gathering in the case of non-Shrotriya Brahmans that is held every year at *Saurath* during the marriage season. There is no specified place where these three castes habitually go for marriage negotiations. Marriage negotiations in these three caste groups, namely, Rajputs, Bhumihara Brahmans and Shrotriyas are carried on between individual families known as *grihakatha.* All the issues regarding the settlement of marriage, like money, dowry, age of the bride and bridegroom, education and others are settled through discussions and negotiations at places convenient to the groom's family. As a matter of uniform rule, it is only the bride's men who move to the groom's house or, for that matter, any other place for proposing and/or discussing issues regarding marriage negotiation.

While this is true of all the three caste groups under study, the Shrotriya mode of negotiations is marked by certain peculiar distinctions. The question of taking money/dowry is rather unthinkable for the Shrotriyas. There is an in-built mechanism within the Shrotriya community that protects the group from any type of money transaction in marriage negotiations. If anybody strays out to ask for and receive money, he faces utter disgrace in his own community and, at times, faces even tacit ostracisation. As a matter of practice, therefore, marriage proposals, irrespective of strata-divide, are frequently made and settled in the Shrotriya caste-group quite easily.

This is, however, not the case with either the Rajputs or the Bhumiharas of this region. They insist that marriages should take place between families having equal socio-economic status. The custom of paying or receiving hefty cash to the groom's party (to the groom's father, in particular) at the time of the ritual of Tilak, or even earlier, is an established tradition. Besides, dowry in different forms, like household goods, jewellery, real estate, etc., is considered as the indicator of superior social status. In contradistinction to the Bhumiharas and the Rajputs, the Shrotriyas ascribe importance to social courtesy, language consciousness, obsequiousness of the bride's group and abstinence from any type of action that may amount to display of affluence. The Shrotriyas do not even prefer gorgeous and exotic dress and make-up materials for participating in ceremonies like marriage. The only material necessity for the Shrotriyas in marriage s*amskara* is the requirement of *panchabhusana* (five ornaments), some cooking utensils, two sets of bedding and thirteen-and-a half grams of gold.

The Shrotriyas cannot and do not take their meal more than once at the bride's place and even that meal has to be purely vegetarian and free from salt. As a result, little expenditure is incurred on feeding the guests in a Shrotriya marriage. At times, if the bride's party has economic constraints, the number of guests forming the marriage party, too, is reduced to the minimum of three or five persons. The Shrotriyas practice strict discipline on such occasions. The guests from the groom's party are classified in order of social/relational seniority and this is acknowledged by the bride's party by washing the feet of each member of the groom's party in accordance with the order of precedence fixed up by the groom's guardians. In the process of feet-washing, each member of both the groom's and the bride's party have to be dressed in *dhoti, kurta, pag* (the special headgear of the Maithil Brahmans), and *tauni* (the wrapper). Every member of the groom's party has to quietly wait in queue for feet-washing. Among the Rajputs and Bhumihara Brahmans, as indicated earlier, the practices in this context differ widely from that of the Shrotriyas.

As a matter of common understanding, entertainment of guests among the Bhumiharas and the Rajputs must be on a very lavish scale. The marriage party of the groom belonging either to Bhumihara or the Rajput family must take at least four meals. Among the Rajputs, non-vegetarian item in the marriage feast is necessity; at places, liquor, too, is served to the guests of the groom's side. It is, perhaps, this reason that often ignites heated exchanges, scuffles and/or even fatal display of physical force (with guns booming —sometimes injuring members of the bride's or the grooms party). In Bhumihara caste, such acts of indiscipline have not been reported. Taking of non-vegetarian food at the bride's place, too, depends on the sect status (depending on whether a family belongs to *Vaisnava* or *Shakta* sect) of the family. Besides, also in the matter of dress, no uniform dress pattern has been observed in both the castes. Note, for example, that in the Rajput marriage party most of the participants were dressed in European style. However, the uniformity of language, *i.e.* Maithili, was found to be common for communication among both the Maithila Rajputs and Bhumihara Brahmans, who, though less conscious about general dress, were found to be very much particular about their headgear—a type of cap (resembling the Gandhi cap) which they use in combination both with trousers and *dhoti.* However, in case the marriage party belongs to a non-Maithili language group, the medium of communication in these castes is usually Hindi.

For the Shrotriya caste group this question has no significance as all the members of this caste speak in Maithili and they practice endogamy. The Shrotriya practice of offering salt-free food to the guests of the groom's side is typical to the Shrotriyas with no other castes in Mithila following this practices. The level of relative austerity in marriage expenses is highest among the Shrotriyas, the lowest among the Rajputs and medium in the case of Bhumihara Brahmans. The Bhumiharas seem to follow nowadays the Shrotriya pattern of taking only one meal at the bride's place (which they attribute to the growing scarcity of time), but the Rajputs still continue the practice of three four meals at the bride's place. These factors reflect a process of change in observing certain practices relating to marriage. In addition, changes have been introduced as a result of matrimonial alliances formed outside Mithila. In contrast to these two castes, the Shrotriyas remain true to the traditional practices.

While all these three caste groups have had to bear some impact of modernisation on their socio-cultural life, the pattern of variation in their ritual practices have been different. The Shrotriyas have shifted from four-day rituals to one single day at the bride's place. In most of the cases now the bride, in Shrotriya castes, is sent along with her husband on the same day and all the essential rituals take place at the groom's house. Except for this shift, the Shrotriyas have been able to continue their ritualistic traditions till date. Their folk/ritualistic songs (possibly representing the folk songs of Mithila as reported in the seventeenth century) still reflect the chastity of notes and text. So is the case of their floor paintings and designs of frescoes in Kohabarghar (northern house). And, since the impact of the commercialisation of tradition (in terms of the sale of fresco designs etc.) has been meagre on this community, these designs have not been much vulnerable to commercial intrusions.

In the case of the other two caste groups, it seems that they have lost, to a large extent, their traditional art forms used in their rituals (practised in their root territory, *i.e.* Rajasthan in the case of the Rajputs and Magadh for the Bhumiharas), and have not been successful in imbibing the Maithil type of traditional art forms (either paintings or songs) in their standardised style. As a result, the ritualistic floor paintings of both the Bhumihar and the Rajput caste-groups are either alien or the distortions of Maithil designs. Since the ritualistic paintings or the songs of Bhumiharas or Rajputs lack in purity and keeping in tune with the substantive significance of the occasion, they have proved to be much vulnerable to the forces of modernisation. These ritualistic paintings/songs, therefore, have gathered incrustations from cheap pieces of fine art and/or popular music from theatre and movies. This apart, the impact of movies has also brought about parodies of *bhangra/dandia* played under the backdrop of film music in these caste-groups. The text of their songs, too, reflect the impact of popular street/film compositions.

9

Overview

The discussion in the preceding chapters have not focused on marriage as a *samskara* alone. In fact, the preceding discussion has been wide ranging in the sense that it has, substantively speaking, covered an extensive territory marked by all those factors which help in understanding the real import of *samskaras* in man's life and social relations. The real import of *samskaras* can be apprehended only when we locate them in their proper context defined by their status in the social world, a cosmion, in the sense that the social world is a small replica of the cosmic order. *Samskaras* help preserve the cosmion character of the social world and are instrumental in keeping man attuned to the need of preserving this character of the social world by performing certain religious rites and rituals as necessary components of *yajna* as a surrogate of the cosmic *yajna* that was originally performed by *Purusha* in order to create the world. When located in this perspective, *samskaras* become quite transparent in their meaning and purpose. Marriage as a part of the whole gamut of other *samskaras* is, again, a forceful reminder of the need of doing what the gods did in producing the cosmos.

In locating the question of what *samskaras* substantially mean in their larger context, it is necessary, first, to make a distinction between types of societies in which *samskaras* play or do not play an important role. There are those societies in which they are by no means completely absent; they might be there in vogue, but, then, they play only a peripheral role because they have been confined to only a small segment of life and do not have any visible impact and effect on the actual pattern of living. In contradistinction to this, there are societies in which *samskaras* still play a vital and important role in almost every area of individual lives in all his life stages and social relations.

This differential relevance and performance of *samskaras* in different types of societies raises an important question: What are the factors that make for this differential acceptance and relevance of *samskaras?* This is the question that we disposed of in the first instance before moving on to discussing some larger issues involved with the meaning and relevance of *samskaras* in man's life. As already pointed out, the traditional way of looking at man and his world treats society as a cosmion; that is, society is treated as a small version of the cosmos itself by virtue of which it shows a remarkable degree of homology with the cosmos.

The substantive significance of the cosmos does not imply that the world is simply a physical accident, something that represents a concourse of cause-and-effect, devoid of any human meaning and relevance. When the world is treated simply as a physical accident, the only meaning and relevance it has for man is that it is the habitat of man as well as the source of his subsistence and the potential means of satisfying his myriad desires. The cosmos, on this view, does no signify a well-ordered world that is also the source of order for those who it provides shelter and sustenance to and becomes the source of meaning and value. In contrast to this view, there is also available another version of the cosmos which is considered to be well ordered; that is, the principles of order are inherent in the cosmos and are constantly operating to keep it on its true course. Needless to say that the order supposed to be inherent in the cosmos is not the order that scientists discover by using the method of observation, classification and generalisation. The principles of order that the scientists discover are not isomorphic in all the realms of scientific inquiry nor are they anything that can have any value other than utilitarian significance. And what is of utilitarian value is inescapably linked with certain material purposes in life.

In contrast, the order inherent in the cosmos takes a definite shape in the process of being created by the God or the Absolute or the Idea as Plato calls it. This conception of order has different ramifications for man and his world. These ramifications have to do with the need of installing order in the interior of man and, through the process of preserving this order in the psyche of man, putting the external world, especially the social world, in order. It is only on this basis that man can initiate a process of well-ordered and salubrious interaction with the external world. In this sense, the cosmic order has a cultural and moral significance for man. The awareness of this significance can be available only by what Cicero calls contemplation. But before one can contemplate the cosmos and the order inherent in it, one must have the awareness that there is inherent in the cosmos an order that has a vital meaning for him which he must understand. Once this awareness is somehow created, one must, then, try to understand what kind of order it is and what are its constitutive principles. Once these principles become transparent, one must take the next step of what Cicero calls imitation, that is, one must translate these "discovered" or transmitted principles into one's life and thereby mould one's life according to the ideal of living derived from the principles of order immanent and inherent in the cosmos.

To derive the ideas of an ideal pattern of living from the principles of the cosmic order is to set in motion a pattern of culture which, in its traditional sense, is also a process of education, that is, a formative process. The education of this type is by no means a surrogate of what we know today as formal education; it is the forming of man in the existential sense of the term. In its existential sense, culture means a definite commitment to certain principles yielded by a primordial insight into the structure of order, the principles that answer to the essential characteristics of man's being and the profoundest laws of human nature. It is these principles that govern the spiritual and material aspects of the individual's life and the structure of society. In other words, these principles are the operationalisation of what Heraclitus calls the universal *logos* which is common to all beings in a particular society. The act of transforming individual lives and social relations in accordance with these principles is what is traditionally known as culture.

Culture is thus the process of educating men in deliberately moulding human character in accordance with the ideal contained in these principles. But to mould one's character is, first, to suppress or eliminate completely those attributes or elements in one's being that are either inimical or outright antagonistic to and destructive of the endeavour of casting one's character in a particular ideal mould. Unless these attributes or elements are 'murdered', so to say, the possibility for opening up for regeneration of man's personality and social order in accordance with the ideal vision of life will never come true.

Thus, the moulding of the life pattern according to the ideal vision of life involves a two-stage transformation. The first stage is defined by the efforts to suppress or completely eliminate those elements in man's being which are proven obstacles in the path of the proper development of man's character and the salubrious functioning of the social order. The second stage is meant to actually make conscious efforts to live up to the ideal of life envisioned in the principles of the cosmic order. As a matter of fact, however, these two stages are but two different facets of a single process, that is, the process of self-transformation so as to rise above the animality that man receives from nature. Only after man has killed the animal in him he can pull himself to a higher level of existence.

The process of attaining a higher level of existence is, by definition, an individual achievement. However, this achievement, although personal, is not possible in a social environment which is either hostile or extremely indifferent to the effort to attain a higher level of existence. Such a society prefers to pursue and evolves institutional mechanisms to support the pursuit of certain other values. This preference discourages, if not altogether rules out, efforts by the members of that society to attain a higher level of existence. There is yet another dimension to it. In many societies, the pursuit of a higher level of existence is considered to be an aristocratic value which only a few have either the inclination matched by the requisite leisure or have the resources appropriate for the pursuit of the ideal of a higher level existence. In contrast, a large number of persons are either unable or unwilling to pursue this value because, as John Locke pointed out long ago, no body is born with loaves of bread, fish and wine. They have to spend their whole life in trying to acquire the bare necessities of life for survival and subsistence. As a result, they have no time to say hallelujah. They are primarily, even exclusively, engaged in pursuing those values that are basically democratic and can be pursued by a large number of people. These values are antagonistic to the pursuit of the aristocratic value of the quest of a higher level of existence. As such, it becomes very difficult for the selected few to persist in their quest of a higher level of existence.

In addition to this, there is entirely a different kind of social system which is decisively opposed to the pursuit of a higher level of existence that is grounded in the traditional ways of thinking and doing. These societies deny the existence of any higher reality, including that of the God, accept the reality of the human person who is considered to be nothing else than a natural being endowed with appetites and desires. As a natural being, he has his naturally imprinted desires and appetites which he must seek to satisfy if he is to enjoy felicity in the Hobbesian sense of the term. In such societies, the fulfilment of biological needs are supposed not only essential for the survival and sustenance of the human race, but are considered to be very important for the realisation of the highest moral aspiration, as Rousseau insists. For the people in these societies, the fulfilment of biological needs is the pathway not only to felicity but also to progress both in morals and civilisation and paves the way for the realisation of human potentialities which may, as Kant observes, remain undeveloped if there were no material interests and conflict caused by the inevitable clash of interests.

It is inconceivable for the two types of societies to prefer or promote the quest for a higher level of existence except the one that involves the progressively raising of the standards of living by continuously expanding the base and the technological capacity for generating ever-larger quantities of consumable goods and services. When the attainment of a better life through the pacification of the appetites and passions and the production of necessary means for it emerges as a dominant value, the quest for a higher level of existence in the traditional sense of the term, is either considered redundant or pushed to the periphery of human existence. As a result, the quest for a higher level of existence is attributed as being of lesser importance or being outright irrelevant. It has, therefore, to face stiff competition from other, supposedly higher values concerned with the fulfilment of ordinary life needs. Or, alternatively, it may exist and people may also acknowledge its existence but may pay only a formal and token respect to it.

All this suggests that the quest of a higher level of existence whose true idea people form by contemplating and imitating the cosmic order is preferable and desirable only in a society that considers itself as a replica of the cosmos, the cosmion. And since its attributes of being a cosmion can be sustained only when men live up to and shape the pattern of their living in accordance with the principles of order immanent in the cosmos which derive their validity and legitimacy from a still higher reality, the reality that is the ground of being, the moulding of human life becomes necessary. Since the reality that is the ground of being is not cognisable, the principles of cosmic order can be derived from a glimpse, a very dim glimpse at that, of the source of the cosmic order. Thus, to contemplate and imitate the principles inherent in the cosmic order substantively means to be attuned to the ground of being itself. It is this attunement that illumines the meaning in human terms of reality and its relevance for the quest of a higher level of existence that enables man to transcend his animal nature.

Thus to be aware of the cosmic order and to contemplate and imitate the principles of the cosmic order in life is to be aware of the ground of being which is the substratum of order and, at the same time, to be attuned to this ground. To be so attuned to this ground is to have the experience of the presence of the ground of being not only in the cosmos but also in the deepest layer of man's interior. This is not something like an object in the external world that can be easily grasped just by extending one's hand and possessed like a thing forever. The experience of transcendence is possible only when men open up their soul to receive the flash of eternity. It is only when his consciousness is touched by the flash of eternity that a person is able to see, if only dimly, the structure of reality and the principles of order immanent in the cosmos. It is this awareness, engendered through a spiritual awakening leading to the experience of transcendence, that constitutes the basis of whatever knowledge we have of the cosmic order. Simultaneously, it is also the source of establishing and installing order in man's interior and the society at large.

But the experience of transcendence is ineffable and beyond the ken of cognition or discursive logic. This experience is based on "*darshana*" consequent upon what, in the traditional Indian perspective, is called *bodhi,* that is, direct experience or enlightenment. As such, *buddhi,* or thinking in concepts is not of much help in having the *darshana* of what is beyond the phenomenal world or *idam sarvam.* It, however, becomes an important vehicle of deliberation and communication only after some knowledge of what is beyond the phenomenal world has already been attained by perception or some other means ending in the discovery of the form of the Beyond. Thinking in concepts furnishes simply a device of argumentative deliberation upon the unknown entity. The vision of the unknown or the experience of transcendence or of the divine ground of reality is thus prior to the act of philosophising.

Thus the object of philosophising is to describe that which is, by definition, essentially unknowable. The truth that we seek to understand and realise is not an object that can be identified through concepts and possessed like a thing. Also, it is not something that can be cognitively analysed and categorised. It is a truth that can only be experienced through participation in reality and realised through a consciousness that is not only attuned to but also illumined by the flash of eternity. Thus, the truth we seek, the God that we try to understand and realise in our own being, can be apprehended only in a particular state of consciousness. To seek to apprehend the divine ground of reality in any other way is to invite the only possible response of "*neti,*" "*neti*" (not this, not this).

This is so because the plenitude of the divine ground of reality cannot be fully described with the help of attributes insofar as each of these attributes falls short of the richness of the plenitude. It is also because the participating consciousness, even when touched by the flash of eternity, cannot express what it experiences in the language we ordinarily use. The reason for this lies in the fact that consciousness itself has no language; it must depend on the thought to articulate and express its experience. And thought itself is inadequate because, lacking the depth, the penetration and the expanse the consciousness is equipped with, it must depend upon speech (*vak*) which is only partly manifest. The obvious reference here is to the *Vedic* concept of *vak* whose three legs –*para, pashyanti* and *madhyama*—are hidden with only one leg, that is, *baikhari,* being visible. But *baikhari* is not at all capable of articulating reality in all its richness.

It is, therefore, not surprising that the *Vedic* seer poets rely not on discursive logic but on what Plato calls the likely story of creation detailing how and through what process the cosmos came into being. The mysterious ways of the Absolute in which it transforms itself into many, that is, *idam sarvam,* can be apprehended only through the likely story or *srishtividya* or *bhavavrittam.* It is, therefore, the *srishtividya* or cosmogony that offers an insight, no more than an insight, not a complete knowledge elaborating the details of how the cosmos came into being which can be checked and tested for its truth value, into the structure of order. It is this cosmogonical account of the coming into being of the cosmos that not only offers some, necessarily dim knowledge of the form of the entity beyond this phenomenal world but also provides the basis on which one can mould his life and relations with a view to coming nearer his Maker, as Mahatma Gandhi puts it.

Thus, the *srishtividya,* as a likely story of the transformation of the One into many, offers not only the map, as it were, of the cosmos but also constitutes the source for deriving the principles of order for putting into order both the interior of the individual and the social system. It is also this *srishtividya* that constitutes the fountainhead of culture in the sense of its essential role in educating men in the ideal vision of a pattern of life that is lived in the presence of the transcendent as well as in providing the ways and means through which the ideal vision of life can be actualised and lived in conscious awareness of man's linkage with a reality that is larger than his limited, contingent life, even larger than the society he happens to be a member of. This is so for the simple reason that even the organisation of society and its constitutive principles are themselves an attempt to imitate in institutional form the ethos of the cosmic order.

Culture in this sense, that is, in the sense of something that authoritatively prescribes what an ideal vision of life is and that it must be translated into a dynamic force in life, is a characteristic feature of all traditional societies. It also has the function of evaluating and penalising any deviation from this ideal pattern of living. In this sense, culture is nothing else but the process of education that teaches man to be truly man and relate himself meaningfully with his fellow beings, his society, the world, and the gods above and beyond this world but not apart from it. It is only by living according to the ideal vision of life as envisioned in culture that a person can truly make the idea of the primordial community of beings. This primordial community of beings binds together God and man, world and society into a quatenarian structure of primordial community which can be lived only when its live awareness is ever present in the minds of men.

Culture in this sense joins together two orders of being, the one relating to the finite existence of man and the other referring to the absolute source of truth, meaning and value. It is this linkage between the finite and the infinite through the medium of culture that functions as a shelter in which man may give to his life a semblance of meaning. In performing this shelter function, culture evinces a permanent general structure comprising three sets of ideas. These sets of ideas are: (a) the ideas concerning the constitution of the cosmos as a whole; (b) the ideas concerning the internal order of the cosmos; and (c) the ideas concerning the status of the cosmion (that is, the social order claiming to be a replica of the cosmos) simultaneously in the cosmos with its graded layers ranging between Prithiwi and Satyam as well as in history. Society as cosmion thus straddes over both the *asak loka* and *asya loka.* While its paradigm is derived from the vision of the order grounded in the idea of the divine society also has its existence in history. If the vision of reality on which a particular social order rests is eternal and unchanging, its actual passage in history is affected by the flex of time that we know as history. It is the combination of these ideas that constitute the essence of culture as a formative force.

Insofar as the idea concerning the constitution of the cosmos is involved, they are, as we have already seen, derived from the *Vedic* likely story based on the spiritual experience of the *Vedic* seer-poets. The beginning of this likely story is the *Swayambhoo* himself whose transformation into *vishwa* through a two-stage *vivarta* occurs in two stages; the first stage, that is, the *purvarddha,* is marked by the development, at the non-material plane, of the possibilities of numerous names and forms as well as the birth of gods as presiding deities of essential elements and processes necessary for the creation to move ahead. The process of creation attains gradual maturation in the second stage, that is, the *uttararddha,* when the possibilities of names and forms get materialised in *pinda* form. The process of creation is, then, consequent upon a constant interaction between two opposite but complementary forces, that is, *Agni* and *Soma.* It is conceived in the *Vedic* perspective as the syzygy between them as the necessary condition of creation. This primordial syzygy finds expression in many different ways and between many figures of divinity in the *Vedic* likely story.

It is this likely story that constitutes the source of apprehending the principles of order in the cosmos. The aggregate of all these principles is called *Rita* in the *Vedic* likely story that imposes on all things, including the gods, a set pattern of functioning without any deviation. Man's physical constitution, too, is governed by certain invariant and fixed rules. However, man also enjoys freedom which, when exercised unthinkingly and abandon, produces disorder, both in the man's psyche and the social system. This disorder can be checked and prevented from occurring when man becomes aware of his divine nature that gets engulfed in the pressing and alluring concerns of the everyday life. Only when man seeks to rise above the allurements of these worldly concerns, that is, above the petty, contingent experiences of his life, he can make his awareness of his linkage with the divine ground of being a real dynamic one. The most efficacious way for man to rediscover his divine nature is, according to the *Vedic* perspective, the performance of *yajna.*

The performance of *yajna* serves some very important functions in man's life. In the first place, the performance of *yajna* is considered to be the one way in which man can establish his link with the gods if it has been snapped and use it as an aid in self-development. In the second place, the world he lives in is only a small part of the cosmos at the apex of which stands the Creator. The cosmos consists of a series of seven *lokas.* Although man forms only a small part of the cosmos, he tends to forget his smallness and acts as if he is the lord of the universe and he thinks that everything in it is meant to serve his needs. This narcissistic attitude toward the world impels him to treat the external world only as a potential means for the realisation of his self-defined purposes. This brings into existence a state of war of one against all others. Thus, man's *hybris* becomes the cause of social unrest, conflict and violence. *Hybris* can be dissolved if man comes to realise his place in the cosmos and becomes aware and conscious of his responsibilities of protecting and preserving the integrity of the cosmos and, through it, that of the lived world as a necessary condition of his own well being.

To be conscious of the need to protect and preserve the integrity of the cosmos is to make it sure that the process of exchange between man and the gods continues uninterrupted. To perform *yajna* is one of the ways in which the process of exchange between man and gods can be protected and preserved. Another way of keeping the process of exchange is to restrain and overcome the tendency towards *pleonexia.* This can be achieved only when man sheds covetousness or cupidity. He must be satisfied with whatever he has or can have with the sweat of his brow and limit his wants so that he is not tempted to get what he thinks he should have beyond what he actually needs either by wile or will power. It is in this context that we can appreciate what *Bhagawat Purana* says: "Men have ownership over only as much as would fill their belly; he who thinks as his own what is more than that is a thief and deserves punishment." *Taittiriya Brahmana* goes as far as to suggest that he who hoards more than what he needs disrupts the cosmic metabolism and invites death.

Lastly, therefore, all these become possible only when man engages in the act of self-development through self-transformation or follows faithfully the proper lines of conduct which conduce to self-development and promotes harmony between man and his external world and himself and the gods. Thus the key to self-development is the quest for a higher level of existence. This is assuredly a personal quest but its pursuit must be collectively safeguarded, promoted and supported. Without this, personal quest faces difficulties or becomes very difficult to sustain. Since the quest for self-development constitutes the basic value implying the performance of *yajna* as a means of self-control, the pursuit of worldly vocations must be subordinated to and are precluded from becoming autotelic realms of action generating their own different principles of operation and assuming the pseudo-objective character of independent forces keeping man subjugated and helpless. The pursuit of worldly vocations, then, becomes the instrument and vehicle of self-transformation and a means of bringing harmony between the inner man and his external existence.

It is against this background that we can appreciate the status and the role of *samskaras* in endowing Indian civilisation with longevity when other civilisations have gone under the current of history. *Samskaras* function as a link between the finite existence of man and the absolute source of truth, meaning and value. They are the ways in which the Hindus seek to do what the gods did. The *samskara* of marriage, as a part of the whole gamut of *samskaras* is one such instance and it is therefore sanctified by religious rites and rituals.

Index